Positive Psychology and Change

Positive Psychology and Change

How Leadership, Collaboration,
and Appreciative Inquiry
Create Transformational Results

Sarah Lewis

WILEY Blackwell

This edition first published 2016
© 2016 John Wiley & Sons, Ltd

Registered Office
John Wiley & Sons, Ltd, The Atrium, Southern Gate, Chichester, West Sussex, PO19 8SQ, UK

Editorial Offices
350 Main Street, Malden, MA 02148-5020, USA
9600 Garsington Road, Oxford, OX4 2DQ, UK
The Atrium, Southern Gate, Chichester, West Sussex, PO19 8SQ, UK

For details of our global editorial offices, for customer services, and for information about how to apply for permission to reuse the copyright material in this book please see our website at www.wiley.com/wiley-blackwell.

The right of Sarah Lewis to be identified as the author of this work has been asserted in accordance with the UK Copyright, Designs and Patents Act 1988.

Library of Congress Cataloging-in-Publication data applied for

HB ISBN: 9781118788844

A catalogue record for this book is available from the British Library.

Cover image: Getty/klublu

Set in 10.5/13pt Minion by SPi Global, Pondicherry, India

Printed and bound in Malaysia by Vivar Printing Sdn Bhd

1   2016

To Jem, Jordan, and Rhia.
who enrich my life beyond measure

Contents

About the Author

Sarah Lewis is a chartered psychologist, an Associated Fellow of the British Psychological Society, and a founder and Principal Member of the Association of Business Psychologists. She holds a master's degree in occupational and organizational psychology, attained with distinction, and a certificate in systemic consultation. She is a specialist Appreciative Inquiry practitioner and an expert at facilitating large group events.

She is the managing director of Appreciating Change and is an experienced organizational consultant and facilitator who has been actively involved in helping people and organizations change their behavior for over 25 years. Her clients include local government, central government, not-for-profit organizations, and private sector clients, particularly in the manufacturing, financial, and educational sectors.

When positive psychology burst onto the scene, Sarah quickly realized that work in this area both chimed with her practice and offered robust theoretical support to Appreciative Inquiry as an approach to organizational change. She integrates these two approaches in her work and is delighted to be able to extend, explore, and share this connection in this book.

Sarah has lectured at postgraduate level and continues to be a regular conference presenter in the United Kingdom and internationally. She writes regularly for publication, is the lead author of *Appreciative Inquiry for Change Management: Using AI to Facilitate Organizational Development* (2007), and is author of *Positive Psychology at Work*, published by Wiley-Blackwell in 2011.

Sarah's work can be viewed on her website (www.acukltd.com) and she can be contacted on ++ 44 (0)7973 782715 or by emailing sarahlewis@acukltd.com

Foreword by David L. Cooperrider

What Will the Future of Organization Development and Change Look Like?

The future is here—in this book.

Beginning in the 1980's one could sense it, that is, the urge to create *a positive revolution in change*. First there were theoretical and conceptual calls questioning the inherently awkward logic—or illogic—of wanting to rally and "inspire" people to change *by focusing the field's most powerful deficit-analytic tools on a person or system's weaknesses, dysfunctions, and root causes of failure*? Really?[1]

Remember, for example, the era in Organization Development (OD) of sophisticated and statistically refined *low morale surveys*: first would come the documentation on a scale of 1-7 of morale among employees, and then the cascading feedback, endless meetings, and subsequent interventions designed to remove the root causes of usually the lowest levels of morale. It was like attempting to remedy a dark room by focusing on darkness.[2]

Well it never, ever worked to inspire and motivate in the sense that people clearly learned tons about the causes of low morale—because that's what the diagnostic process set out to document—but the analysis or search rarely if ever surfaced any kind of substantive (and inspiring) new knowledge, for

---

[1]Cooperrider, D. L., & Srivastva, S. (1987). Appreciative inquiry in organizational life. In *Research in Organization Development and Change*, Pasmore, W., Woodman, R. (Eds.), (Vol.1). Greenwich, CT: JAI Press.

[2]For the first articulation of *Appreciative Inquiry: Toward an Applied Science of Social Innovation*, see the Cooperrider Ph.D dissertation defended in 1985. Download the pdf: http://www.davidcooperrider.com/wp-content/uploads/2013/06/Dissertation-Cooperriders-1985.pdf www.david.cooperrider.com search for the blog post "Rare Admiration" June 18, 2013.

example, about surprising "hot teams" or extraordinary times of "enterprise flourishing" or times when people were so turned on and called by a powerful purpose greater than themselves that they would contribute far beyond their job descriptions. Even if those exceptional moments were fleeting and rare, it still never occurred to the field of OD and change management that layered into the narratives of those positive deviations were the most *natural and most consistently powerful* cognitive, positive emotional, imaginative, and supercooperative seeds of human system change available. If there were debilitating patterns of problematic dysfunctions and breakdowns in an organization, of what possible use could it possibly be to go off on a tangential search of times of peak performance, positive deviance, or a deep dive analysis into the positive core of all past, present and future capacity in a system? It was *as if this material—this universe of strengths and understanding of history as positive possibility—was irrelevant and of little use for human system development, change, and elevationary transformation.*

Paradigms are like that. They are stubborn. They can blind us. Perhaps that's why we still thrill to it, that is, Einstein's often-quoted words when he said:

> *"No problem can be solved from the same level of consciousness that created it. We must learn to see the world anew."*
>
> —*Albert Einstein*

Sarah Lewis, in this volume, not only helps leaders and managers, change agents, and even parents and coaches, *to see the world anew* but she helps us *to see change anew*—in and through a vibrant and vast integration of the new OD. The new OD, as it is illuminated here, is one that serves systemically to bring out the best version of a person or organization *most naturally, easily, and consistently* and yes, all of this, in the service of pressing, totally real, and complex change. Years ago Sarah sighted it all, a sea change—from the earliest writings in Appreciative Inquiry (AI) to the strengths revolution in management, and also from the new sciences of complexity and dialogic construction to the positive psychology of human flourishing—and then she began to mix and resonate all of it like a maestro. The result: Sarah Lewis brings together the strongest streams of an entire revolution into a one integral and remarkable portrait of the new OD— what it is, how to do it, and why its so powerful – better than any other *evidence-based* book I've seen.

The signature of this volume rests upon Sarah's rich and real storytelling from the frontline of organizational and leadership life, and how she draws us into both the evidence based research findings—for example what good are positive emotions such as hope, inspiration, and the joy of design-thinking and co-creation—while brilliantly illustrating practices, principles, and tools you can use. And the insight that I will never forget from this book is that people actually love change. They don't resist change. Think of the infant in the crib and, if you were lucky enough to be there and see it, think about what you saw *the moment the infant took hold of the railing for the very first time, lifting his or her own little body to an upright position all at once.* What you likely saw was a beaming smile, a sparkle in the eyes, and the squealing sound of delight. Human beings love change—for example in rites and rituals of moving from childhood to adulthood, when being elevated to a new job, or in pushing oneself into some never before used maneuver while kayaking in wild white-water—in these situations resistance to change is *not* the hallmark.

People don't resist change. They resist being changed—always have and always will—until when? Its that special moment where being changed is transformed into being charged, being commissioned, being called authentically into *co-creation*. Sarah's call, complete with how to do it, is unmistakable.

What this book is about is creating the leader*ful* company, in ways that serve to heal "the scar tissues" or eras past—where people were treated as machines; where what managers mostly attended to was breakdown and disrepair; and where change was a push-and-imposed type, not a co-created positive emotional attractor where people will unmistakably see and experience their signature *in* it.

I've used every method in this book in my own work with organizations, communities, cities, whole industries, and UN level world summits.[3] And what's been my experience? In a word: it's all about the power of hope.[4] My hope about what we are capable as human beings has gone up and up, every time for example that we've used the World Café method of dialogue, or the

---

[3] Cooperrider, D. 2012. The Concentration Effect of Strengths, Organizational Dynamics, Vol. 42, No. 2, April-May 2012, p. 21–32.

[4] Cooperrider, D. (2013) A Contemporary Commentary on Appreciative Inquiry in Organizational Life. In Cooperrider, D.L *et al.* (2013) **Organizational Generativity: The Appreciative Inquiry Summit and a Scholarship of Transformation**. Volume #4 in *Advances in Appreciative Inquiry*. Bingley, UK: Emerald Group Publishing Limited.

life-centric and strengths-inspired philosophy of Appreciative Inquiry, or have tapped into the magic of macro—where we do planning, strength-finding, and designing in whole system configurations of strengths in groups of 300 or more internal and external stakeholders. Sound impossible? Read this wonderful book carefully.

What serves to make it all possible are the conditions that bring out the best in human systems. It's when we bring together expertise *and* emergence; it's when we bring together positive discovery mindsets *and* design-prototyping; it's when curiosity velocity and the search for the true, the good, the better and the possible is at least a 5:1 ratio over dogmatic answers; and it's when we actually *love* bringing people out of silos, separations, and stereotypes into moments of supercooperation.

Two comments from CEO's stand out in my memory bank as I've approached change just as Sarah illuminates here. The first, from a company in the Netherlands, is "What was all the fuss about" said the CEO, "we've got such good people here why were we so afraid?" and then the second was a President of a major telecommunications company who used the appreciative methodologies and said, "This has implications for every aspect of our business, everything we do as a company (long pause)… but I *only* wish now I'd heard of these ideas when I was raising my children."

This book is a doorway into generative, strengths-inspired and solutions-focused change. It gives leaders the gift of new eyes and teaches how humility might just be a leaders greatest strength. It brings front and center the joy of high quality connections—and the sustainable effectiveness of it all—back into the field organization development. And it reminds us all that we can create conditions—the evidence base is there—to confirm our deepest conviction: that human beings are good.

And this book shares the wisdom into why and when this is nearly always true: *it's when we bring the best versions of ourselves, our communities, and our organizations to the task of co-creating our better future.* As for the how? That too is simple: just start turning the pages of *this* book!

David L. Cooperrider, PhD
Honorary Chair, The *David L. Cooperrider Center
for Appreciative Inquiry*
Stiller School of Business Champlain College

Fairmount Santrol Professor of Appreciative Inquiry
Weatherhead School of Management, Case Western Reserve University

David L. Cooperrider

David is the Fairmount | David L. Cooperrider Professor of Appreciative Inquiry at the Weatherhead School of Management, Case Western Reserve University where he is faculty chair of the Fowler Center for Business as an Agent of World Benefit and Co-director of the Strategy Innovation Lab. David is best known for his original theory on Appreciative Inquiry ("Ai") with his mentor Suresh Srivastva, and has served as advisor to senior executives in business and societal leadership roles, including projects with five Presidents and Nobel Laureates such as William Jefferson Clinton, His Holiness the Dalai Lama, Kofi Annan and others. David has served as strategic advisor to a wide variety of organizations including Apple, Verizon, Johnson & Johnson, the Boeing Corporation, National Grid, Smuckers, Sloan-Kettering, Fairmount Minerals, Green Mountain Coffee Roasters, McKinsey, Parker Hannifin, Sherwin Williams, Dealer Tire, Wal-Mart as well as American Red Cross, American Hospital Association, Cleveland Clinic, and United Way. The United Nations called on the Appreciative Inquiry large group method of planning to grow the UN Global Compact to over 8,000 of the world's largest corporations advancing the global goals: eradicating extreme poverty through business and creating a bright green energy future.

David has published over 20 books and authored over 100 articles and book chapters and served as editor of both the Journal of Corporate Citizenship with Ron Fry and the current research series for Advances for Appreciative Inquiry, with Michel Avital. In 2010 David was awarded the Peter F. Drucker Distinguished Fellow by the Drucker School of Management—a designation recognizing his contribution to management thought. His books include *Appreciative Inquiry: A Positive Revolution in Change* (with Diana Whitney); *The Organization Dimensions of Global Change* (with Jane Dutton); *Organizational Courage and Executive Wisdom* (with Suresh Srivastva) and the 4-volume research series *Advances in Appreciative Inquiry*. In 2010 David was awarded the Peter F. Drucker Distinguished Fellow by the Drucker School of Management—a designation recognizing his contribution to management thought.

Most recently, Champlain College, with the support Bob Stiller, the Founder and former Ceo of Green Mountain Coffee Roasters, honored David with an academic center in his name. It is called the *David L. Cooperrider for Appreciative Inquiry.* For the center's dedication Marty Seligman wrote: "David Cooperrider is a giant: a giant of discovery, a giant of dissemination, and a giant of generosity" while Harvard's Jane Nelson at the Kennedy School of Leadership said: "David Cooperrider is one of the outstanding scholar-practitioners of our generation."

Preface

When meeting an organization interested in commissioning some work, an interesting question to pose is, "Why this now? Why is the now the moment at which you have decided to invest time and money in this?" I thought I might ask the same question to shape this preface. Why this book now?

I have been a psychologist for 30 years, for 10 years as a social worker and for 20 years as an organizational consultant, and it's all about change. Life is about change. We are expert at change, we are the most adaptable species on the planet and yet it causes endless problems and challenges in organizational life. Many books have been written about how to successfully change things in organizations. Many of them are very good. Fewer have really called on the psychology of people and groups to explain why the plans don't always work out quite as, well, planned, or to explain how our very humanness is our greatest asset when it comes to working together to influence our own futures.

I am moved to put the time and effort into writing this book now because I believe that positive psychology, combined with co-creative participatory approaches to change such as Appreciative Inquiry, offers very effective ways of helping organizations and people to change. Having said that, all change initiatives take place in a context, and that context is all-important in influencing how any change activity is interpreted by those involved. So this book doesn't present a "recipe" for achieving more successful change as many change books do. It is more about the processes that can help with change. It is about how the context and history of an organization affect how the announcement of change initiatives is experienced. It is about working with big action events and tiny micro-moments to help achieve change. It is about applying some of the latest thinking and practice from positive psychology and dialogue-based organizational development to the age-old organizational challenges of performance, culture, and working practices to make change as positive an experience as possible for all involved.

I am not an academic. I am not affiliated to a university. I don't do original research. Instead, I try to put the work of others to the test, in practice, in the field. A book like this is an attempt to create a mosaic drawn from the best of the brilliant work of others. It is a labour of love, intended as homage to those who painstakingly do the research or generously spell out their practice in detail. The researching and writing of this book was challenging, rewarding, engrossing, thought-provoking, and fun. I hope you find reading it to be a similar experience.

I have written two previous books about positive psychology and Appreciative Inquiry. I have tried on the whole not to repeat myself here. I have tried to balance the possible frustration of those for whom some concepts are new and are not fully explored here against the possible sense of déjà vu for those who came across these ideas in depth in previous books. I wanted to take the opportunity to more fully explain concepts that didn't make it into the last book. My intention is that the books stand alone, yet are complementary.

This is a book of two halves. The first five chapters are focused on ideas, concepts, and theory in positive psychology and organizational development. The second half of the book gives much practical guidance, although you will notice a high degree of overlap. This means that sometimes practices get mentioned before they are explained in full; for example, Appreciative Inquiry is explained fully in Chapter 6, and yet mentioned in probably every chapter.

Along with the core content are some added extras. A highlight of the book is my husband's kindly donated cartoons to "lighten things up a bit." They make me laugh, which is always good for the soul, and I hope they do you too. I have included stories from my personal experience to try to illuminate the practices I am talking about. I hope they also break up the density of the text from time to time. Your privilege as a reader is to skip those bits that don't "do it for you." I encourage you to do so.

As ever, choices have to be made when putting a book together. The most challenging, I find, is that of referencing. I know that references in a text can trip up those not used to them, although I assure you that with a little practice your eye will learn to gloss over them and you will hardly notice them. On the other hand, I get frustrated if a reference isn't readily available when I want it. I like to know on what basis an assertion is being made. I want a reference to hand, not buried in a footnote linked by a miniscule number somewhere in the text, nor at the end of the chapter that I have to flick back and forth to locate, but in the text right next to the relevant information and easily accessible in a combined reference section at the back of the book. So that's what I have provided for you.

I wrote in the preface to the last book, "I can only hope that you buy this pristine volume and rapidly deface it with underlining, exclamation marks, question marks, comments, dog ears and coffee stains. Such, to me, are the signs of a useful book." Some people were kind enough to contact me to tell me just how coffee bespattered their book had become. I was thrilled, and I can't better this as my wish to you.

Acknowledgements

A book doesn't come out of thin air. The invitation to write this book came from Darren Reed and Karen Shield of Wiley-Blackwell following the modest success of the first book we produced together. I was delighted to oblige. It has taken a year longer than we originally hoped, and their response when I had to divert my attention to various family matters was so graciously supportive that I truly felt I could take the time it took.

This book is built on the work of so many other people: people I've read, people I've talked to, and people I've worked with. I have made every effort to acknowledge the original researchers and practitioners whose work I have called upon. On the other hand, I have granted my clients the cloak of anonymity in an attempt to protect their reputation, if not my own, and so trust that they are only recognizable to themselves. That they allow me and people like me to come into their organizations and workplaces and "do creative things" with their people is a wonderful privilege and I am eternally grateful to them all. Practitioners, like trainee doctors, have to start somewhere, and so even further back in the midst of time are all my earliest clients from whom I learnt so much about the art of engaging productively with organizations. I thank them all.

On a more practical level, at the behest of the publisher, this time I have written every word of this text myself, quotes excluded. It's a lot of words! Jem Smith, my eldest son, has been much involved of late, spotting the convoluted sentences and esoteric modes of expression in a last-ditch attempt to improve its reader-friendliness. He is also helping with assembling the references and spotting those typos that fool the spellchecker. In addition, he kindly lets me know about any boring bits so I can have another go at making them more interesting. He has done all within his power to ensure that you find this a readable read; thus liability for any sleep-inducing sections and other errors that have slipped through are to be laid at my door alone. I am truly grateful for his help.

In turn our efforts have been ably supported by Giles Flitney, whose attention to detail as copy-editor was exemplary: no fudge of referencing or "near enough is good enough" laziness of expression got past his eagle eyes and sharp brain. To Giles must go the credit for clearing the way of the last stumbles and trip-ups so that the meaning could flow freely through the text.

And last but not least, I want to thank my husband, Stewart Smith, who, ploughing through text about a world to which he is not connected except through me, managed to spot a variety of opportunities for a joke or a laugh that he could shape into a cartoon. Of itself this book isn't a bundle of laughs; his ability to spot such opportunities as arise is a true talent. We are all extremely grateful for the light relief thus provided.

1

The Legacy of Twentieth-Century Ideas about Organizational Change

Picture the scene. I'm watching Boardwalk Empire *on DVD with someone who came of age well into the twenty-first century. We get to the scene where a young "gofer" is asked his name by another gofer. He replies, "Al, Al Capone." My young friend says, "Wasn't he a real person?" I don't answer immediately, pausing while I wait for a suitable gap in the dialogue. She answers her own question: "Yes he was." She reads a few sentences about Al Capone from her iPhone. She then asks, "Are any of the other characters real?" "I don't know," I say. A slight pause and then, "What's Nucky's proper name?" "Enoch." She looks up "Enoch Thompson" on the phone. "Oh yes, he's real too." Throughout our programme-watching her phone whistles at her intermittently, and each time she attends for maybe 30 seconds, smiling, pouting, texting.*

There is nothing new in this account, and everything. My dinosaur ways, such as watching a DVD rather than viewing content direct from the internet, my assumption that all relevant information is present in the vision and sound on the screen, my distance from my electronic "work" devices (it is the weekend, my mobile phone is in a bag somewhere, undoubtedly still on silent from the last meeting on Friday), all mark me out as essentially from the pre-digital age. My young friend engages with the world differently. Her phone lives in her hand. She is a cyber-person at one with the internet. It is always on and so is she. Any curiosity, mild or strong, can be instantly gratified. When she cooks a meal, before we are allowed to eat it a picture must be sent to friends. Arrangements with friends are so fluid as to be at times indiscernible to the naked eye as commitments. Fraught and loaded conversations with the boyfriend about "the state of the relationship" are conducted in 20-word text bites. She truly lives in a different world to me.

Positive Psychology and Change: How Leadership, Collaboration, and Appreciative Inquiry Create Transformational Results, First Edition. Sarah Lewis.
© 2016 John Wiley & Sons, Ltd. Published 2016 by John Wiley & Sons, Ltd.

STEW
SMITH

"Say cheese!"

Introduction

My young friend and her colleagues are the inhabitants and creators of future, as yet unrealized, organizations. These organizations need to be fit for the changing world. At present we are in a state of transition from the solid certainties of the latter half of the twentieth century (the programme is shown once, at 9.00 p.m. on BBC1 – make it or miss it) to the increasing fluidity of the twenty-first century (watch it now, watch it later, on the TV, on a tablet, legally or illegally – whatever, whenever). This isn't only the case in the media world; it can be argued that the organizational development world is in a similar state of flux.

Many of the organizational development approaches and techniques that are in common use in organizations today were developed in the1940s and 1950s. Most of the theorists were male, European and living in America. Their ideas are located in a specific time and context. Their ideas and theories are not timeless truths about organizations and organizational life; rather they are a product of, and are suited to, their time and context. This chapter examines the key features of these organizational development models and their influence on current beliefs about how to produce organizational change. First though, a reminder of how much the world has changed since the 1940s.

A Changing World

The jury is still out on whether the recession of the last six years (as experienced by most of the Western world at least), is a temporary glitch in the upward path of increasing productivity and affluence, or the dawning of a new economic world order. What it has brought into sharp unavoidable focus is the interconnectedness of the world, and the complexity of that interconnectedness. Michael Lewis's books *The Big Short* (2010) and *Boomerang* (2011) spell out in words of few syllables how the US property and financial markets came crashing down, bursting property bubbles all over Western Europe, and bringing other markets down with them. One of the many insights to be drawn from this calamitous tale is that the level of complexity developed in the money market obscured the connective links between actions. One of the few who seemed to understand something of this before the event is Nassim Taleb, who, in his book *The Black Swan* (2008) (a somewhat more challenging read than Michael Lewis, and not for the faint hearted), essentially says that the real threat isn't what can be predicted, precisely because we can prepare for that; it is what can't be predicted. And his argument essentially is that the degree of fundamental unpredictability, for organizations, is growing partly because of the increasing level of complexity and interconnectivity of the world at large.

Unpredictability and complexity create challenges for change initiatives. When there is a high degree of unpredictability and complexity it becomes more obvious that not all the variables relevant to a situation can be known. Not all the likely consequences of actions can be predicted in their entirety, and the effects of our actions can't be bounded. Cheung-Judge and Holbeche note that "overall the challenges for leaders relate to dealing with the complexity, speed and low predictability of today's competitive landscape" (2011, p. 283). And yet we all, leaders and consultants, frequently act in the organizational change context as if we can control all the variables and predict all the consequences of our actions. A contributing factor to this misplaced sense of omniscience is that many of our change theories and models are predicated on the idea that organizational change *is* predictable and controllable. To understand this, we need to recognize that many of them are the direct descendants of ideas developed over 60 years ago, when the world was a very different place.

The Roots of Many Change Models

In the 1940s Europe was busy tearing itself apart in the second large-scale conflict of the century. It managed to drag in most of the rest of the world through alliance and empire as the war ranged over large parts of the globe. Every continent (barring the South Pole) and almost every country was involved. The German Nazi party gave itself the mission of purifying the German race by removing various Nazi-defined undesirable or foreign elements that lived among them. This desire to eradicate perceived threat was focused mainly on the large German and later Polish and other annexed countries' Jewish populations, but it was also aimed at homosexual men, Gypsies, and the mentally deficient. As the reality of the Nazi ambition became apparent, many under threat sought to leave Europe. America was a place of sanctuary before and during the war for those under threat of death, particularly the European Jewish population.

The genocidal intent of the Nazis and the industrialization of death through the extermination camps were a horrific and terrifying new reality in the world of human possibility. After the war the phrase "never again" encapsulated the ambition of many to understand and prevent such a tragedy from ever happening again. Many people devoted their remaining lives to trying to understand how it was possible for people to persuade themselves that such ambition and activity was not only acceptable but desirable and to be actively pursued. For some this expressed itself in an interest in understanding group dynamics. Organizations are a particular expression of social grouping. One German American Jewish refugee in particular wanted to understand how what had happened had happened, and more particularly, how to prevent it happening again.

Kurt Lewin was an immigrant German Jewish psychologist who found employment at Cornell University and then MIT. An applied researcher, he was interested in achieving social change and he developed the research methodology known as action research as a way of creating practical and applicable knowledge. As part of his work and research, Lewin developed models to understand and effect organizational change which still reverberate in organizational thinking. His three-step model of organizational change (1947), namely, unfreeze, change, freeze, is at the base of many more recent change models. This model understands organizations to exist in an essentially stable state, one that is periodically interrupted by short episodes of disruptive change. The use of the "frozen" image to describe the before and after state around the period of change suggests not so much stability as a deep stolidity, like a block of ice. This suggests that change is not something that might grow internally from within the organization, but rather something external that needs to be applied to organizations to encourage change, to create the necessary unfreezing of the present state to allow change to happen. Lewin also described these external forces as a force field, and advocated force field analysis.

He suggested that at any point a stable organizational state is held in place by a force field of restraining and driving forces (1947). The field is revealed through the creation of a vector analysis diagram of any particular context, identifying the pertinent forces. The restraining forces, things such as organizational norms, structure, and so on, he argued, hold the situation in place. Driving forces, such as managerial desire or the consequences of not changing, are those that push in the direction of the desired change. While they are in balance the situation is in stasis. To achieve change, he argued, one needs either to reduce the restraining forces or to increase the driving forces. He argued that the restraining forces offer comfort to people, being familiar and habitual. He argued that a measure of discomfort needs to be introduced to get people to move towards a new situation. In this we can see the origin of the idea of the need in change to "get people out of their comfort zone." Similarly, when considering how to achieve change, the question frequently asked is, "So what are the driving forces for this change?" The force field model is one of analysis, suggesting that the total situation can be modelled and that all the forces for and against change can be identified. Integral to these ideas is the notion of resistance to change (1947, p. 13). As French and Bell explain it, "Identification and specification of the force field should be thorough and exhaustive so that a picture of why things are as they are becomes clear" (1999, p. 175). Some characteristics of old paradigm thinking are outlined in Box 1.1.

Box 1.1   Ten Indicators of Old Paradigm Thinking

1. How will we get buy-in?
2. How will we overcome resistance to change?
3. What are the driving forces for change?
4. We need to force people out of their comfort zone.
5. People don't like change.
6. Share information on a "need to know" basis.
7. Just tell them what to do.
8. I'm just a hired hand, they're head office.
9. I'm not paid to think.
10. Cascading communications.

Table 1.1   How the world has changed.

Twentieth century	Twenty-first century
National boundaries	Interconnected world
Jobs for life	Zero hours working
Data search	Data swamp
Fixed communication points	Portable communication points
Local competition	Global competition
Poorly permeable organizational boundaries	Highly permeable organizational boundaries
State-based world economy	Business-based world economy
Manageable rates of change	Unmanageable rates of change

Organizational development as an approach was built from these early foundations. Some of the early tools of organizational development, stemming directly from Lewin's early work, include T-groups, action research and participative management. These ideas can be seen in their present form in such common organizational development practices as team development, various forms of action research including Appreciative Inquiry, and employee involvement in decision-making. His research into human and group behaviour during change, and insights expounded about people and change, remain sound and indeed are fundamental to some of the ideas discussed in this book. Unfortunately, his engineering-based approach to understanding organizations has proved to be a stronger legacy when it comes to approaches to organizational change. While they may have proved illuminating in the world of the 1950s, the context within which human organizations exist and function has fundamentally changed (see Table 1.1). This means that some of the assumptions evident in various change models based on the application of his basic thinking are open to challenge. Specifically, we might now question the appropriateness of the idea of periods of stability between those of change; the idea that the whole situation is somehow "knowable"; and the idea of planned change as being sufficiently fast, adaptable, and flexible to achieve sustainable organizational change.

Legacy Thinking about Organizational Change

In line with these ways of thinking about how organizations develop, change in organizations is often characterized as hard, painful, and unwelcome; a process frequently feared and resisted both by those implementing it and by those experiencing it. The most common explanation of the "emotional journey of change" is taken from a study of the bereavement patterns of those coming to terms with a loved one's dying and death (Kubler-Ross, 1969). Two of the most common topics for managers or leaders contemplating making organizational changes are "how to sell the change" and "how to overcome resistance." The need to identify and quickly manoeuvre out those who are deemed unable to "get on the bus" of change is a close third. This way of thinking encourages the belief that change is a huge drain on managerial energy as people are pushed through their resistance into new patterns of interacting and ways of working. Lewin's three-step model of change, now over 70 years old, is behind many of our current approaches to change.

'how to sell the change' and 'how to overcome resistance'.

STEW SMITH

For instance, it encourages the idea that it is possible to "finish" the job of change, that is, that it is possible to arrive at the most "perfect" organizational form that won't need any further attention. In this way, since hope springs eternal that this will be the last time this level of disruption will have to be experienced, change tends to arrive with a fanfare of announcements that it is "the answer." In addition to solving current issues, it will revolutionize the work, the company, and your life. All this reinforces the "this time we've cracked it" attitude to change as a one-off solution to the problem of organizational design. Lewin was not the only one to apply an engineering eye to organizations, he was preceded by Taylor (1912). Between them they have created quite a legacy.

The Legacy Beliefs of Lewin and Taylor in Our Understanding of Organizational Change

1. Organizational life is essentially stable with necessary periodic episodes of disruptive change

This belief has particularly pernicious effects on how organizations approach change as it contains within it an understanding both that change is a discrete event and that it is an ongoing process. It is the former belief that encourages the idea that the many challenges of organizational design can be successfully resolved "once and for all," while the later reality means that in the longer term every change initiative is doomed to failure. Small wonder that this second implication gets overlooked in the enthusiasm for solving the issues right here, right now. This characterization of change as an occasional necessary disruptive event encourages three frequently observed beliefs among managers. First, they regard change as a discrete event that only needs to be attended to periodically (and the rest of the time can be ignored). Second, they regard change as an interruption to the normal running of things (that therefore isn't real work or their core work but rather a resented addition or distraction). Third, and this tends to be a more subtle, less overtly obvious belief, they frequently believe that the current necessity for disruptive change is an indication of some past failure to "get it right," the blame frequently being laid at the door of the last big change effort.

In addition, this belief discourages innovation or adaptation. Once the dust has settled from the most recent "change" there is a tacit understanding that "that's it" – problem solved. So what need for constant innovation? This is the best way; we can all breathe out and get back to work. However, over time the downsides of whatever the last solution was become apparent. As Senge said some time ago, "Today's problems come from yesterday's 'solutions'" (1990, p. 57). Over time, the benefits of the current organizational form become less and less obvious, and the downsides more so, until at last there is a huge effort made to swing the pendulum to the other extreme, solving the current downsides, and yet also sowing the seeds for the next "readjustment" in a few years' time.

Today's problems come from
yesterday's "solutions"

STEW SMITH

2. There is a "right" answer to the challenge of organizational design

In essence there is no definitively correct answer to the challenge of organizational form and so all attempts predicated on the supposition of a right answer are doomed to fail. Indeed, in contrast, constant adaptation within an organization is healthy, as is a certain "untidiness." For example, exceptions to the generally accepted or standard ways of working may add value for a time, while a complexity of organizational forms under one roof may aid local performance and create flexibility. These are valuable organizational assets that can be destroyed during "big bang" change when the focus on consistency and a drive for efficiency frequently militate against flexibility and adaptiveness.

3. Logic is the route to achieving change

Leaders and managers frequently hold an unarticulated image of the organization as a machine (Lewis, Passmore, & Cantore, 2007; Morgan, 1997), subject to the rules of logic. This leads them to believe that the way to solve organizational problems is to apply their powers of rational and logical thinking. Logic is a philosophical or mathematical discipline. However, few of us are trained philosophers or skilled mathematicians, and consequently, as many authors have shown (Kahneman, 2011), our "logic" is full of time- and energy-saving heuristics (that is, assumptions and shortcuts) and fallacies. In practical terms, this means that an appeal to "logic" to indicate the best solution to a challenge doesn't necessarily act to unite all in agreement. Apart from the general human difficulty in actually being logical in the strict sense of the discipline, there is also the challenge that each person's substitute, their idea of what "makes sense" or "seems logical," is based on their personal understanding of the world. In general terms, we make sense of things differently depending on our context, history, current drives, and so on, meaning that what seems an eminently sensible, indeed the only logical course of action to me may well, equally logically, seem like madness to you. In other words, our own particular beliefs are likely to seem perfectly "logical" to us.

While logical thought is defined as being free of emotional contamination, we humans are constantly assailed and affected by emotion, which affects our judgement. Even if something is accepted as logical, our feelings about a situation might affect our ability to act on that logic. To take an extreme example, starving people in desperate situations have been known to eat the flesh of their dead companions. Perfectly logical, assuming it is accepted that the main goal is the preservation of life.

I don't think you can argue the logic, but we are by no means all persuaded by it. Indeed, some in those desperate situations have refused to eat the flesh of their dead companions, so condemning themselves to death. And returning survivors rarely seem confident that all will understand and be persuaded by the logic of their decision. In an almost analogous organizational situation, an argument to cut cost by cutting back on staff may be perfectly logical, assuming the priority is to preserve the life of the organization, yet may still be anathema to some present, even though they can see the logic.

The point that is sometimes missed is that just because something is logically correct it doesn't mean it is morally right. Organizational decisions, involving people, cannot be separated from moral decisions. In social situations, decisions based on "logic" are, a priori, no more valid than those based on values or beliefs. However, in many organizations logic trumps almost every other argument, and moral argument in particular is not always even allowed a seat at the table. When doing what is logical goes against our values, we can experience a sense of betrayal, of wrongness. Sometimes people find it hard to put their counter-argument to the "logic" into words, ending up with "I can't explain; it just feels all wrong." The experience of wrongness can be very visceral and embodied. Such feelings drive behaviour, frequently the behaviour that is labelled, harking back to Lewin, as "resistance" to change.

Psychological research in fact suggests that whatever we might declare to be the case, our choices in situations are rarely driven solely by logic; rather they are heavily influenced by emotion and values (Damasio, 2005). This suggests there isn't a neutral logical argument that will ensure that all see the light of the need for the change; rather there are more and less powerful voices in organizational systems, the "logic" of the more powerful tending to hold sway.

4. There is no need to take account of what has gone before

These change models are based on beliefs of the organization as a mechanical entity, and this sense of change as an engineering problem can be traced back to Taylor (1912) and is present in Lewin's work. For more on this see my earlier book (Lewis, Passmore, & Cantore, 2007). These models are frequently ahistorical and acontextual (Collins 1998). That is, they take little or no account of what has gone before, and they take no account of the "special circumstances" of the particular situation. Instead they are universal cures or panaceas. They can be applied anywhere, anytime, to any organization regardless of the particular organization's history or current state. This is essentially the big bang understanding of change: life starts anew at this point. This makes them particularly attractive to new brooms, of whom more later in Chapter 2.

5. People patterns can be engineered without psychological or social impact

If people are considered part of the change at all, they are considered as parts of the machine that can be moved about to predictable effect. Productivity is not supposed to be affected. There is little or no understanding of the cognitive and social energy that goes into reconfiguring mental models to accommodate or adapt to the changes. There is little to no understanding of the energy needed to learn new behaviours, and to suppress or override old patterns and habits. As a general rule, there is very little awareness of the many and varied emotional impacts of change, including glee, envy, excitement, frustration, or relief, as well as despair or uncertainty.

Yet, paradoxically, at some level it is understood that people may be affected by change, although the conversation about this is shaped by the idea of resistance to change. Those trying to implement change can, unconsciously, conceptualize resistance as a conscious choice that some people make in order to be difficult and obstructive. The reactions of the "resisters" are usually viewed through the prism of their perceived self-interest, allowing their objections to be dismissed by the change implementers as "they would say that, wouldn't they." In this way those resisting can be held responsible for their reactions and the demand is often made that they "shape up or ship out." Rarely are "resister" reactions to change recognized as psychological processes not always under conscious control, as fundamental adjustments of identity and purpose that take time and mental energy to assimilate. Neither are they often recognized as a spirited defence of valuable and vulnerable aspects of organizational life and culture. Even more rarely is an accommodation made allowing that performance may suffer as organizational energy is diverted to adjusting and reconfiguring.

6. The whole situation can be modelled

There is often a belief that the organization in its current state can be "mapped." The changes can then be imposed on the map. However, the map is not the territory. Any map of an organization is going to contain inaccuracies. Therefore, any plan based on that imperfect map is going to be subject to corrective feedback where the assumptions of the map proved faulty. Unexpected reactions or effects of implementing the plan therefore should be embraced as giving useful information about how things are, rather than interpreted as a mistake in the planning. More usually though, they are regarded as mistakes or errors leading the organization to divert energy into "clampdowns" to reduce "deviations" from the plan, or into playing "the blame game," where they decide who to blame for a lack of omniscience.

7. People dislike change and have to be sold it

It is true that, on the whole, people aren't widely enthusiastic about change that is forced upon them without consultation, especially if it also appears to make their life or working conditions worse. It is also true that people will often quickly become aware that if they point out the problems that the proposed change will cause, they will be labelled as a troublemaker or worse. Given this, they may passively comply rather than actively resist. This compliance is often confused with "buy-in."

People aren't widely enthusiastic about change

Stew Smith

The much repeated and highly prevalent belief that people are resistant to change often leads to a defensive and fearful approach to organizational change, inducing much girding of loins by managers before they go out to face the anticipated wrath of those affected by the change. However, if this were true, none of us would emerge from babyhood. We spend our whole lives in a state of change: allow me to welcome on to the stage at this point the process of aging. We often change our family set-ups (marry, leave home, have children), redecorate our homes, plan to be elsewhere (holidays, etc.), or embark on voluntary activities; or decide to write books. We are creatures of change and growth as well as creatures of habit. We are the most adaptable species the planet has yet produced. What is true is that change takes energy, and people don't necessarily always have the energy or inclination to engage with change. Frequently it is not change itself that is the issue but the effect imposed change can have on things that are important to us: autonomy, choice, power, desire, satisfaction, self-management, sense of competency, group status, sense of identity, and so on.

8. It is necessary to build burning platforms to achieve change

This belief is a natural successor to the one above. Since people don't like change, they have to be motivated into it through fear. Hence the often expressed need to "build a burning platform" to energize people towards the change. However, we might note that a natural response to a burning platform is blind panic or paralysing fear. People do not make great team decisions when they are panicking. They don't even make good personal decisions. Creating fear and anxiety as drivers for change can have unhelpful consequences in producing self-orientated, unthinking survival behaviour.

9. Resistance to change is a problem

Resistance to change is often labelled as problematic. Instead it should be viewed as a sign of engagement, of commitment. There are many truths in organizational life and they don't always align well. Some people may hold a different view about what is best for the organization. If they are prepared to risk conflict then they care enough to let you know.

10. Change cannot be implemented until you have thought through every step and have every possible question answered

This belief more than any other causes organizations endless problems as the expressed goal of perfect planning is unachievable yet the change process can't "begin" until it is achieved. This familiar "omniscience of the leader" (or leadership group) belief leads to exhaustive energy going into detailed forecasting and analysis of every possible impact and consequence: in the worse cases leading to paralysis by analysis. It slows things down, allows rumours to fill the information vacuum, and feeds feelings of disempowerment. Walking into an organization where there is huge awareness of "the need for change" and much talk about the change, yet where there is at the same time a sense that nothing can be done until "the plan is finally released" and where the release date of the plan has been delayed once or more already, is to encounter a readily recognizable state of "engines revving and no movement," or "wheels spinning and no traction." It is, in my experience, an undesirable state of anxiety, disempowerment, disengagement, and falling morale and productivity.

11. *The path to the future is just waiting to be uncovered*

Sometimes in change, leaders and planners act as if the future lies there waiting for us; that we have only to uncover the path and follow it. To believe this is to misunderstand the nature of time, and to confuse uncovering with creating. The future is in a constant state of creation, it doesn't exist until it is now. Our actions today affect or create tomorrow. How we understand the past affects how we conceive possibilities in the future. In this way we begin to see the creation of the future as an activity that takes place in a constant present. Creating the future starts with what we are doing today.

12. *You can control the communication about change within the organization*

This prevalent and mistaken "control" belief leads to embargoes on information sharing, "until we have decided everything" (see belief 10), and much investment in finding "the right words" to convey the story of the change. Meanwhile, people are free to make their own sense of what is happening, uninhibited by any corrective input from management.

Adherence to this belief can cause considerable difficulties for organizations, and particularly for leaders. For example, recently I was with the Group IT board of an international organization. Recent activity would make it clear to any observant member of this division that changes are afoot. For a start one of the big four consultancies is visibly around and involved in a large, future-oriented project. Sub-projects have been set up to examine alternative possible futures. Visits have been made to India, renowned for cheap and skilled IT labour. The team leaders present know their people are already putting two and two together and coming up with future scenarios that involve outsourcing and redundancies. They may well soon start asking difficult questions. What are the team leaders to say? This question, articulated at a team day, led to an interesting discussion illuminating how people navigate the boundaries between the story told and the story lived: trying to comply with the secrecy requirements while also accommodating the emerging group need for information.

In this situation, as is frequently the case, the official management line is that nothing has been decided, therefore there is no point in worrying about anything, and no need for a discussion as there is nothing to discuss. We can label this the *story told*. All well and good, except that people are active sense-makers who will come to their own judgement about whether the signs add up to anything significant. We can call this experience the *story lived*. By denying the necessity for a conversation about the difference between these two experiences, the organization also denies itself the chance to actively influence the sense being made of the things being observed. Without conversation it becomes impossible to reconcile the story lived and the story told since there is no acceptable meeting point. Prohibition of discussion is rarely an effective response to anxiety, working only to push things out of sight and out of reach of the leader's influence.

This group leader knows this and chooses to break organizational proto- col by coming clean with her team, giving a full, nuanced, and contextual account of activity, current thinking, and plans as she understands them to be at present. It is a complex picture, full of potential, hope, possibility, political sensitivities and uncertain outcomes. While trusting them with this confidential information she also articulates her sense of vulnerability at doing this, since by doing so she is privileging their need to know over confidentiality obligations to other colleagues. They, in turn, make it clear that they have found this sharing of what is presently known (and what isn't) immensely reassuring even in its uncertainty. In general, knowing is better than not knowing, as a lack of definite knowledge does not prevent the imagination from running riot. It is clear that this has been a very helpful conversation for everyone present.

Each team member is in turn leader of another team of people, the people most likely to be affected by future changes and whose anticipated questions partly stimulated the debate in the first place. Yet the guidance she gives in response to their concern about how they answer direct questions such as "Are we going to be made redundant?" is not to do as she has done, that is, to address that fear as a legitimate point of discussion, but rather to repeat the official line that "nothing has been decided yet." She expresses her hope that maintaining this line will "not set hares running about redundancies" that may or may not come to pass in the future. So the people she knows intimately, her team members, are treated as responsible adults who can manage ambiguity, uncertainty, and complexity. The others, less "real" maybe to her as individuals, are to be treated as those that can't be trusted in this way. This, of course, is not entirely her decision. It is more that her sense of obligation to her senior colleagues is greater than her sense of obligation to these "others" and so overrides it.

However, this attempt to keep specific information "out" of the system puts those now in possession of that specific information in an invidious position – something the people in this particular meeting were well aware of. The talk extends into an ethical space. How can I feel I am behaving ethically when I am withholding information? At what point does just following the corporate line slip into actively misleading people? What will this do to my relationship with people I know and like and who I believe trust me? Then, as the practicalities of different scenarios emerge, so does another question: "Is it right to earmark some people as 'the talent' who must be retained during this uncertainty (and so implicitly label others as 'not the talent')?"

Once people know, there is no unknowing. Unintentionally, the group leader has passed the burden of managing this balancing act of being party to privileged information from herself to them. And in these situations the danger of informal leakage is very high. The group leader herself knows this. As she said in a reflective conversation after the event, "my fear is that even if they say the right things they'll give things away." And she is right. The momentary hesitation in answering the straight questions "Are they considering outsourcing?" and "Will there be redundancies?" is all people need to have their question answered, whatever words may follow.

The intention behind the desire to stick to the party line is honourable. The group leader wants to honour her commitment to her senior colleagues; she also wants to spare people the pain of worry and uncertainty. She wants to protect the organization from the disruption of distracted people worrying about a future that may not happen. The trouble is people may well be doing this anyway, but underground.

Stew Smith

In many ways, it is easier to work with uncertainty when it is named and in the public space. We can't legislate for the sense people will make in situations, we can only hope to influence that sense-making. And we can only do that if we and they are part of the conversation. The danger in the very typical scenario outlined above is that the conversation goes on within the divisional membership and the leadership team are excluded from it. Two disconnected conversations emerge: the official leadership conversation and the hidden organizational one. When these become too disconnected it creates organizational problems.

13. You can control meaning created

Meaning is created, not dictated. I can *not* dictate to you how you are to understand things; I can only suggest. If I am unable to create a shared meaning with you then we are not aligned. All too often organizations try to dictate how their actions are to be interpreted by all.

14. To communicate about change is to engage people with the change

This belief leads to an over-emphasis on communicating about "the change." Staff hear managers talking endlessly about how important this change is, how big it is, how transformational it will be, yet no one seems to know what the change actually means for people. To be part of this scenario is to suffer a confused sense of "but what are we talking about?" This in itself is usually symptomatic of the fact that at this point there is only a fuzzy picture of what this much-heralded change will mean for people.

15. *Planning makes things happen*

This belief in "plan as action" fuels a plethora of projects and roadmaps and spreadsheets of interconnection, key milestones, tasks, measures, and so on. People can invest time and energy in these plans and activities fondly believing that they are "doing change." The plan is not the change. It is, at best, a connecting link between a dream of the future and present day action. All too often those involved in creating the plan for change believe this to be the most essential part of the process, worthy of extended time and effort, while implementation is seen as "just" a matter of communicating and rolling out the plan.

Plans are predicated on stories of hope and dreams of the future. Plans are lifeless without the charge of hope and dreams. Their production is indeed a change in the world and the experience of planning can be very changeful for those involved. However, when organizations talk about change they mostly mean the visible effect of people doing their work differently. In this sense, for organizations, change happens when people change their habitual patterns of communication and interaction in a meaningful and sustainable way.

16. *Project management is the way to achieve change*

Charles Smith (2007), an experienced project manager turned organizational psychologist, has performed a fantastic analysis of how successful project managers actually do project management compared to how they tell us they do it. In the process he has discovered some very useful ways of thinking about projects and the role they perform in organizational life. In particular he notes that successful project managers have an unrecognized project-craft that they call on to aid the delivery of the "formal plan." I highly recommend this very readable book and meanwhile have picked out 10 juicy gems of insight and wisdom that resonated with my experience (see Box 1.2).

Box 1.2　Project Management Insights

Effective project managers:

1. Help the organization develop a local language for talking about change, above and beyond PRINCE2 language: talk of swimlanes and stop/go gates doesn't cut it.
2. Recognize that projects are about managing uncertainty and complexity; they create stories of order to help keep chaos at bay.
3. Understand that the project is not real; it is a social construction.
4. Think in terms of negotiating among tribal loyalties rather than the blander "stakeholder management."
5. Know that tribal identities are strong and permanent; project identities are weak and temporary: projects are political alliances.
6. Understand that project action and talk is all about sense-making.
7. Appreciate that project artefacts – diagrams, maps, risk registers – are physical enactments of sense-making and are important for this purpose.
8. Know the people affected by, or involved in, the project in a meaningful way to be able to influence or negotiate with them, acting to enhance their sense of identity.
9. Are aware that the risk register is a political document reflecting power and choice, not a neutral record of fact.
10. Understand that a project is a social process.

Adapted from Smith (2007)

Conclusion

Change conceived in, and implemented from, this perspective runs a high risk of creating what Cheung-Judge and Holbeche refer to as "scar tissue" (2011, p. 200). This scar tissue being "resentful, cynical and disengaged 'survivor' employees who no longer trust the organization or its leaders and are unlikely to give of their best to the organization in the future" (2011, p. 200). This approach to change, predicated on mechanistic metaphors and a mid-twentieth-century appreciation of work, organization and the interconnectedness or otherwise of the world, is out of date, ineffectual and at worst positively harmful to organizations and all who sail in them.

2

The Challenge of Leadership

Recently I was working with the leadership team of a medium-sized UK business. They had been in decline for some years and, at the time I was briefly involved, were making a 0.5% profit on a turnover of £26m. The business was struggling and the managing director had led heroic efforts to sell their way out of trouble. By the time I was asked to help them he was working all hours and the senior staff were running on adrenaline. All activity was reactive, fire-fighting. Quite apart from the complicated history and politics of the organization, one of the things that became clear very early on was that there was no sense of a leadership team. The MD felt it was on his shoulders to "rescue" the organization, which he had done time and again by finding another sale. The trouble was the business he procured was not necessarily producing profit because the margin was very low and the factory operated in a very inefficient manner, meaning that any potential profits could easily be lost in damaged goods or quality errors. And so on they struggled, not quite on life support but getting uncomfortably close.

So the two first priorities seemed to me to be to create a leadership team from the other directors and senior managers, who were presumably being paid to take some of the pain, and to develop a strategy for the future. (There was no sense of a future, only an endless panic-inducing present.) At the same time "Group" started to take more interest in this subsidiary and sent the company a marketing specialist to help them. To begin I assembled 10 senior managers and we had a first development day together, which achieved a number of things. First, it introduced the idea to those present that they were the leadership team and so were, collectively, the people who needed to start the change. Second, it explored, using Appreciative Inquiry, the current status,

Positive Psychology and Change: How Leadership, Collaboration, and Appreciative Inquiry Create Transformational Results, First Edition. Sarah Lewis.
© 2016 John Wiley & Sons, Ltd. Published 2016 by John Wiley & Sons, Ltd.

hopes, aspirations, and beliefs about possibilities for the future, culminating in a first draft aspirational vision statement. Tentatively, hope was born that things could be better and that a difference could be made.

When we met for our second day together three months later, I was highly impressed by the shift in the group. It became apparent that people had made real changes in their working practices to help align their departments better with their colleagues' needs. Independently, the operations director was trans- forming the factory through the application of lean manufacturing principles and other efficiency technologies. The ship was moving. The finance director shared information about the financial picture, creating further common understanding of the challenge of the situation. However, many thorny questions were still being skirted around. Essentially these were to do with the identity of the company. Who is our customer? Who are we? Therefore what is our brand? How do we present ourselves? How do we target our marketing efforts? How do we best invest our energy? You might say that some of the key strategic questions were beginning to be identified by the group, with possible answers being tentatively discussed. However, these were questions that hadn't been named before, let alone discussed as a group. It seemed to me we were poised to head into a very productive third day that would flush out and engage with this core challenge of identity. I was keen to get the day set up fairly soon after this one, to maintain the good momentum.

As the day ended, with these questions to a large extent still open, the group- loaned marketing consultant put pressure on the MD to "make a decision about the vision, and the brand identity" and to write the plan and just tell them. There had been enough consultation (the implication was "time wasted") and now "someone," that is, the leader, "had to make a decision." The consultant wanted "the line drawn," and a shift from talking to decision-making and action. This way of thinking is, of course, predicated on a model of the organization as an entity of two parts: head and body. Within this model the body is not involved in thinking or decision-making, it is just there to follow orders (you can read more about these outmoded ways of understanding organizations in Lewis, Passmore, & Cantore 2007). This thinking, combined with a general understanding that leadership resides in individuals rather than being an active organizational dynamic, led her to believe that all leadership in the organization resided in the MD.

Unintentionally and potentially unhelpfully, she and I were offering two very different ideas of what effective leadership looked like. On the one hand, I was offering a vision of leadership as a consultative and collaborative process, one that initiates change more slowly to begin with but gathers momentum as the story of who we are, what we are about and what we need to do begins to cohere within the group and as the shared commitment to action develops. On the other hand, she was offering the model of the leader as the decisive person who takes the lead from the front and tells his or her leadership group how it is and what is going to happen, needing only compliance to achieve action. This encounter epitomizes the clash between a psychological view of leadership as a relational activity and an organizational science view of leadership as a formal position of power. Both of course are true. But it seems to me that the effectiveness of the second is dependent on the strength of the first.

"We'll be with you in a minute!"
Stew Smith

Introduction

Questions about leadership continue to fascinate us. What makes a good leader? How much influence do they really have? Is good leadership some sort of innate talent or is a trainable skill? What do we really value in our leaders? Do we value the right things? In this chapter I want to briefly examine some of the dominant ideas about leadership, then explore alternative metaphors of leadership before outlining the new thinking about effective, relational leadership undertaken from a positive psychology and Appreciative Inquiry perspective.

First, let me tell you about a piece of research that caught my eye recently. Early in 2014, British newspaper *The Guardian* ran a small piece entitled "MPs pick decisiveness as key trait in a prime minister" (2 January 2014). Further reading revealed that "MPs believe that being decisive is a more important trait than principles, honesty or intelligence (in leaders) …" Of the 156 MPs surveyed, 75% had chosen it as "one of the top three require- ments for being a successful occupant of 10 Downing Street [Prime Minister's office in the UK]." The survey, run by the Department of Politics and International Relations at Royal Holloway University of London (i.e., a repu- table institution), identified being principled as the second most important quality. Of course, this is a survey about what a rather select group want from their leaders rather than what actually makes a good leader. However, I believe this desire for decisive leadership is widespread. One might argue that it reflects rather poorly on the rest of us who just want someone to make the difficult decisions for us. The question this survey interestingly raises is, should decisiveness in leaders be the priority quality?

Should Decisiveness Be the Priority in Leaders?

Here is an example of decisiveness in action. I was one of four people meeting in a restaurant to have a meal and exchange some information. Three of us were there, discussing the options, whether to have starters and if so separately or shared, in a desultory manner, when the fourth person arrived. As she was taking off her coat, she picked up the menu and said "let's have the antipasti for starters," glanced briefly around the group, presumably saw nothing to dissuade her that this was a great idea, and, even as she was shaking her other arm out from her coat, attracted the waiter's attention and ordered it. That settled that then! In this situation this decisiveness was reasonably helpful to the group since this decision was incidental to the purpose of our being there; but on the political questions of whether to go to war, or to cut benefits, or to reorganize the health service, or the organizational ones of whether to restructure or to acquire a new business? Some might say that a little more appreciation of the complexity of these challenges, and a little less decisiveness, might be a good investment of time.

But such thoughtfulness might not have left our political leaders looking so decisive and so convincingly in charge. And here is a key leadership dilemma both in politics and in organizations. Among other things, leadership is a performance with multiple audiences. Different audiences evaluate leadership differently. Which audience is our leader to play to? How can he or she balance the demands of different audiences? The question and the responses to it make up a big part of the drama of organizational life.

So to return to the story that opened this chapter, in this instance, the leader was caught not only between two "advisors" with different mental models of organizations, but also between two advisors working for different commissioners, and so two different audiences. The marketing consultant was working for "Group," who were demanding decisive individual leadership action. Something needed to be seen to be done, and that something looked like a decisive written plan right now, if not yesterday. I, on the other hand, felt my commissioning agents to be "the senior management team." I believed strongly that they would benefit most from more collective development to allow them to continue their journey of developing clear collective accountability for the future of the organization. From my perspective, change was already happening and, in a short time, an account of intended future direction and activity could be written (a plan). From her perspective, nothing had yet happened, nor would it until there was a plan, and time was marching on in a situation of some urgency. Once there was a plan, only then could change begin. I attempted to suggest that it was possible to act in a sophisticated way that would meet the needs of Group for evidence of "action" and allow the senior team to continue on their co-creation of change journey. In this I failed and I was not invited to return to the organization.

Leadership is a performance with multiple audiences that takes place in a dynamic and changing context. It is a complex, challenging, highly visible organizational role and we struggle to understand how it can be done well. Over the years many different leadership models have been put forward, none answering our questions entirely satisfactorily. At present we seem to have reached some agreement that different approaches to leadership are appropriate for different situational, organizational, or leadership challenges. This is known as a contingency theory of leadership, which in itself contains various different models (Shackleton & Wale, 2000). This is an understanding of leadership that rather suggests that any leader needs to understand the context he or she has entered before trying to make any changes. However, one of the consequences of leadership being a performance behaviour is the perceived demand to be "seen to be making a difference." This need frequently militates against a leader having the opportunity to truly understand a situation before trying to change it.

The Need to Make a Difference

The demand that leaders demonstrate leadership by making a difference, and quickly, is exemplified by the emphasis on the importance for newly appointed leaders of the first 100 days of leadership. While this is a key transition time worthy of careful attention, the perceived value of decisiveness, combined with an acute awareness of interested audiences, can, and frequently does, become expressed as "a need to be seen to be doing something." This demand to be seen to be doing something means that very often new leaders go in ablaze with excitement about the new things they can bring and the changes they can make. This is known as the ability to "hit the ground running." Unfortunately, this can lead to a disregard of the value of what is already present in the organization, resulting in a number of common, unhelpful, new broom behaviours (see Box 2.1). What other ways do we have of understanding leadership that allow us to conceptualize and enact it differently? If our current metaphors based on "organization as machine" and "organization as army" are no longer fit for purpose then how should we think of organizations?

Box 2.1   Common New Broom Behaviour

The pressure on new leaders or senior appointments to make an impact, and quickly, is tremendous. The organization has spent time and money attracting, selecting, and securing the chosen candidate; now they want to see the value they have bought. It's a brave person who can hold fire while they take time to look and learn; take time to find out what works here, and how it does; to find out who the people are who really ensure the work gets done; to find out who is brave enough to deliver bad news. This knowledge is often hidden, while, to new eyes, what doesn't work, who doesn't look or behave like management, and who too often isn't at the end of their phone or at their desk, is all too obvious.

In their attempts both to improve things and to make a mark quickly, new brooms frequently commit one or all of these mistakes:

1. *They believe in year zero.* New brooms often act as if everything that happened before their arrival is irrelevant. They have no interest in why things are the way they are, they know only that they are wrong. The wholesale change that follows as they (re)create the organization in the image of their last organization, or a textbook organization, tramples over history, accidentally throwing out precious babies with the bath water.

2. *They create tomorrow's problems.* "Today's problems are yesterday's solutions," said Senge (1990). It follows that today's solutions are tomorrow's problems. New brooms, in their enthusiasm to create new solutions, often inadvertently create the foundations for the next set of problems, for the next new person to solve. The experience on the ground can be of repeated extreme pendulum swings.

3. *They create ground zero.* This approach often accompanies the year zero mentality: since nothing created before I arrived is of value, nothing will be lost in its destruction. Creating ground zero usually starts with the drawing up of a new organizational chart followed by frenzied activity restructuring, firing, and rehiring, redrawing all paper work (job descriptions, etc.), and retraining to create the brave new world. All too often the map changes but the terrain remains the same.

4. *They have the answer.* At last our leader is in a position of power where they can put this great new idea they have come across into practice: lean management principles, team-based working, business

(Continued)

Box 2.1 *Continued*

process reengineering (BPR). The list of management fads from which to choose is endless. The trouble is that there is no one right way to organize. Organizations are full of irresolvable tensions, they are dynamic entities that flux and flow, seeking to resolve the irresolvable. In this way they can keep everything in play. Once there is only one answer, only one way, the benefits of equifinality and fluidity are lost.

5. *They love tidiness.* This approach is often related to having the answer. To the newcomer the evolved solutions are messy. The organizational chart is not neat, things aren't arranged logically, the rationales for the way things are done are idiosyncratic, it doesn't seem equable, and everything is an acceptable exception. Like Kim and Aggie, of British TV programme *How Clean is Your House* fame, they tear through the mess, creating order, boxing things up, cloning and standardizing. Everyone must start at 8.30, no exceptions. Bang goes the best customer service girl we ever had, who can't get in until 8.45. Tough!

6. *They cut through the Gordian Knot.* Our new broom doesn't have the time or the inclination to engage with office politics, so pretends they don't exist. As they set about finding out what's what, they dismiss any notion of being manipulated by the players. It's easier to take everything at face value and then apply their own superior 20/20 vision to get to the truth. Often the people who lose out are those who really don't know how to play politics and who strive to deliver a truth, as everyone else angles to demonstrate their irreplaceable value.

7. *They believe context is irrelevant.* Leaders who believe they are impervious to office politics often also believe that context is irrelevant. They have a plan for change. There will be winners and losers. It's very cold out in the employment market at present. The leader is in a very powerful position, determining people's futures. Without a lively awareness of this context, it is very easy to mistake people's quest to retain job security for the expression of a heartfelt endorsement of the new leader's genius and a real desire for change. From here it is all too easy to get rid of dissenting voices.

8. *They fire the opposition.* The new leader is insecure: they need to prove their worth. They don't want to hear that their plan has flaws, that there are benefits to the current, irregular, way of doing things. Expression of such thoughts is heard as disloyalty; it is easier to label such dissenters as resistant to change.

9. *They devalue social capital.* The new leader is seduced by the organizational chart and all the paperwork that dictates who must report to whom, how the job must be done. Focused on this, they fail to notice the intricate and delicate patterns of relating communication, information flow, and informal problem-solving that facilitate effective working. Seeing such informal networks as essentially irrelevant to achieving the task, they (re)arrange people without regard to these informal relationships and patterns of communication. The social capital of the organization is reduced, its efficacy damaged.

10. *They disregard sense-making as a powerful change process.* Too often a new broom is overly focused on the behaviour change they require, and they work hard to "make" people do things differently. Failing to appreciate that our behaviour is related to how we make sense of the world, they invest little time in working to change people's mental maps, their experience of reality. They work to drive new behaviour into people rather than release the potential for new behaviour that resides within people.

What Does Shifting the Organizational Metaphor Mean for Leaders?

Cheung-Judge and Holbeche reviewed the leadership literature over a seven-year period from 2003 to 2010, examining the emerging trends in how leadership was being thought about, viewed, and prescribed. From this review they note that "leadership is increasingly defined not as what the leader *is or does* but rather as a process that *engenders and is the result of relationships*" (my italics) (2011, p. 282). This chimes with Wheatley's quantum physics metaphor of organization, where she notes that "In the quantum world, *relationship* is the key determiner of everything" (1999, p. 11). Cheung-Judge and Holbeche also note that there is "a growing challenge to the 'one size fits all' normative approaches to leadership against which leaders can be developed and measured" (2011, p. 282). And further that "emphasis is shifting away from the 'heroic' leaders towards the leadership system that makes it possible for people at all levels to exercise leadership" (2011, p. 282). In this they further agree with Wheatley, who wrote, "The era of the rugged individual has been replaced by the era of the team player" (1999, p. 39). These different sources seem to be observing a similar phenomenon, and are arguing for change. Particularly, they are suggesting that we need to make a shift from a concentration on the individual leader to a focus on the "leadership system." What does such a shift mean for our understanding of leadership, and how might it be defined?

New Definition of Leadership

In an issue of *AI Practitioner* devoted to exploring positive and appreciative leadership, Campbell and Radford suggest that "More than at any other time, the ability to lead is about standing back from the traditional view of leading; it is about being open with everyone about the complexities of a situation, making visible the uncomfortable options, supporting others in recognizing and grappling with the ethical dilemmas involved in facing difficult decisions, and more than anything discovering and staying true to one's own core values so that actions are transparent and authentic" (2014, p. 4). If we take this as a temporary statement of what "fit for the C21st" leadership may look like, then we can ask, how is it achieved?

Doing Leadership Differently

Cheung-Judge and Holbeche note that leaders lead through their "words and deeds" (2011, p. 281), in other words by what they say and what they do. The simplicity of this observation belies its profundity. Words and deeds are all any of us have. Leadership is not some mystical force; it is a product of the patterns of our words and deeds in relationship with others. In the same vein, Wheatley argues that words and deeds create "fields" within which behaviour takes place. The idea of fields in this sense comes from quantum physics. Wheatley offers a case study to illuminate what she means. During a retail assignment, she noted how a strong sense of customer service was present in some stores but not others. This sense of service was intangible but quickly recognizable to all. It was created through the store managers' "words and deeds" for they "filled space with clear and consistent messages about how the customers were to be served" (1999, p. 55). She notes that "The field was strong in its congruence; it influenced behaviour only in one direction" (1999, p. 55). She offers a strong argument that leadership is about creating fields of influence that make certain behaviours more likely, with congruence as a key determiner of effect.

I saw this in action in a school once. As the Deputy Head and I were walking along a school corridor, the bell rang and young people shot out into our path like grapeshot from a cannon. Even as we continued our conversation and ambulation, he broke off every few seconds to inform someone of the discrepancy of their behaviour (running, for instance) from the expected standard (walking, in this case). His deeds were a live embodiment of the words in the school rules and charter. He created a consistent field that influenced behaviour in one direction.

Stew Smith

This definition highlights leadership as a visible, relational, influential set of processes that produce probabilities. It emphasizes the phenomenon of leadership as lying at least as much in the moment-to-moment small interactions and decisions as in the big set pieces of strategic planning announcements. The question of interest becomes: What is different about some leaders' words and deeds? How do some inspire followership and commitment even in difficult situations while others find this hard even in good times? What do they do differently, or do that is different? Much of our understanding of alternative conceptions of leadership comes from the emerging study of appreciative and positive leadership; the leadership associated with successful Appreciative Inquiry activity and explored through positive psychology studies. Both these fields have identified some of the common characteristics of "new" styles of leadership.

Characteristics of a New Leadership Style

1. They work with and through relationships with others

We recognize many admirable qualities in those who survive experiences as isolated castaways, but leadership isn't usually one of them. One of the reasons for this is that leadership is a "social act" (Lewis & Moore, 2011, p. 4). Interestingly, it can be seen as a social act of two parts: leadership is both claimed and granted. DeRue, Ashford, and Cotton (2009) note that leadership claiming acts include taking the seat at the head of the table or asserting one's expertise in a particular domain, while leadership granting acts include deferring to the leader's opinion or seeking out his or her help or expertise. Both sets of behaviours contribute to an individual's develop-ment of a leadership identity. Followership behaviour is important in creating leadership.

"Effective leaders are likely to increase followers' commitment to shared goals and also enhance follower satisfaction" (Greene-Shortridge & Britt, 2013, p. 571). This is a point worth stressing since historically in the "people management" arena the ability to "manage direct reports" has been seen as the key skill to concentrate on, certainly more important than some ill-defined notion of "relational ability." Yet "managing" direct reports suggests a very particular type of relationship: one based on order, direction and monitoring. It says nothing about mutuality, trust, or the complexity of human relationships. It is located firmly in the historical, Tayloristic perspective of organization being the art of managing a rational set of resources, including the people. (If you are unfamiliar with Fredrick Taylor and the long reach of his thoughts on organizations, please see Chapter 1 of Lewis, Passmore, & Cantore, 2007). This perspective is at the root of the longstanding debate about the difference between management and leadership.

This debate becomes an increasing irrelevance as all "management" roles that include responsibility for people and their work or performance by default require the operation of a leadership/followership process. Whatever level of management we are referring to, attending to people, and their needs, is the job. It may sound obvious but it can involve a huge mind-shift for some people, especially those who have been promoted on the basis of their individual skill and expertise and not their relational abilities. There are many who, ill-suited to people management yet unable to resist the allure of promotion, cling desperately to the hope that the heart of their job is still fixing machines (or manipulating figures, or designing IT systems, etc.), at which they are exceptionally good, and not having to deal with people and their endless stream of problems and needs, at which they are exceptionally bad and about which they know little and, to be frank, care even less.

Wheatley quotes a friend of hers who noted that "Power in organizations is the capacity generated by relationships" (1999, p. 39). This is exactly the point Cooperrider makes in his call for us to refigure our understanding of organizations and their wider systems as a strengths economy (Cooperrider & Godwin, 2012). When we can reconfigure the way we work through combining and recombining our strengths, we produce greater capacity. However, this ability to co-create greater capacity in this way is predicated on relationships. It is through relationships that we know the strengths of others, negotiate their support, and create the desire of people to work together.

Baker, Cross, and Wooten identified positive energy networks in organizational systems, with particular individuals at their heart (2003). Later, Baker found that high-performing organizations have three times more positive energizers than average organizations (2004). Positive relationships are "a generative source of enrichment, vitality, and learning" (Dutton & Ragins, 2009, p. 3). The quality of relationships will affect the quality of leadership, the two are inseparable. It is through the quality of their relationships with others that leaders get things to happen. However, effective leaders don't just attend to the relationships between themselves and others, they also attend to relationships between others across the organization.

2. They work to create and influence the social context of the organization

Relationships don't occur in a vacuum, they exist in a social space. Social spaces have their own rules, norms, and ways of behaving. Within different social spaces people behave together differently, and this is also the concern of the leader. Whitney, Trosten-Bloom, and Rader suggest that the appreciative leadership task is "to become relationally aware, to tune into patterns of relationship and collaboration – that is, to see, hear, sense and affirm what is already happening in order to best relate to it and perform with it" (2010, p. 6).

Cameron talks about this as the leadership activity of creating a positive climate. He gives a case study where a popular leader, expelled in a power shift, is recalled a few years later when the organization is in difficulty. He finds, on his return, decimated finances and job eliminations (redundancies) in place. Rather than letting a negative climate develop in this situation, he works to develop strong relationships, open and honest communication, and a focus on the meaningfulness of their hospital work. The organization institutionalizes forgiveness, optimism, trust, and integrity as expected behaviours. This emphasis on organizational virtues is correlated with the turnaround in the organization's fortunes, its rapid recovery from the difficult redundancies, and its emergence as one of the top 25 best places to work in the Fortune rankings (Cameron, 2003). A positive work climate has also been found to enhance decision-making, productivity, creativity, social integration, and prosocial behaviours (Bolino, Turnley, & Bloodgood, 2002; Rhoades & Eisenberger, 2002). Positive social relations are also good for people, positively affecting hormonal, cardiovascular, and immune systems (Hefferon, 2013; Lewis, 2014).

3. They encourage leadership as a distributed organizational phenomenon

Positive and appreciative leaders understand that leadership potential, possibility, and actuality don't lie only with formal leadership positions: leaders can emerge in many and any different social group situations. However, in many organizations any perceived bid to offer leadership by those outside the formal hierarchy is regarded as a threat, an organizational challenge to power. Even at best it is likely to be regarded as misguided activity rather than as resourcefulness. However, some leaders have begun to realize that other acts of leadership within an organization can be regarded as an expansion of the leadership capacity of the organization rather than as a dangerous alternative leadership pattern. Things happen so fast in most organizational sectors that organizations need to be adept at noticing changes, and at responding in an appropriate and coordinated way. An expanded leadership capacity enhances this responsiveness: organizations that adapt through lots of little acts of leadership that occur simultaneously in a coordinated and coherent manner are likely to be more nimble at change than those that rely on big acts of directive leadership by a few people. Leadership needs to become an abundant property of the organization.

Such an organization, identified by Raelin (2005) as "leaderful," is collaborative rather than controlling and is compassionate rather than dispassionate. Its effectiveness is also highly dependent on the co-creation of a strong shared sense of direction, purpose, culture, vision, and so on that holds the field together so allowing discrete acts to be collectively coherent.

Gastaldi shares a story that reveals the power of relationship to encourage connection and release leadership. He was working with a high-quality meat and related foods producer in Italy, Pineda Carni, S.p.A. The pace of growth was creating some strain on the organization; in particular there was increased internal conflict between the sales and warehouse function. Customer service was being adversely affected. With some encouragement the organizational leaders set up some system-wide working days. These days were attended by people from all across the organization. Gastaldi describes a pivotal moment during this process when "Massimo [a front line staff member] stood up and asked for the microphone. While looking intensely at his colleagues (sales people), his boss and everyone else, he said, 'We must realize that our friends in the warehouse, and the others who drive our trucks every day, 70 people … have some damn hard problems and we have been ignoring them! It is about time we do something with them!'" (2011, p. 24).

This was a call for coordinated action issued by a member of the organization from a different department, not one of the formal leaders. Their problem had become our problem. Gastaldi identifies Massimo's leadership act as one that triggered a deep change in the organization by offering a new model of organizational member behaviour where everyone can take the lead to resolve or improve things. In this way, a leader becomes redefined as someone able to offer leadership, that is, is someone who listens, who brings forward difficult issues, who considers him- or herself accountable for challenges across the whole organization not just in his or her own section, someone who supports those in need and connects people across organizational divides. The significance of this is huge. In many organizations there persists the strong belief that leadership (and so the power to change things) lies always with the next layer of management higher up in the organization. This concrete sense of disempowerment is certainly observable in nominally "senior management teams" and sometimes even at board level. It is usually expressed as, "We would love to do (or stop doing) something but its *they* who hold the power to change it." "Who," I ask these senior position holders, "is the *they* of whom you speak?" After some debate I find myself asking, for them, "Who are they if not we?" Frequently an eye-opening moment, it can be a hard question to answer and takes us straight into the challenge of organizational culture. Leadership is a cultural issue.

When leaders begin to grasp the idea that they can call on the "distributed leadership" of their organization to help with the challenges of leadership, they sometimes lurch from trying to do it all themselves to bailing out completely. Kimball and her team, working with a hospital, found that when they encouraged leaders to step back a bit to make space for others to come forward "a few leaders had difficulty letting go of their familiar role of telling people what to do." However, "to our surprise, a bigger problem was leaders who 'got' the idea that they needed to create a more bottom-up process but thought that meant staying away from the initiative altogether" (2011, p. 37). It doesn't. Rather, as Marcia Worthing, one-time Senior Vice President of Human Resources and Corporate Affairs at Avon Products, explains, it means becoming "a proponent of letting things evolve while still maintaining strategic direction" (Schiller & Worthing, 2011, p. 20). This can be seen as another expression of the core Appreciative Inquiry concept that co-creating a shared "dream" of the future is a way of creating a motivating force for change. The Appreciative Inquiry dream process can be seen as contributing to the development of an imaginative, multi-faceted strategic direction.

4. *They use their attention to focus organizational effort*

Not all leaders understand the powerful ability they have to shape things purely through the exercise of their attention and the investment of their time. Kimball, discussing the leadership behaviours that make it possible for leaders to support others to take initiative and leadership, identifies "showing up" as one of the key behaviours. She notes that you "demonstrate that you value and respect what other people are doing by simply being there" (2011, p. 38). In this way the focus of leaders' attention can be seen as a primary culture-embedding process (Schein, 2004).

However, many leaders don't see attention in this dynamic, influential, proactive way but rather as a reactive or neutral thing: they attend to what needs their attention, or to what is there. To understand the influence of something as seemingly intangible as attention on organizational processes such as growth, change, and development is to understand the organization as a social phenomenon, as something socially constructed. This understanding is an important underpinning principle of Appreciative Inquiry.

Social constructionism, as this understanding of social realities is known, argues that social reality is constructed by the people in the social system. In essence what this means is that the things we, as a group, pay most attention to are the things that loom largest in our understanding of the world. Other groups, who pay more attention to other things, will see, and experience, the world differently. Very importantly, we act on our projection of the world: the world as we understand it to be. In this sense "reality" is constructed in our conversation. This view of socially constructed reality stands in contrast to the idea that reality exists "out there" in some immutable form that everyone sees and experiences in the same way.

I know that if you haven't come across this idea before it sounds a bit bizarre. Yet a moment's thought demonstrates that we really can't pay equal attention to everything that exists in our world. There is just too much going on in terms of sensory input: sounds, vision, smell, touch, and so on. We filter out stuff all the time so that we can concentrate on particular things. We make choices all the time about what to attend to. Tom Rath reports that we experience 19,200 moments in a day (2015) and Shawn Achor reports that "scientists estimate that we remember only one in every 100 pieces of information we receive; the rest effectively gets filtered out" (2011, p. 94) In that sense our brains, as he puts it, are like "spam filters" (p. 94).

Leaders in the new paradigm understand this. They recognize they can consciously choose what they attend to. They can choose to take a world view that is positive and life-affirming, focused on spotting success and abundance, rather than one focused only on spotting deficit and failure. They also recognize that the focus of their attention will influence the focus of the attention of others. Schiller expresses it well saying, "Attitude is a choice. A hundred times a day we can look at things one way or the other" (Schiller & Worthing, 2011, p. 20). Cameron notes that positive leaders are unusual in that "they choose to emphasize the uplifting and flourishing side of organizational life, even in the face of difficulty … In the absence of such an emphasis, negative inclinations overwhelm the positive and a negative climate is the default option" (Cameron 2008b cited in Cameron 2008a, p. 21).

Appreciative leaders choose to look appreciatively. Positive leaders choose to look for the positive. In this way they grow the best of their organization. However, the ability to do this, and the realization of the necessity of doing so, can't be taken for granted. Too often I've helped an organization with a development event in which much time and money has been invested, only to return a few weeks later to find that management don't know how the energy and agreed actions from the day have had an impact. They don't know because they haven't asked. They haven't asked because it's not in their day job, which they understand to be managing problems. It is assumed that as people have said they will make changes, fired with the energy of the day, they will. Sadly, this doesn't follow. They will want to, they will intend to, but the forces ranged against their ability to do so are considerable. To ensure that the fire lit on the development day continues to burn, the leadership needs to be paying attention. They need to be, as Bushe puts it, "tracking and fanning" activity (2001, p. 125). That is, tracking initial small changes and fanning these initial small embers of evidence into a belief in their ability to really make a difference. In this way leaders amplify early signs of change so it can be seen and heard around the organization. One way leaders can direct attention to the things they want to grow is to keep asking good questions about those things.

5. They believe that asking questions is more important than giving answers

Good leaders ask good questions, of themselves, of others, and of the context. A good question helps people think new thoughts, which is a necessary precursor to doing new things. They are generative. Good questions can also help people appreciate other people differently by bringing different aspects of their life, skills, experience, or personality into the room (see Box 2.2).

In more general terms, appreciative leaders set the agenda by focusing attention "through the questions they ask" (Whitney *et al.*, 2010, p. 31). "Asking a question is an act of engagement" (p. 43) and when people from different parts of the organization interview each other inquiry can be a "silo buster" (p. 52). Cooperrider describes this focus on the appreciative

**Box 2.2   Characteristics of Appreciative
and Generative Questions**

Appreciative and generative questions are questions that:

- direct attention towards the positive
- unleash new accounts so creating generative stories
- focus attention on what you want more of
- bring different aspects of organisational life into focus
- identify strengths
- identify the positive core of the organization
- are context specific, resonating with language meaningful to the organisation.

and positive as an organizational "appreciative mindset" and talks about the "exponential inquiry effect" of asking positive and appreciative questions that works by "establishing the new" while simultaneously "eclipsing the old" (2015). To leaders brought up on a model of the leader as the one with the answers, accessing this mindset does not come easy. As Whitney and colleagues note, "Inquiry requires daily practice: to ask more and to tell less" (2010, p. 29). Yet it is such an efficient use of the limited resource of leader time and energy. Taking the time to frame a provocative, positive, connecting, generative question can spark off a virtuous circle of innovative thinking, connections, and excitement that generates new thinking and motivation to change something; so much less energy-depleting than having to have the answers to everything. This ability to see leadership as the art of asking questions rather than as the art of having the answers might seem like a small thing but it is huge with many virtuous circle spin-offs.

6. They see human imperfections as an asset

People drive other people mad. They are so imperfect: they don't listen, they don't remember, they get distracted, they have their own priorities … the list of human imperfections is endless. We see these as imperfections because we mistake people for machines. Machines are very good at doing what they are designed to do; they don't need reminding, or refocusing, or re-motivating, they are set to go and they go.

People just aren't like that. And the human things that get in the way of being machine-like are what make us great: we have lively minds and are curious, we care about things, we have imaginations and we have feelings. We need to recognize that people are, from a machine perspective, imperfect and be grateful that, from a human perspective, they are human. All of these deviation-inducing features – excitability, emotionality, distractibility – are part of the human ability to sense-make, to create new things, to be tenacious in the face of challenge, to add value and generally to be extraordinary. So, either we fight against human imperfection, or we accept it or even embrace it.

It is only when we embrace it that we are truly able to appreciate, and work with, diversity. Diversity at its best isn't tolerance for difference; it's wonderment at the talents, strengths, and abilities of others. Clearly, to be able to wonder at these features we have first to be able to see them. To be able to see them we have to stop looking for what isn't there, and start looking at what is. The human desire to "change people" is endemic. Many of us marry someone "for who they are" and spend the next 20 years trying to make them someone else: someone tidy, or thoughtful, or financially astute. Similarly, with our staff we can spend a lot of energy trying either to make them fit the role-shaped gap left by the previous incumbent, or into mini-models of ourselves. It can take a long time to truly realize that these projects are doomed to failure, that they frequently lead instead to conflict, eroded morale and motivation, and poor performance.

7. They work with what they've got

A while ago, on a radio programme, someone said that research had shown that, "The happiest married women aren't those with the best husbands, but those who make the best of the husband they've got." And so it is with organizations. When people are recruited they are generally thought to be at least fit for the job if not the best person for the job, yet somehow, even a short time later, the appeal and fit may not be so obvious. It is not uncommon to find managers in a position of really wanting to "fire the whole lot of them and start again," so frustrated are they with some aspect of work or performance. Many things may have contributed to this state of affairs, but given that such wholesale "fresh starts" are rarely available as the answer, another way forward must be found. A great place to start is in discovering the best of what you've got, and how what you've got can be at its best. This means focusing less on job descriptions and what they "should" be good at, and more on their actual abilities. It means less telling and exhortation of how things "should" be, and more inquiry and listening to find out how things are. In particular, it demands a focus on what in their work is motivating, what is facilitating their progress and what is obstructing their efforts to get the job done.

While I have discussed strengths in more detail elsewhere (Lewis, 2011, 2012), we can note here that the idea of working with strengths rather than job descriptions can be remarkably challenging for organizations conceptually. In addition, since managers are rarely practised in such strengths rather than role description-based conversations, even when the spirit is willing the ability may be weak. Despite the growing evidence that conversations between managers and subordinates about strengths increase performance, still 68% of managers are having the wrong conversation with people (Polly, 2015). Given the proved difference it makes, developing the strengths conversation is a key organizational priority. When individual and organizational strengths are pulled together in intelligent ways then organizational diversity becomes a key feature of an organization's collective intelligence. Such an organization is operating as an economy of strengths.

To my mind this phrase conjures up a vision of an organization where people's strengths are well known, where job roles are built around people's strengths, where asking for help with the bits of your job you aren't energized by is encouraged and seen as a sign of maturity not of laziness, and where people spend most of their time motivated by opportunities to apply their strengths at work. Positive and appreciative leaders recognize individual strengths and weaknesses and work to combine them effectively.

For example, by studying great organizations, Cameron identified that one of their defining characteristics was that of affirmation: they demonstrated an affirmative bias (2008a). What he means by this is that they work to affirm the best in people. To be able to do that you have to be able to spot the best in people. And to be able to do that you have to look for it. From the Appreciative Inquiry literature comes the notion of developing an appreciative eye, that is, the ability to notice what is good, what is going right and what is working, whether in a situation or in people. Whitney and colleagues identify that "Appreciative leaders ... look through appreciative eyes to see the best of people" (2010, p. 7). The best in people is connected to their strengths. Somehow we are all very good at spotting what is missing in people, what they aren't so good at; somewhat fewer of us are good at spotting what they do bring and what they are good at.

8. They have a moral compass

Avolio, Griffith, Wernsing, and Walumbwa identified four key characteristics of authentic leaders by referring to historical accounts of what had been recognized as good leadership (2010). One of these was having a strong moral compass (the others being: relational transparency, adaptive self-reflection and balanced processing). Schiller and Worthing point out the relationship between this strong moral sense of right and wrong and values: "Values provide us with a 'true north'. They point us in a direction. We all have some non-negotiable values; those things we will not do or say 'no matter what'. They are the values that define our core" (2011, p. 18). Burnes and Cooke note, "Only leaders and organizations with a strong moral compass are likely to be able to resist the siren call of short-term expediency in order to promote long-term sustainability" (2012, p. 1417).

Integrity, another way of describing a moral compass, is one of the five key appreciative leadership qualities noted by Whitney and colleagues (2010). They suggest that followers know when leaders are on the path of integrity. I think their characterization of what happens when people sense a lack of integrity in leadership is worth quoting in full.

> When you are off the path of integrity, people sense it. They see it in your actions: when the way you relate to people minimizes them, belittles them, or even harms them. They hear it in your words and the tone of your voice when you make promises you cannot deliver upon. They feel it when you are short on emotional intelligence, avoid conflict, blame others, or express

anger inappropriately. When you are off the path of integrity, people move away from your ideas, your way of working, and you. They seek out others whom they can respect. When you are off the path of integrity you become a role model for what not to do. People learn and perform in spite of you. (2010, p. 158)

When you are off the path of integrity, people sense it.

Stew Smith

Maintaining integrity as a leader is not easy, especially in the politicized power-driven atmosphere of many higher organizational spheres. It is equally a challenge in highly changeable and uncertain conditions. One of the ways we demonstrate integrity is to ensure that words, body language, and actions are clearly in alignment. It is this alignment that gives words their power. The old adage "sticks and stones may break my bones but words will never hurt me" is often interpreted as denying the power of words to have impact. It is more helpful to understand it for what it is, a defensive cry of pain against the power of words by someone who is really hurting: a magic incantation to lessen the pain. If words really had no impact we wouldn't need to declaim against their power so vehemently. Make no mistake, words really matter.

9. *They understand the power of words*

Appreciative and positive leaders use words to help create the workplace culture they want. Such leaders truly understand the power of words; they understand how their use influences the sense we make together, the social context we create. This is not always obvious to people who somehow assume that words just carry predetermined messages; that words are in no way creative or generative.

Appreciative and positive leaders recognize the importance of using words wisely for they create feelings, motivation, and connection which impact on engagement, behaviour, and performance, not to mention wellbeing. Cameron notes how positive leaders pay attention to language so that terms such as "reconciliation," "compassion," "humility," "courage," and "love" are acceptable in the organization's vocabulary, as well as "ambition," "drive," and "competitiveness" (2008a, p. 29). Cameron identifies positive communication as one of the distinguishing features of positive leadership, arguing that such communication "occurs in organizations when affirmative and supportive language replaces negative and critical language" (2008a, p. 51). Which isn't to say that course correction feedback can't be given – of course not, it is essential – just that it is delivered rather differently. Whatever they are doing, leaders need to use positive talk, minimizing criticism and negativity, and instead using positive feedback and expressions of support.

Being conscious of the effect of language on organizations has two main facets. What matters is not just *what* you talk about together but also *how* you talk together. As was noted earlier, it is possible to choose what to focus on: problems or opportunities; causes for despair or hopefulness; what can be done or what can't be done. These choices are expressed through the medium of words and language. We noted earlier that leaders use words and deeds to achieve cohesion, direction, and coordinated action with their followers. Of this duo, words are often dismissed as the lesser powerful, and it is true that actions can drown out the power of words when they are not aligned; that when the chips are down actions speak louder than words. However, it is the alignment with actions, with positive purpose, and with good intent, that amplifies and magnifies the power of words to help us make good sense together. The approaches we will be looking at later in the book are predicated on the power of words to create movement and change. However, they are only truly effective when they are genuinely aligned with personal and organizational intent.

10. They use stories

Appreciative leaders understand the power of stories. In an organizational context stories can be read as "accounting," that is, a process for giving account of what is going on, what has happened, or what we desire. Organizations are full of stories, potentially different accounts of different realities. They are a tremendous organizational resource for understanding and sense-making, for motivation, for dreaming, for innovation, and for connection. The art is in choosing which of the many available stories to focus on, to repeat, to amplify, and to broadcast. People often don't fully appreciate the choices they have in this regard. We mistake stories for truth. Think of it like this. Reality is a many-faceted diamond. It is something real, hard, immutable, yet it has many different, connected faces. At any one point one "face" is, as it were, staring us in the face, and yet there are many others, above, below, behind where we are looking, hidden in shadow, or blinding us with dazzle. We only have to shift our gaze, or move, to see a different face, yet we are still looking at the same thing, only from a different perspective. So it is with the connection between truth and accounts of truth (stories). We can talk about the same thing differently and still be in the realm of "truth"; we are choosing to take a different perspective rather than just accepting the one that stares us in the face right now. The stories an organization values, chooses to tell and repeat are an important aspect of its culture.

The use of stories, legends, myths, and parables about important events and people is one of the cultural reinforcement mechanisms mentioned by Schein (2004) in his exploration of organizational culture. Stories are a fantastic way to convey information, aspiration, example, emotion, values, and many other important things in a way that is much more compelling, for most, than a list of statements. Stories hold culture. The stories the organization tells about itself create its reality. Bushe points to the inspirational quality of stories: much of the generative power of Appreciative Inquiry resides in the effect of hearing the stories of other people's successes, achievements, and dreams. Somehow this experience can open the gates of innovation (2007).

The stories may not offer something directly relevant to our situation, but they act as a springboard to a new, unexplored area of possibility. To have this effect, the stories need to be neither too similar nor too dissimilar: ideally they resonate with the person's own situation yet offer a different view, slant, or perspective. Stories generated by a group working together in an Appreciative Inquiry process generally fit the bill perfectly. "Hearing other people's stories enriches our sense of possibility and builds the confidence to face uncertainty" (Whitney *et al.*, 2010, p. 132). Whitney and colleagues consider the ability to "talk story" (p. 131) as key to providing inspiration and name the courage of inspiration as one of the five key qualities of appreciative leaders.

11. They make sense, with others

Appreciative and positive leaders recognize the changeability of the world, its high level of unpredictability (Taleb, 2008), and so are wary of being too decisive about what the future holds or the way forward. They recognize that the future is created out of the actions of the present and the past. Future progress is not immutable but is influenced by what is done or not done, said or not said, today. Therefore they balance the need to have a general sense of direction with a need to attend to the moment-by-moment decision-making that happens all the time in organizations. They try to create with their members a shared sense of direction and a set of guiding principles and priorities. In this way they constantly create and re-create a culture that encourages flourishing, positivity, appreciation, and growth, allowing a positive future to unfold. For, as Quinn notes, organizing is always breaking down (2015) and so needs to be constantly recreated. This, he argues, is the essence of leadership.

In this unfolding context situationally sensitive leaders approach decisions differently. They recognize that decisions "make sense" in a particular context. So, as the context changes, as new information arrives for instance, they recognize that a different decision may need to be made. This pattern of situation-evaluation, action, further evaluation has been described as sense-making (Sutcliffe & Weick, 2007). Sense-making is predicated on situational awareness within a context of long-term objectives. This micro-decision-making, sense-making-oriented adaptive leadership is better fitted to our fast-changing, highly interconnected world than big bold decisions that are expected to hold for years.

12. They make effective use of micro-moments

Many of the leadership behaviours outlined above are played out through an attention to the micro-moments of organizational interaction. In defining appreciative leadership Whitney and colleagues note that a central measure of success that appreciative leaders use is that they have contributed "good" to the day. "What this means is that at the end of the day, appreciative leaders can describe what they did that day to add value to others, to bring out the best of people or situations, and/or to set positive ripples in motion" (2010, p. 9). These are the criteria of achievement they bring to every interaction, meeting, or conversation of the day. As they say, once we understand the organization as a living process, a conversation in progress, then "every conversation in every location could affect – for good or ill – the future of the organization" (p. ix). Positive and appreciative leaders are mindful; and as we have seen, they use words with care.

13. *They recognize the power of emotional states*

The precision of the statistical underpinning of Fredrickson and Losada's (2005) and Losada and Heaphy's (2004) identification of 3:1 positive to negative emotional experiences as the point at which flourishing states emerge has been questioned recently (Brown, Sokal, & Friedman, 2013). However, in general the evidence of the benefits of a predominance of positive to negative states to human functioning and flourishing is well established (Achor, 2011; Lyubomirsky, 2007). The benefits of a high ratio of positivity has recently been affirmed by Robson in her doctoral research during which she gathered data on the discourse positivity ratio of 10 organizations undergoing change. This included examining their written documents as well as recording meetings. Her data revealed that the poorest performing organizations demonstrated a 1:4 deficit-bias in their discourse patterns, while the high success change efforts demonstrated a positivity bias of over 4:1. (Robson, 2015, cited in Cooperrider & Godwin, 2015) This ratio also occurs in research into couple relationships and into mental health and functioning. It is widely accepted that most of the time we do experience more positive than negative emotional states, and that most people most of the time describe themselves as generally happy. However, workplaces, with their particular emphasis on performance and the elimination of error, can become over-critical in all spheres, unintentionally shifting the normal balance of these experiences for people. And since we spend a lot of our lives at work, this can spill into other spheres of life, influencing us to stop noticing the good and to only focus on what is wrong in our lives.

Cameron suggests that positive leaders need to create a positive work climate. This is defined as the predominance of positive emotions over negative emotions in the workplace (2008a, p. 17). Positive climate is characterized by employees with optimistic attitudes and positive outlooks as opposed to employees experiencing stress, anxiety, or distrust. The leaders' emotional state has a strong effect on the development (or otherwise) of a positive climate (Fredrickson, 2003). Emotions are contagious and positive emotions produce upwards spirals of "optimal functioning and enhanced performance" (Fredrickson, 2003, p. 169).

Positive and appreciative leaders effect a degree of self-management of their emotional state. This doesn't mean they deny difficult emotions, or that they are inauthentic in their presentation. Rather they recognize the wide influence of their mood states and attempt to maximize the benefit and limit the damage of their own emotional journeys for others. No one is saying this is easy and it is one of the reasons many leaders value a "safe space" such as a coaching or mentoring relationship where they can experience and explore less positive emotional states and reactions without infecting others.

While all of us can influence others through our mood, leaders' emotions are especially influential. Leaders' positive emotions predict the performance of their entire group (George, 1995). Compassion, forgiveness, and gratitude are particularly important positive emotions that help create a positive work climate (Cameron, 2008a, p. 23). Working on mistakes produces competence, while focusing on forgiveness and high standards frees up individuals and organizations to become positively deviant (Cameron, 2008a, p. 29). Positive deviance is defined as "intentional behaviours that depart from the norm of a reference group in honourable ways" (Spreitzer & Sonenshein, 2003, p. 209). We might think of it as something of a licence to innovate or experiment. In coercive work environments it is this willingness to try something a bit different that might improve things that is missing. The costs of making a mistake are perceived as being too high. We often characterize this as a "blame culture." Those working to lessen the blame culture they have perhaps inherited from their predecessor's behaviour need to focus on building a positive work climate. And finally, positive and appreciative leaders look after themselves.

14. *They look after themselves*

Leadership is generally challenging. While the rewards can be great, at times leadership can be a very difficult place to be. Leaders who attempt to do everything themselves run the risk of exhaustion, not to mention stress and depression, or physical ill-effects like cardiac or stroke problems. Inappropriate coping behaviours such as excessive alcohol or drug consumption only increase these risks. Effective leaders recognize that they need to look after themselves. At a basic level this includes the obvious things like relaxation, sufficient rest, healthy nutrition, and exercise. Less obviously, it also includes proactively looking after and managing your emotional state.

The relationship between emotional states and physiology, and so mental and physical health conditions, is well established (Lewis, 2014). For example, gratitude facilitates better physiological health, cognitive functioning, and performance at work, not least because the heart rhythms associated with a state of appreciation (or gratitude) are much steadier and slower than those associated with states of frustration (Cameron, 2008a, p. 31). Research also demonstrates that willpower or ego (to some extent this can be understood as our energy for decision-making) is a limited resource that becomes depleted through use (Achor, 2011). It is a resource that needs replenishment through regeneration. Different things will help different people to re-energize so they are at their positive, appreciative, flexible, adaptable, complexity-engaging best. Effective leaders find ways during the day and when not at work to replenish themselves. In the same way that the organization needs to become a self-regenerating system, so does the leader. Joep de Jong is an appreciative leader who has given this considerable thought over the years and has distilled his practice for remaining effective in ever more challenging roles into five key daily practices (see Box 2.3).

Box 2.3   Daily Disciplines of an Appreciative Leader

The practice of appreciating

This involves putting one's own ego aside to truly appreciate what is (as opposed to what I hope, believe, want, think, should be). It includes recognizing that the leader's perspective is one among many and that other perspectives may offer greater value.

The practice of courage

This involves working with others to co-create new ways of working and learning. It is the courage of not having all the answers, the courage of involving others in a way that might be challenging. It opens up the possibility of generative, unexpected new ways forward.

(Continued)

Box 2.3   *Continued*

The practice of humility

This involves genuinely recognizing and accepting that there is so much that you don't know. Moving from "knowledge is power" to "shared knowledge" provides strength.

The practice of discipline

This is about clarity of purpose and a focus on the important and meaningful. It means not getting too distracted or diverted by the many aspects of organizational life into working from a perspective other than that of "doing good" and moving forward towards a desired state. For de Jong, practices such as yoga and meditation help him empty his mind of the important yet essentially trivial to refocus on his dreams for people, organization, and future.

The practice of reflecting

De Jong now believes that one of the most important functions of leadership is that of reflecting. That is, reflecting on what is happening in the organization and its wider context. Note the emphasis on thought over action. The operational demands of fast-paced business can easily become the context within which decisions get made on an ad hoc, knee-jerk, firefighting basis. The practice of reflection is in part a counterbalance to that pressure.

De Jong says, "If you spend some time every day to grow your skill in mastering each of them you'll see two things happening. Firstly, the community you work with will greatly appreciate the openness and space that you provide; and secondly, you will start to feel a greater balance in your own life."

Adapted from de Jong (2011)

Conclusion

The different context of the world today and the different challenges organizations face demand a different model, style, and understanding of leadership. Tomorrow's leader needs to understand that organizing is held together in relationship. The most successful leaders today are describing their relationship to the world as one of love (Sisodia, Sheth, & Wolfe, 2014, pp. 4–6). Love has not been a standard part of the vocabulary of many organizations; maybe it is time it became so.

3

Helping People Engage Positively with Imposed Change

Recently I received a call from a human resources director who wanted to offer some support to a leadership team charged with bringing about some change. They thought they wanted a day's training on "doing" change. As I spoke to them all beforehand it became clear that what most of them wanted and needed was something much more experiential that allowed them to make sense of and engage with their specific change. Everyone agreed that the changes they had been charged to make were "logically" a good idea, and they were pretty convinced that everyone else would agree that "you couldn't argue with the logic." Yet they also knew in more or less well articulated ways that this might not be enough to make the changes happen. And somehow, although they could all recite to me, in some detail, the "plan" of the changes needed, they couldn't get started on making any changes. The day ended up being a slightly odd hybrid of "teaching" as commissioned and experiential sense-making as required.

There were two particular points of interest about this day relevant to this chapter. Late in the afternoon I had created a space to "dream" about how the organization could be once these proposed changes were operative. The two groups tackled this very differently. One discussion was all about inspired service for customers and the group involved were getting excited and passionate about the good they could do in the world and what a great place the organization could be to work. Their flipchart was full of images and inspiring phrases. The other group focused on the practicalities of how the service changes would be delivered and their flipchart was a complex picture of boxes and arrows. Both ways of thinking about the future are of course valuable. The interesting part was when a guy in the second group, rather impressed

Positive Psychology and Change: How Leadership, Collaboration, and Appreciative Inquiry Create Transformational Results, First Edition. Sarah Lewis.
© 2016 John Wiley & Sons, Ltd. Published 2016 by John Wiley & Sons, Ltd.

if taken aback at how the first group had interpreted the exercise, after we had been discussing the two outcomes for a while, said, "So you're saying that we are doing this back to front. We should have had a vision first, then worked out what changes we needed to make." This was a "Bingo!" moment. We talked about the difference it made to how they felt, and how able they felt to engage with the challenge of change once they had created the "attractive image of possible futures" for themselves. We were able to discuss how if it was so for them then maybe it was so for others: How could they help other people generate "positive images of the future" that would draw them forward?

This group's experience up to that point, of the push of an imposed change with no corresponding pull of an attractive future, is not uncommon. In this way the changes get pushed from the top down through the organization as for a task that must be done. Change viewed as a task that must be done becomes hard and often distasteful. And of course the whole "resistance" phenomenon is an integral part of this approach. This group of leaders were struggling to "get going" on this change partly because all they could feel was the disruption and the upset it was going to cause, despite the "logic" of its necessity and appropriateness. Somehow the speech from the top introducing this need for change had managed to introduce the metaphor of a "dishwasher." The changes would mean that the organization would be more like a dishwasher. Not surprisingly, this metaphor had stuck. It was certainly a new way of thinking about the organization, yet it was neither inspiring nor useful.

In the time we had available we could only begin to create the "pull" factor of a sense of how these imposed changes could be key to creating a future great place to work. It is this belief in future possibility that gives people the energy to engage with the often challenging, and definitely ethically loaded, process of affecting other people's lives.

The second point I want to mention is that when the group re-measured themselves against the targets for the session all had moved in the right direction, that is, positive progress had been made on items like understanding planned and emergent change approaches; understanding the individual and collective strengths we bring to this change challenge; and identifying the positive core of the organization to bring forward. However, one item had a strong outlier. While most of the group agreed that they had more of a "shared appreciation of the complexities of change" than when they had started the day, the leader's score was in stark disagreement. He explained he had scored this item highly at the beginning of the day as he had thought it was all simple and straightforward since everyone understood (i.e., could recite) the changes needed and that therefore there was a high shared appreciation of the complexity of the change: that it was straightforward. He was now aware that other people in the group saw it in a much more challenging and complex way than he did and so he saw less agreement.

They finished the day with some concrete plans that suggested they were starting to take ownership of this change rather than just being a conduit for it. They were resolved to engage in conversations with their senior management to negotiate more about how much autonomy they had to do things "their way," that is, to take some leadership of this change in their area. And they were resolved to start engaging the people who were going to be most directly involved in this change in conversation about "how change could be introduced" as well as about "what needed to happen."

Introduction

The approach to change outlined above is not unusual. Organizations are awash with interesting beliefs about change and people, including the belief that change is just a matter of planning and that people are naturally resistant to change, to which one is tempted to reply "Up to a point, Lord Copper" (Waugh, 2003 [1938]). In reality we experience change without experiencing "resistance" all our lives: we move from crawling to walking, from riding a bike to driving a car. We change our hairstyles, our house, and our partners. We can't get through life without making changes and very often we embrace them: getting married, having a baby, getting a promotion. People are not, on the whole, resistant to change. What many people do find difficult, and may resist, is having change imposed upon them, and imposing change can easily become something of a habit in organizations.

Typical Experience of Imposed Change

In my experience a typical organizational change scenario runs as follows. Senior management become aware of the need to make changes in the organization. This perceived need can be promoted by any number of things: new blood in the boardroom; changing market conditions; changing economic conditions; regulatory changes; some internal incident that exposes a major weakness, such as a serious workplace accident, fraud, or poor performance; the introduction of new technologies, whether hardware (i.e., new machines) or software (e.g., new IT system or process); or maybe awareness of a new technology such as lean working. And so it is decided that something in the organization needs to change, and a small group of people start making plans. At some point those who will be most affected, those who work the machines, use the IT programmes, or make up the process workflow, will get to hear about these plans, sometimes through a formal announcement and sometimes not. The immediate reaction isn't always the ecstatic embracing of the new dawn for which the executives were hoping.

Instead what tends to hit people smack between the eyes when wholesale, large-scale change is announced is the high immediate cost to them: the disruption; the inconvenience; the uncertainty; the loss of value of their hard-won skill in the present system or process; the likely rupturing of valued relationships, whether with clients or with colleagues; the loss of privileges once seen as basic necessities, like their own desk space; the learning curve ahead of them, and so on. Of course, people have many choices about how to respond to or engage with the imposed changes. Some will quickly see the advantages of the new system or process and will be keen to get going; others may become vocal in their disagreement with either the change or the way it is being done; many, however, become rather passive and disempowered (see Box 3.1).

Box 3.1 Different Ways People React to Change

Emotional (feelings)
   Worried, scared, angry
   Excited, enthusiastic
Cognitive (thought processes)
   Distracted, preoccupied, dull
   Fired up, creative, focused
Social
   Isolated, withdrawn
   Outgoing, connecting
Contextual
   Loss of sense of identity, rewards, satisfaction
   Enhanced identity, new rewards, new satisfactions

Unintended Consequences of Imposed Change

Feeling that they have no control over all this "change," people can enter a "waiting" state. Waiting for the powers that be to tell them exactly what the future holds; waiting to be told exactly what they are going to do; waiting for illumination about what the new job looks like; waiting for clarity regarding what the priorities are and so on. Frequently, they believe that "senior management" has this change all planned out, right down to who will sit where. In some organizations, with vast resources, this may be the case (not that I have ever experienced it!), although having all the answers won't necessarily endear them to those for whom they have so devotedly planned. More often senior management has only the vaguest idea of how this is all going to look in the end, never mind every step along the way. Rather, driven by necessity, advancing with hope, keeping the faith in an uncertain future, and at the mercy of reassuring experts, they endeavour to maintain the illusion of certainty and control.

This approach to change seems frequently to produce a situation where the change-makers are working flat out to make the change happen while those affected, having no say in the process, have little option but to wait. While waiting they become less and less effective as they find it hard to know what to do for the best in the present. They are no longer sure what to be doing *now* to help create a great future; they know only that what they have been doing is apparently not what will be wanted. Frustration can grow on both sides. It is worth looking at this worst, but not uncommon, experience of organizational change through two particular psychological lenses, emotional and cognitive, as they reveal how we can intervene to re-energize and re-motivate those adversely affected by the organizational changes.

Understanding the Psychological Impact of Imposed Change on People

The effects of imposed change viewed through an emotion lens

An unintended consequence of the change scenario described above is that the working world can become emotionally negatively charged, by which I mean the ratio of difficult, unpleasant, or upsetting feelings, such as confusion, uncertainty, anxiety, worry, or stress, against pleasant feelings, such as satisfaction, achievement, or affirmation, can shift. Once the ratio shifts below 3:1 (i.e., less than three pleasant feelings to every unpleasant feeling) then a downwards spiral of dissatisfaction is likely. This is often an unintended consequence of the announcement of change because, however management frame the announcement, the initial impression for many can be a barrage of bad news. Regardless of how carefully the message is couched, often in jargonistic management-speak, what people immediately hear is disruption and uncertainty, if not threat (e.g., to their job, status, values, sense of professional identity, friendship networks, etc.).

The announcement raises unanswered questions and the level of uncertainty rises. Many people find this unsettling in itself, especially when it involves the question "What is to become of me?" Doubts and uncertainties can plague people: "Will I be able to learn the new system? Will I still have a job?" At the same time the supply of established sources of mood enhancement, the reliable little blips of spirit-raising pleasure, can dwindle. For example, front line managers have their own anxieties to deal with in this change process and may have less time for their staff, so unintentionally reducing the amount of management rewards of time, attention, praise, smiles, and so on. The general mood may become more tense and uncertain, with less laughter and ease at work as the general diffuse anxiety contaminates everyone. People may find themselves in competition with their colleagues for jobs or resources (like desks!). Most importantly though, and often unnoticed, the work can become less rewarding. By this I mean that the things people did that used to win them rewards (approval from others, status, satisfaction in a job well done, etc.) are often displaced in the "new system" and it's not always immediately clear where the rewards now lie. The opportunity to exercise personal strengths on a daily basis, which is highly motivating for people (Seligman, 2003), may be reduced. Hence the work environment can become reward-poor rather than reward-rich. All of these subtle factors can add together to shift the ratio of positive to negative work experiences in the wrong direction so that the whole experience of being at work develops a more negative emotional tenor (see Box 3.2). Morale begins to fall.

Box 3.2   Rewards Lost during Change

Certainty, routine, and predictability
Positive managerial attention – praise, shared jokes
Satisfaction of a job well done
Technical knowledge status
Organizational knowledge status (status due to knowledge about how
   the organization works)
Organizational network knowledge status (status due to the "knowing
   everyone" ability to get things done)
Ability to get things done quickly and easily
Secure sense of future
Secure sense of identity
Friendship networks
Daily use of strengths
Satisfying use of well-honed skills
Sense of expertise
Worker identity
Group ease of being, laughter
Clarity of what good looks like

The effect of imposed change viewed through a cognitive lens

One key emotion that keeps us upbeat, resilient, and able to meet life's challenges is hope. Hope is a future-oriented emotion, essentially a belief that in the future things can be good. Zimbardo's work on the psychological aspects of time offers an interesting perspective on what can happen to people's cognitive state when confronted with imposed change, which in turn can affect their emotional state. First, though, we need to understand some key aspects of Zimbardo's theory.

Zimbardo's work suggests that we can identify six different time-oriented states of mind. These are future-oriented, past-positive-oriented, past-negative-oriented, present-hedonistic-oriented, present-fatalistic-oriented, and future-transcendental-oriented. All of us are capable of adopting all of these time-oriented cognitive states at different times; at the same time we tend to have different profiles of how often we visit each (Zimbardo & Boyd, 2010). Let us examine them in more detail.

Future   transcendental   orientated

To be in a future orientation state is to be highly aware of the implications of today's actions for tomorrow; for example, "I'm studying hard now so I can earn more money later," or, "I'm working hard on this project to enhance my CV and to improve my promotion prospects." A past-positive orientation is to appreciate the best of the past, to enjoy shared memories – what we might call happy reminiscing – while a past-negative orientation leads to rumination on opportunities missed, wrong paths taken – regrets, in other words. A present-hedonistic orientation is expressed in the ability to enjoy the present moment through indulgence, relaxation, or thrill-seeking, for example. While present-fatalistic is characterized by a belief that nothing one does can make a difference so why bother to try. The future-transcendental orientation is predicated on a belief of life after death, allowing a calm acceptance of the inevitability of death and perhaps a different relationship to today's trials and tribulations (Zimbardo & Boyd, 2010).

All of these time orientations are useful to us at particular times and ideally we develop a balanced temporal perspective that allows us to cherish the past, relish the present, and invest in the future (Boniwell & Zimbardo, 2003). A balanced time perspective is the state, and ongoing process, of being able to switch flexibly between these time frames as most appropriate to the demands of the current behavioural setting (Zimbardo & Boyd, 1999). Our ability to experience or enter these different time orientations is influenced by our current context. As Zimbardo notes, "As our ancestors succeeded in eliminating threats, they were free to look further into the future without the fear that they would be killed if they took their eyes off the present" (Zimbardo & Boyd, 2010, p. 36). When change is experienced as a threat to our wellbeing it may well make it harder for us to be future-oriented, just at the point that the organization is demanding this of us.

"I gave you one simple task....."

Instead, the change process can encourage both a past-negative and a past-positive time orientation, neither necessarily in a helpful way. So while one group might cast the past as having been somehow "wrong" in order to justify the change (past-negative), another may be busy creating the "golden age" myth of a time when everything and everyone worked well in the absence of this level of management interference (past-positive). The greater challenge though is the spread of a present-fatalistic mindset. In this state people feel hopeless and express beliefs that immutable outside forces control their lives. Both past-negative and present-fatalistic mindsets are associated with strong feelings of depression, anger, anxiety, and aggression (Zimbardo & Boyd, 1999). In addition, present-fatalistic orientation is related to a perceived lack of control, negative affect, and a great degree of emotional distress and hopelessness. None of these are particularly helpful to the challenge of change.

Although Zimbardo's work in this area has mostly explored these ideas at the level of the individual, I think we can legitimately extrapolate these ideas to groups of people. If we think of the organization as a living system, then we can hypothesize that the organization, or groups within it, can develop particular time orientations. Experience on the ground with groups experiencing imposed change suggests that the development of the present-fatalistic mindset (we have no influence, they don't listen to us) often expresses itself in a mixture of active anger and passive resignation. This is expressed in organizational terms as a sense of disempowerment.

Accessing Psychological Resources to Increase Efficacy and Resilience

This is not to suggest that imposed change always produces these effects or that everyone reacts the same way. However, faced with a group of people feeling demoralized, disempowered and stuck in an endless present, the challenge becomes to reintroduce a sense of optimism and a future orientation. Working from this emotional and cognitive perspective, there are a number of possible ways to help people stuck in a depressing and demoralizing present become once again their active, engaged, and optimistic selves.

1. Create hopefulness

A key psychological or emotional state that helps motivate people to engage with creating and influencing the world is that of hopefulness: a state of being full of hope. Hope, while self-evidently generally a good thing, is a tricky concept in many ways, being rather ephemeral and difficult to quantify. Yet we refer to it in countless ways and are understood as we do so: "We hope to be there by 7 o'clock," "I'm feeling quite hopeful about our prospects at the moment," "I hope we have put all that behind us," and so on. Hope is key to our ability to engage positively with the future and so is particularly important during imposed change. As we saw earlier, hope can be an early casualty of imposed change.

Hope is good for us as individuals: an individual state of high hope (for the future) is favourably associated with positive outcomes in the areas of athletics, physical health, psychological adjustment, and psychotherapy (Snyder, Rand, & Sigmon, 2005). Meanwhile, organizational research has demonstrated a link between hope and favourable organizational outcomes such as profitability (Adams *et al.*, 2002). Peterson and Luthans' research found that high hope leaders had more profitable work units, better retention rates, and better subordinate satisfaction than low hope leaders (2003). Other studies indicate a link between hope and job satisfaction, organizational commitment and performance (Luthans, Norman, Avolio, & Avery, 2008). Hope, in my opinion, is the singular most important positive emotion to pull people from apathetic inertia into becoming proactive in their own futures.

However, hope isn't a monolithic concept. Carlsen, Hagen, and Mortensen (2012) identify *opening-up* hope as a general feeling of optimism or positivity about opportunity or possibility that has opened up due to some change. This is distinct from Snyder, Rand, and Sigmon's more *goal-oriented* concept of hope (2005). For example, recently I worked with some parents of children in a children's hospice. We spent time experiencing and talking about positive emotions and identifying strengths. At the end of the session, one young mother said how much better she felt, how refreshed, how optimistic. Life had been tough over the past two years. Something in our time together had created a sense of possibility that things could get better. This could be seen as the emergence of opening-up hope. There was some talk of finding a way to take up running again, maybe to enter the London Marathon. Maybe in time this would coalesce into an attainment goal of completing the marathon in a certain time. But for now the experience of opening-up hope was sufficient to allow her to imagine a different future from the current endless present.

These theories of hope suggest that to move forward after a sudden or unexpected disruption people need to experience both opening-up hope and attainment hope. These theories of hope suggests that to advance directly by trying to generate goal-attainment hope might be premature; instead people need an opportunity to become more hopeful in general, to become "open" to the idea of hope or better futures before laying down plans. Appreciative Inquiry as a process enables the emergence of both forms of hope. Appreciative Inquiry is explained fully in Chapter 6 and I shall be referring to it extensively throughout the rest of this chapter.

Opening-up hope is a co-created, shared, relational, emotional experience. This experience of generalized, but as yet untargeted, hope can be characterized as the ability to believe that the future will be different in ways not yet specified from the past and somehow freer than the past or the present (Rorty, 2000). Such opening-up hope is a condition of growth. In this way opening-up hope is a necessity for life in general and for change in particular. The positive, relational, and generative focus of Appreciative Inquiry processes helps create this more diffuse yet powerful motivation. It is this opening-up hope that allows groups paralysed by uncertainty to start to step into the unknown. Such hope cannot be commanded by imprecations to, for instance, "Buck up!" It can only be generated or released. It is a motivator and as such is drawn out of people, not pushed into them. It is both an emotion and a vital coping resource. As well as releasing or creating this kind of hope, Appreciative Inquiry also supports the creation of goal-attainment hope through the evolution of dreams into action.

2. Create dreams of positive future states

Dreaming of the future and experiencing hope are inextricably intertwined. So much so that in everyday life we barely notice ourselves either dreaming or hoping. Yet all projections of ourselves into a positive future that has not yet arrived, such as the idle thought of "Later I'll go for a swim" or "At the weekend I'll get going on that vegetable patch," are essentially dreams and imaginings that create both hope for a positive future state and motivation for action in the present that makes that future state more likely. I might be motivated, for example, to crack on with this writing so I have time for that swim, or to buy those seeds today so they are ready for the weekend. There is a powerful dynamic between hope, imagination, and future-oriented action. It is this dynamic that is accessed by the "dreaming" stage of Appreciative Inquiry. In Appreciative Inquiry these visions of attractive future possibility are known as dreams. To contemplate the future with any enthusiasm we need to harbour some positive expectations, or dreams, about it. During imposed change this process needs to be more consciously managed than at other times.

3. Focus on what can be achieved

During change we need to help people focus on solution talk over problem talk. The emphasis in solution-focused conversation is on what we can do, rather than what we can't do. Appreciative Inquiry as a process is particularly well suited to facilitating such talk. Through the use of appreciative questions, people and groups can be guided to redirect their attention and focus from the things they can't influence to those they can. With an increasing sense of the possibility of influential future-oriented action comes increasing hope. My experience of working with groups to help them move from a sense of hopelessness to one of hopefulness is that this is an almost tangible process as the seeds of hope become apparent in the group. Glimmers of light appear in the doom-laden conversation, suggesting that, tentatively, people are daring to hope, daring to believe in possibilities of a better future. And daring is the right word. It takes a certain courage to believe in an uncertain possibility. To "get your hopes up" runs the risk of having them dashed. Yet to not take the risk of being hopeful makes it incredibly difficult to find the energy to do things differently. By positively affecting people's emotional state we make it possible for them to begin to think differently, while thinking differently they begin to feel different. In this way an upward virtuous circle of improving mood and expansive creative thinking can be initiated that helps militate against the adverse effects on motivation and morale often experienced during imposed change.

4. Create empowering narratives

For groups to create new ideas about themselves and their possibilities in the future something needs to change or shift about their conception of themselves in the present. It is the discovery interviews in the Appreciative Inquiry process that feed new information into the system, allowing new conceptualizations to emerge. During the discovery process people are asked to share stories of themselves, or their organization, or their group at their best in the past. As a group of people share stories of themselves at their best, many of which will be previously unknown to the majority of the group, something begins to shift in the group's conception of themselves. It is almost a tangible rearrangement of the atoms in the room. Essentially, as person after person reveal hidden strengths, determination, tenacity, moral courage, effectiveness, and other virtues, values, and abilities, people begin to re-evaluate the nature of the group of which they are a member, and the potential of the group to achieve change. Hope, goals, dreams, possibilities, imagination, and creativity are all interlinked and interdependent and can be held together powerfully by narrative.

a) Narrative to create positive mood
We spend a lot of time in organizations, and sadly also often in life, focusing on what people do wrong and complaining about it to others, and pre-cious little in noticing what they do right and celebrating it with others.

Appreciative Inquiry discovery interviews invite us, for a relatively short period of time, to turn our attention to discovering the best in our colleagues. In normal organizational life we rarely extend the invitation to others to share those moments when, just for once, they knew they were at their best doing something good. The results can be electrifying. Just as the outsider listening in to the stories as they are shared, I regularly find myself very moved, often indeed close to tears. People can be just so damned impressive! Ordinary-looking folk turn out to be capable of extraordinary things. One is humbled. Good discovery stories have an emotional impact in the moment. Among other effects, they often work to rekindle embers of hope as the amount of resourcefulness in the room becomes apparent – and as it becomes apparent that other people also care about important things.

b) Narrative for resource identification

Beyond this, of course, the group can analyse the stories for resources. They can be analysed for the strengths evident in the stories. They can be analysed for useful ideas. They can be compared to similar yet not quite so impactful experiences to yield the small things that make a difference between OK and great. Appreciative Inquiry also uses narrative for resource identification in the dream phase. In this phase, groups of people create dreams or images of the future. These imagined futures aren't plucked out of thin air; rather they are created in the context of the discovery about the best of the past. People use their imagination to create images, and accounts, of how the future can be, at its best. Once again people are telling stories, but while in the discovery phase these might be stories of things that have happened in the past, this time they are of things that might happen in the future. These dreams often contain useful resources not yet present in the world. During the design phase, key future resources can be identified as development projects.

c) Narrative to create dense future zones

One thing that stories of future possible states do is create "dense future zones" which are connected with a future time orientation, as mentioned earlier. To have a dense future zone is to be full of ideas, plans, hopes, and aspirations for the future; to have a rich picture of a positive future that pulls you forward. When engaging with this temporal perspective we tend to operate with an eye towards "consequences, contingencies and the probable outcomes of present decisions and actions" (Boniwell & Zimbardo, 2003, p. 169). In addition, we are "dedicated to working for future goals and their attendant rewards" (p. 169). This is essentially how dreaming of the future positively affects the likelihood of it occurring. Dreaming encourages us to act now in ways that are in line with the desired future. Dreaming acts to draw people out of the passivity associated with a present-fatalistic mindset and helps shift behaviour from short-term survival mode to longer-term investment mode.

In addition, having a dense future zone is good for us. The density of the future zone, usually measured by the number of plans, commitments, and anticipated experiences, has been found to be positively correlated with wellbeing (Kahana & Kahana, 1983), while "a positive future orientation is often viewed as the essence of personal optimism" (Boniwell & Zimbardo, 2003, p. 173). Future orientation is related to higher levels of perceived control and positive wellbeing or affect, and to persistence (p. 173), and it allows for a sense of possibility of being agentic, that is, taking responsibility and making choices. A dense future zone can be highly motivating: "When you want to achieve something and believe that you can, you work harder" (Zimbardo & Boyd, 1999, p. 137). All of which helps with the motivation and energy needed to make changes. However, for the narratives to be effective at producing change, they also need to be generative.

5. Create generative images

Gervase Bushe notes that achieving positive energy in Appreciative Inquiry interventions is not enough, there also needs to be a generative element (2013). By this he means that something new needs to be created or to emerge during the process. This something new need only be a realization, conceptualization, image, or idea that is new to this particular group, not to the world at large. More important than world-shattering innovation, what is needed is a novel expression or image that captures the new thinking in a nutshell, a cohering symbol. Over uniqueness what's needed is connection. The "new thing" needs to be something to which the whole group is connected, something that speaks to them all, something that encapsulates the group's best image of themselves and their hopes for the future. For example, for one group I worked with the emerging image was of a "one stop shop." This is hardly new, but for them it expressed a multitude of ideas and aspirations in a simple phrase. The conversation jumped forward once they could express all these things in this simple image.

6. *Redefine success*

In times of change what we have to do is build, and help others build, new definitions of success. This can be particularly important during imposed change when people probably haven't had the opportunity to think about this. We need to help people set new goals and we also need to help them administer rewards differently in line with the new success criteria. I had a conversation with someone about this in a workshop only the other day. The workshop was on leading through uncertainty and change. One participant agreed with the points I was making but was having trouble applying them to her situation, a team that knew it was going to be disbanded. How, she asked, could she maintain morale? This is a perfect example of a situation where success needs to be radically redefined. Adhering to the old definitions of success, which in this case were to do with amount of work done, would clearly lead to an increasing sense of failure as the team diminished through attrition. Instead what was required, I suggested, was that they ask themselves questions such as, "Given this situation, what is the best kind of run down we could have?" "How will we know if our run down has been successful?" and "How can we both continue to work for the good of the organization and attend to our own futures?" Only by asking themselves questions of this nature could she and her team begin to create goals and targets that were relevant and achievable and against which they could experience success. In this way they are using narrative to create dreams and hope.

In more general terms, it is usually important to help groups identify "what success looks like" in the emerging new order. In project-oriented environments this is particularly important. If you wait until the project is completed before declaring success and allowing celebration you may never reach the point of being able to say "job well done." Project completion dates have a habit of receding over a horizon. And when a project does come to an end, it is rarely a very clean and clear end: it can be more of a straggle of activity slowly fading out rather than a decisive dividing point. For these reasons project-based change activity is particularly susceptible to "success lag." Groups need to create their own accounts that allow them to experience moments of achievement and success along the way.

By the same token, we need to drag people's attention away from the blindingly obvious things that are being broken and are not working, to the hidden parts of the system that are working. Sometimes this is a difference between a surface and a depth perception. So, on the surface, teams are being broken up, processes are being dismantled, walls are being removed – all highly visible, disruptive, and sometimes distressing. Yet at the same time there will be important things that aren't changing or are still working. For example, it may be that, in all the confusion, people are still focused on achieving good customer service or that people still find time to look out for each other. In addition to finding success we can amplify it.

7. Amplify success

We create our own social environment by the way we interact and talk together. Out of the many things that are happening in our environment we can choose which ones to focus on. As I said earlier, Achor (2011) estimates that we are able to attend to one in every 100 "bits" of information that come our way. We filter out the remaining 99% without even noticing. For many of us our default filters are set on noticing problems, errors, mistakes, faults and flaws and so we unintentionally filter out success. It is of course important to notice these things. But if these are all we notice, then our world becomes full of nothing but errors, mistakes, and flaws. During times of change, without conscious effort it is easy to slip into the mindset where everything is wrong (see Box 3.3).

To counteract this we need to consciously seek out things that are right, and beyond that to amplify them. That is, to take the weak signals that exist of things that are working, that are improvements, that are signs of quality, that demonstrate commitment or important values and to boost them through active and deliberate amplification processes. These might be activities such as an entry on the company blog or the creation of a specific "good news" newsletter. Taking opportunities to share things your team are achieving, even if it seems as mundane as continuing to provide a service among all the chaos, is important because under these circumstances "just doing our job" can be a major achievement and worth shouting about. So we should encourage people to take the opportunity during meetings and so on to tell others about the good things their team are still doing. Introducing a "good news round" at the start of every meeting can be an effective way of counteracting a growing story that everything is difficult or uncertain or going wrong.

Box 3.3   Hunting for Leopards

I recently had the good fortune to spend a day on safari in Kruger National Park. I had never been on a safari before and was thrilled to see all these animals in their natural habitat. Every sighting – and they were continual – was a delight. "Oh, an elephant!" "Oh, a giraffe!" "Oh, warthogs!" Not so a group of my companions. They had already been on safari a week and they had one goal in mind. They wanted to see a leopard. They dismissed my delight with, "Oh you'll see plenty of those; nothing to get excited about," and similar comments. They had the driver, who they clearly already knew, racing around the park in a fruitless leopard search. In the end I had to have words to ensure that we took the time to look at what was there, not at what wasn't. What became crystal clear to me was that, when focused solely on seeing a leopard, everything else available to see became classified only as a "not-leopard." While I saw cute baby elephants, they saw only "not-leopard," where I saw wallowing hippos they saw only "not-leopard," and where I saw lion and lioness they saw only yet another "not-leopard." The moral of the tale is: beware of getting caught up in leopard hunting!

8. *Encourage savouring*

Related to this is the idea of savouring. Savouring can be defined as "the capacity to attend to, appreciate, and enhance the positive experiences in one's life" (Bryant, Erickson, & DeHoek, 2013, p. 857). It describes those moments when we pause briefly to notice that we are having a good experience and to enjoy that moment. It also refers to our abilities to do that. We can savour experiences in the present, and can also recall experiences to savour from the past through reminiscing, or conjure them into the future through pleasurable anticipation; either way, the experience is a here and now pleasure. As the researchers in the field put it, "savouring requires a conscious meta-awareness of one's positive feelings while one is experiencing them" (p. 857). Savouring facilitates the access of positive emotions; for example, marvelling accesses awe, thanksgiving accesses gratitude, basking accesses pride, and luxuriating accesses physical pleasure. I noticed savouring in other people before I had a name to put to it. I saw it as the ability to take pleasure in small things. For example, my husband turning a penknife over and over in his hand, examining all the blades and pull-out extras, "tweezers!" My father pausing in the Sunday task of mowing the lawn to settle down to enjoy his morning treat of a "flake cake." It was a bit of a puzzle to me: it's just a penknife, just a cake. Yet research shows that the occurrence of minor positive events is associated with increases in daily self-esteem and perceived control, and decreases in daily depressive cognitions, above and beyond the effect of negative events (Nezlek & Gable, 2001). All of this is of course relevant to the effects of change on people.

I realize now that I had for many years a tendency to "dampen" rather than amplify possible positive feelings. And of course I was too busy to notice these brief moments of pleasure. More fool me. Taking a moment to savour the good things that occur during the day is a sure-fire way to help keep the world a better place and maintain better mental health (see Box 3.4). The difference between flourishing and non-flourishing people is their positive emotional reactivity to everyday events. Their ability to create a ratio of between 3:1 and 5:1 positive experiences in their daily life sets them apart from the mass of others (Fredrickson, 2015). One way to encourage savouring is through constructive responding.

Stew Smith

> ### Box 3.4   10 Savouring Strategies
>
> Sharing with others – women use this more than men.
> Memory building – particularly associated with perceived rarity.
> Self-congratulation – particularly associated with internal causal
>   attributions (i.e., I created this experience).
> Sensory – perceptual sharpening.
> Comparing – better than other experiences.
> Absorption – fully focused on the experience.
> Behavioural expression – women use this more than men.
> Temporal awareness – being in the moment.
> Counting blessings – particularly associated with greater perceived
>   event desirability.
> Marvelling and awe – recognizing the accomplishment or achievement
>   involved.
>
>   Bryant *et al.* (2013, p. 858)

9. Encourage constructive responding

Constructive responding is a way of capitalizing on good events. It can take on a particular importance during imposed change when people can lose sight of anything good that is happening in their work environment. It is important to note that the benefits of attending to and capitalizing on good events are over and above those of not experiencing negative events. In other words, the two processes that allow us to notice and respond to positive events and negative events are separate, independent processes. Which means we can do both at once. Thus someone in the middle of telling you of their woes is quite capable of switching momentarily to remark on the sunset. In the midst of the difficulties at work we are not denying their reality by focusing on positive things, rather we are consciously shifting to a different emotional space to reap the benefits of so doing, which will probably help us with the challenge of the difficulties. Recent research has discovered that we can greatly amplify the impact of good news or positive events by the way we respond to them. Box 3.5 lists the benefits of sharing good news with others or of capitalizing on the positive events in your life.

These benefits only accrue if two conditions are met: that a positive response to good news is offered, and that it is perceived as such by the

---

Box 3.5   Sharing Good News

Sharing good news with others, or capitalizing on positive events in your life, generates additional positive affect over and above the positive affect associated with the event itself. This happens through seven processes:

1. Sharing a positive event requires retelling the event, which creates an opportunity for reliving and re-experiencing the event.
2. By rehearsing and elaborating during the telling, we can prolong and enhance the experience by increasing its salience and accessibility in memory.
3. This means that positive events that are communicated to others are more likely to be remembered.
4. The sharing may foster positive social interaction, which is reinforcing in and of itself.
5. Sharing good news may act to strengthen a relationship through a shared moment.
6. It may allow us to see that others are pleased for us, thus offering a boost to self-esteem.
7. It may allow us to experience a positive reflective appraisal, perceiving ourselves positively in the eyes of others.

Adapted from Gable *et al.* (2004)

---

receiver. The nature of the relationship also makes a difference: the more connected we are, the more likely we are to experience the other's good fortune as our own. For example, my partner is an artist and a highlight experience for him is holding an exhibition of his paintings. He is very clear that while it would be lovely to sell some, the real pleasure comes from people's appreciation of the work. Seeing him having a wonderfully positive experience also makes me feel good, for him and for myself.

Responding constructively to another's good fortune can work to build intimacy. This may seem a strange concept in the workplace, but given our emphasis on the importance of teams and building trust, maybe not. Recent research on organizations that do well both financially and by all the stakeholders is identifying love as a key ingredient of their success. Such organizations combine an emotive dimension with operational efficacy (Sisodia, Sheth, & Wolfe, 2014). To refer to love in the workplace is quite bold; usually we use different terms for similar things, referring to close working relationships, "tight" teams, or high levels of trust. Understanding the importance and the art of constructive responding can help build all these things.

Research by Gable, Reis, Impett, and Evan found that on the days people shared the occurrence of a positive event with others, they reported significantly higher positive affect and life satisfaction (2004, p. 231). Yet negative affect was not significantly diminished by the sharing of a positive event. The independence of the concept of positive affect from negative affect is quite hard to grasp; perhaps an example will help. The period immediately before my mother's death was stressful and difficult. Her accelerating deterioration caused me anxiety, stress, sadness, frustration, and a sense of loss, inadequacy, and other appropriate, yet not usually defined as positive, emotions. These didn't go away just because I also savoured some of the pleasant things in my life, such as watching my garden grow, reading exciting research, sitting in the sun during an unexpectedly excellently sunny June, or spending a lovely hour reading poetry to and with my mother. The experience of one doesn't preclude the other, and the experience of the other helps with the experience of the one.

The way we respond to the good fortune of others can be classified into four categories: active-constructive, active-destructive, passive-constructive, and passive-destructive. Active constructive means responding actively, enthusiastically, and supportively; for example, "That's great, tell me more" or "You must be very excited." It means asking questions that encourage the person to talk and think more about the good news in a good way. It means being genuinely interested and obviously pleased for the other person. Passive-constructive, on the other hand, is quietly understated support. While not actively destructive, the passive-constructive response is likely to be characterized as, "tries not to make a big deal out of it" or as "silently supportive." The recipient reports that the person they told says little, but that they know that they are happy for them. It's a dampening down kind of response, an "OK let's not get too excited here" response. The important finding from the research is that such unvoiced pleasure has no positive effect on the positive mood of the news sharer. This low-key non-destructive response doesn't build positive affect or boost self-esteem.

Then there is the active-destructive response. Here the recipient finds problems with the good news, reminds the good news sharer that good things have bad aspects as well, and points out the potential downsides of the good event, suggesting for example that "It will mean a long commute," or asking, "Won't you feel a bit disloyal?" While finally, a passive-destructive responder just quashes the whole thing: they seem disinterested, to not care very much. They don't pay the news much attention, and may even abruptly change the topic instead. Of these, only an active-constructive response is positively associated with better relationship quality.

Telling the person who is likely to respond best first and telling lots of people both result in higher positive affect and life satisfaction (Gable *et al.*, 2004, p. 239). It seems that this active constructive response has these positive effects through three processes: it offers a validation of the importance of the event; it confirms the significance of the event; and it demonstrates, reveals, or creates affective investment and caring (Gable & Gosnell, 2011). Interestingly, these boosts to positive affect and life satisfaction are above those created by the news itself. In addition, positive events shared with others are more likely to be recalled (Gable *et al.*, 2004), providing a source for future positive-past reminiscing. I believe these findings about the many beneficial aspects of sharing good news are very important as they offer a very positive alternative approach to building strong relationships to that offered by the also effective "we're all in this mess together."

An example of what these different responses look and sound like might help. Imagine you came into the team meeting reporting that you had just landed a big order. An active-constructive response might be: "That's fantastic, how did you do that? How are you feeling about it, excited? I'm really proud of you." A passive-constructive response might be: "Well I knew you would." An active-destructive response might be: "How big? How are we going to service that? Did you speak to production? That's going to put a real pressure on our cash flow." While a passive-destructive response might be: "Really, I see XYZ just landed an order twice that size. I wonder why we didn't get that one. Hey Johnson, you used to work at XYZ. What do you know about …"

While these may seem obvious and distinct, an important point to note is that the defining factor is how the news sharer perceives the response. So, depending on the people involved, the context, or the history, what sounds like genuine enthusiasm to the uninvolved bystander may be heard as sarcasm by the receiver, reminding us once again that achieving good effects isn't a tick-box process of saying the right things, it is built on a longer-term process of creating an atmosphere of trust and authenticity. All of these tactics, amplifying, savouring, and constructive responding, help to create positivity, even in difficult situations. This in turn helps to create resilience, another work attribute at a premium during change.

10. Promote resilience

Resilience is often referred to as "the bounce back factor," reflecting its importance in allowing us to recover quickly from life's slings and arrows. More formally we can say, "Resilience generally refers to positive adaptation in the context of risk or adversity" (Cutuli & Masten, 2013, p. 837). Resilience is key in enabling people to recover quickly from unexpected events, of which imposed change may be one, and to spring back into life. The more resilient we are the better we can cope with shocks or surprises.

The property of resilience in people has been much studied and is seen as having three key components: the ability to function well during times of significant adversity (stress resistance); the ability to return to a previous level of good functioning following a traumatic or severely disturbing experience (bouncing back); and the ability to achieve new levels of positive or normal adaptation when severely adverse conditions improve (normalization) (Cutuli & Masten, 2013). All three of these abilities are useful on a personal and organizational level to help people deal with the more traumatic impacts of change programmes when they can, as it were, be knocked off balance.

Resilience, the ability to bounce back from setbacks, emerges from dynamic processes over time. In other words, it is a product of our previous history. Developmental psychology has been interested in resilience as a personality trait, exploring what it is, how we recognize it, and how we develop it. Most research has been on individuals, particularly children, and has been focused on the effect of adverse life events. In particular, people have been interested in the relationship between life events and the likelihood of developing poor mental health, or experiencing developmental delay. More recently, resilience has been recognized as patterns of behaviour of individuals or groups that affect their capacity for resilience. We might think of this as a system understanding of resilience. We can consider the organization as a system and so extend the research to our purposes.

Resilience is seen as a product of both promotive and protective factors. In developmental psychology healthy brain development and good parenting are seen as promotive factors that predict many good outcomes regardless of risk exposure. In organizational terms we can think of this as general good organizational practice: safe working environments, role clarity, career paths, work satisfaction, and so on. We can also include the presence of the factors demonstrated by Kim Cameron (2008a) to promote a flourishing workplace: positive deviance, affirmation, and virtuous practice. These things all help to promote a happy, healthy workforce.

Protective factors, meanwhile, are those that moderate risk, showing special effect when adversity is high (Cutuli & Masten, 2013, p. 841). They have no function until they are activated by the threat and then they serve a protective role. Examples given in the literature are things like child protection services or counselling. In the workplace this suggests that while general good practice will help promote resilience, in times of particular organizational stress or adversity *we may need to do some extra things to activate protective resilience*. When we note that the most frequently reported factors that promote resilience (from studies around the world) are the attributes of individuals, their relationships, and the context (and indeed research on organizational resilience has underlined the critical role of relationships in fostering resilience at the collective level (Gittell, Cameron, & Lim, 2006)), then we can see where we need to focus our efforts to create protective factors that promote resilience during change.

Social relationships help buffer people from the effects of traumatic events and also help prevent workplace burnout, yet organizational change often damages social relationships. The various co-creative methodologies promoted in this book, and Appreciative Inquiry in particular, all work to strengthen social relationships. They are resilience-building approaches to change that operationalize the challenge of accessing assets and protective factors, as well as identifying risk factors when embarking on disruptive change. As such they fit with a shift within resilience research towards a strengths-based approach (Cutuli & Masten, 2013). For organizations, taking a strengths-based approach means focusing on creating promotive resilience factors such as a flourishing, resilient work culture during the good times; and on adding in protective factors when things get difficult.

Conclusion

This chapter has considered the common situation of imposed change in organizations. It has suggested that positive psychology offers both an understanding of the adverse effects of imposed change, and positive action that can be taken to promote active and healthy engagement with it. It has also introduced Appreciative Inquiry as a methodology particularly well suited to ameliorating the adverse effects of change. In later chapters Appreciative Inquiry and other co-creative methodologies that offer an altogether different approach to change are explained in detail.

4

A Different Approach to Organizations and Change

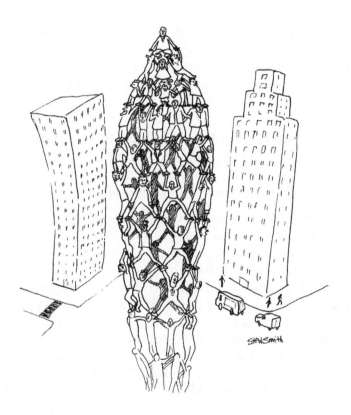

Positive Psychology and Change: How Leadership, Collaboration, and Appreciative Inquiry Create Transformational Results, First Edition. Sarah Lewis.
© 2016 John Wiley & Sons, Ltd. Published 2016 by John Wiley & Sons, Ltd.

Introduction

In the last 20 years a new understanding of organizations has been developed, understanding them as living human systems of enterprise and creativity. It offers an alternative to the dominant view of organizations as large and complicated machines of production. The methodologies described in Chapters 6–9 are all predicated on this new understanding of organizations. They allow the whole of the organizational domain to be approached from the living human system perspective. They allow us to address all organizational challenges, from recruitment to redundancy, within the same living human system frame. And while as methodologies they may be relatively new, they do also build on what went before. For example, Lewin (1951) noted that it was the *learning* produced by group activities in action research that was the most important outcome of the process. Learning is the basis of behaviour change.

Key Factors that Create Living Human System Learning and Change

1. The importance of learning for behaviour change

Learning means that something shifts in our understanding of the world; and understanding the world differently allows us to engage with it differently. The methodologies introduced in this text all effectively enable the system, that is, the people who make up the organization, to learn about itself. These methodologies facilitate increased understanding of how the organizational system behaves, what it believes, what it thinks, and its assumptions about both itself and the outside world. They facilitate greater understanding of how things connect, and of how the organization collectively understands forthcoming change. They facilitate identification and connection of the many different beliefs within the organization about what the changes mean. These shifts in the mental *maps* of the world held by those that make up the organizational system contribute to the organizational system's mental *model* of its environment, which in turn influences ideas about how to engage with it effectively.

2. The importance of participation for system behaviour change

Participative Management was a core component of organizational development in the 1960s. The methodologies presented here build on this awareness of the importance of active participation. The key difference is that such participation is extended beyond the management cadre to the whole organizational membership. This is one of the many aspects of these ways of working that leaders can find very challenging.

3. The importance of dialogue to behaviour change

Dialogic approaches to organizational change emerged in the 1990s, the most notable being Appreciative Inquiry, as coherent yet different approaches to organizational development. The key distinguishing feature of these approaches from what had gone before was the recognition that "reality is socially constructed and socially negotiated and that organizations are (seen as) meaning-making systems" (Burnes & Cooke, 2012, p. 1411). Around the same time, Schein developed his process consultancy model, built on a recognition that "all organizational problems are fundamentally problems involving human interactions and processes" (Schein, 1988, p. 12).

These dialogic approaches were accompanied by the emergence of complexity theories of organization. These attracted attention because they suggested that using these approaches could lead psychologists to understand the complexity of organizations in the same way that natural scientists grasp complex natural systems (Wheatley, 1999). From this perspective, organizations are seen as dynamic non-linear systems, the outcome of whose actions is unpredictable, but, like turbulence in gases and liquids, is governed by a set of simple order-generating rules (Burnes, 2005). That is to say, they are complex but not chaotic.

4. The emergence of co-creative methodologies

The large group methods that are explained more fully in the rest of the book are also known as co-creative approaches to change. They are a separate and distinctive collection of approaches, not to be confused with some other communication methodologies such as town hall meetings, or even Work-Out sessions. While these processes might look similar, in that they gather a large number of people together in a room, they are fundamentally different in process and reflect different sets of underlying beliefs about organizations and change. The co-creative or transformational collaborative approaches that feature in this book have some distinctive features.

Distinctive Features of Co-creative Approaches to Change

1. The nature of their interaction is many-to-many rather than one-to-many

A key feature of these approaches is that conversation, discussion, and communication take place simultaneously within different groups of people for a large part of the process or event. So typically there will be a lot of pairs of people, or small groups, all talking simultaneously either in the same large space or across the organization. This contrasts with, for instance, town hall meetings where typically a few people on stage address the silent majority. The simultaneous conversation present in the co-creative approaches leads to some interesting sub-characteristics.

- No one hears everything that has been said.
- No one has a superior overview of what happened at the event.
- Different people will make different sense of the same event.
- Achieving sufficiently shared understanding to allow broadly aligned activity to take place takes precedence over achieving consensus.

In essence these approaches are predicated on a belief that we don't all have to be singing from exactly the same hymn sheet to be able to move forward.

2. They are predicated on an understanding that the social world is socially constructed

Social constructionism (Gergen & Gergen, 2003) is a philosophical understanding of the nature of knowledge that, broadly speaking, suggests that what we know and accept as truth is an emergent feature of our interactions and communications. It's very easy to disappear in a miasma of qualifiers and circumlocutions when attempting to talk about or explain social constructionism – just take a look at any of the key texts. However, the concept does offer the idea that it is possible for a group of people to each see the same things differently. Accepting this we can see that shifts in perception may open up new possibilities for action. In other words, we might not be able to change the facts but we can change how we view things. Some fundamental social constructionist ideas are important to understanding how these co-creative approaches enable groups to effect change *in the moment* as their understanding of the situation they are in changes.

a) We see what we talk about/we hear what we listen out for

For many of us our default belief position is that we see what is in front of our eyes and we hear what is going on around us. Interestingly, much research has concluded that this is not so. What we hear or perceive is a function *both* of what is there *and* of the focus and preconceptions we bring to it. As we have already mentioned, we only attend to about 1% of what is going on around us (Achor, 2011). Many mindfulness exercises are about increasing this 1%. In this way attention is a crucial component of change: refocus our attention and we refocus what we can see. It also means that directing attention is a crucial leadership activity. These co-creative methods enable the system to focus its attention on a specific topic or question in a new way to bring new information into the light.

b) Reality is socially constructed and we create our realities
in relationship and communication

This means that if we are trying to affect a whole system, then the whole system needs to create the new reality. Together we discover information by focusing our attention, together we negotiate the meaning of the information, together we identify some implications for action, and together we act to change the world. An individual trying to change a system in a directive way is almost certainly doomed to failure as the system is stronger, unless of course they use coercion. An individual working to *create the conditions* for system change is on a much better wicket. This is achieved by focusing the system's attention so it "sees" new things and so adapts its behaviour.

c) Meaning is context bound

Words have a dictionary meaning, a formal definition, while at the same time their meaning is slippery, shifting with the context. Thus the same word can be comic, tragic, or ironic in its meaning depending on the context. In a more subtle way, some organizational words, such as strategy, change, and culture, will take on different meanings in different contexts. Organizations need to understand that the functional meaning of words in the specific context of their organization is a product of how they are used, by whom, and in what context.

For example, I am sometimes involved in helping organizations to "drive our values throughout the organization." A typical scenario is that the senior team have spent some time working out the organizational values. To them the words have deep and specific meaning, although to an unbiased outsider they look fairly standard fare for such an endeavour, featuring, for instance, "respect," "customer focused," "striving for excellence," and so on. Telling the rest of the organization that these are the values may mean that the people become able to recite them, but it doesn't of itself ensure they can live them, or that they become deeply embedded in the organizational life. For that to happen the organization needs to have extensive conversations where the meaning of the value word is explored. Then their active function, their influence on behaviour and their meaning is negotiated in each individual's context of work.

d) Language contains moral order

How we talk about someone or about a situation contains ideas about what might be an appropriate action to take. In this way we can't separate talk from action. Action potential is contained within and created by talk. This is because when we talk we are making sense of things: we are constructing meaning. How we understand things affects how we feel we should act. From this perspective language is fateful and impactful; very powerful, in fact, and to be used with care. As we construct motive in conversation so we construct response. How we interpret the world affects how we act in the world; and we have choices about how we interpret the world, particularly regarding the actions of others. In this way morality is contained within the way we converse about the world.

e) Organizations are networks of conversation

I find this a very succinct expression of a powerful idea. Our "organization" is socially constructed, that is to say, the patterns of interaction and communication of groups of people create and recreate the thing we call our organization. All the artefacts, desks, machines, and so on would have no meaning if it weren't for the meaning we create around and about them. This means that to change our organization we need to change the patterns of interaction and conversation, because it is these that hold our "organization" in place.

f) Information lies in difference

This idea articulates the value of diversity. Comparing two apples we learn little about apples; comparing an apple with an orange we learn something about both of them. Sometimes the more mechanistic planned approach to change strives for consistency; it requires, for example, "everyone to sing from the same hymn sheet" or for the organization to "have all its ducks in a row." Too great an insistence on this can stifle the expression of different perspectives and experience that might be brought to bear on the challenge. It achieves simplicity and clarity at the cost of innovation and resource. Finding a constructive way to work with difference enhances the resource available to an organization during change.

g) We seek always to make sense and go on

We are social animals, we are wired to make sense of things so we can continue to act in the world. This has two important connotations in this context. First, as we have already touched on, it means that people don't wait passively while you finesse that communication document. They are continually involved in a conversation that seeks to make sense of what is happening around them. When their attention is caught by a new feature in their environment, and we are wired to notice the novel, then that will be the focus of some sense-making. It also means that people only need to make "enough" sense to keep going, not necessarily complete sense. We can and do work from a place of "a working hypothesis" to enable us to continue to act in the world. The co-creative methodologies outlined here are all predicated on this ability of social groups.

h) The future is socially constructed

The future isn't out there waiting for us to plan our way to it, nor is it in some way preordained. It is created by the actions we take today. In this way the future is contained in the present. To create a different future tomorrow we need to do different things today. We can influence how the future unfolds.

All this means that, as Shaw says, when working from a social constructionist perspective we are working with "the assumption that the activity of *conversation* itself is the *key process* through which forms of organising are dynamically *sustained and changed*" (2002, p. 10; my emphasis). Understanding this we "try to shift people's perspective to see that organizational change *is* this process rather than an end product of it" (p. 33). However, as Stacey, Griffin, and Shaw say, "… the dominant voice in organization and management theory [is that] which speaks the language of design, regularity and control. In this language, managers stand outside the organizational system, which is thought of as an objective, pre-given reality that can be modelled and designed and they control it." (2002, p. ix). This

Box 4.1   Perspective Is All

A contemporary reviewer wrote this ...

This fictional account of the day-to-day life of an English game-keeper is of considerable interest to outdoor-minded readers, as it contains passages on pheasant raising, on apprehending of poach-ers, ways to control vermin and other chores and duties of the professional gamekeeper. Unfortunately one is obliged to wade through many pages of extraneous material in order to discover and savour those sidelights on the management of a Midland shooting estate. This book cannot, however, take the place of J.R. Miller's *Practical Gamekeeping*.

... of *Lady Chatterley's Lover*.

Zern (2004)

dominant view, they argue, is not aligned with an understanding of human life as "the co-evolution of jointly constructed reality" (p. x). I would agree. Box 4.1 gives an illustration of how our perspective affects what we see.

3. They recognize that conversation is a systemic process

Given the above, it's easy to see why these methodologies focus on conver-sation, communication, and language. They recognize that conversation is a systemic process and that organizations are systemic contexts. A word here about a confusing word: *systemic* means how one thing unfolds in the context of another. On the whole, conversation is a systemic activity. These co-creative methodologies are context-sensitive systemic approaches to change. In other words, they don't offer a one-size-fits-all approach, they take a systemic approach: the approach is responsive to the system it is work-ing with; it will unfold differently each time within some broad parameters.

Systematic activity, on the other hand, is not context bound. It is a way of doing something that is thought to be transferable anywhere. It is driven by routine, not by context. For example, you will have your own systematic way of tying your shoelaces. There are a few different variations of this around, but you are likely to have one way you tie your shoelaces whatever lace-up shoes you are wearing and wherever you are. It's quick, easy, mindless activity that you do the same way every time and it works for you. You don't do it differently in the bathroom and the bedroom, or at work and at home: it is not context specific. Systemic and systematic, although only differing in two letters, are almost opposites in meaning. In my experience, the close correspondence of these two words means that people often "hear" a word they know (e.g., systematic) when one says one they don't (e.g., systemic).

Planned change approaches are sold as being systematic: a series of steps that, if followed correctly, will produce the same result everywhere. David Cooperrider faced a dilemma related to this distinction as he attempted to explain Appreciative Inquiry practice: how to produce a sufficiently informative template that facilitated people to practise *systemically* without producing a rigidly prescribed *systematic* process. The answer was to produce a model of the process, and some guiding principles, and to ignore the invitation to produce a systematic, step-by-step guide.

The beauty of this approach is that it fully accommodates the abilities of the particular practitioner and the circumstances of the particular context. How you do Appreciative Inquiry in any particular setting is always going to be dependent on who you are, your resources and abilities, and the situation or context. The model and the principles create a frame within which to act. At its heart Appreciative Inquiry is an etymological choice, it is a philosophical approach and it is an ethical act. The other co-creative methodologies explored in later chapters, while more prescriptive in some of their detail, are also at heart systemic.

4. They recognize that organizations are about patterns and that change is about changing patterns

These methodologies are focused on disrupting the established patterns of organizational life by inviting different people in different configurations to have different conversations about different topics, framed differently. Since the organization is "a network of conversation," as explained above, this creates change.

5. They are focused on effecting change at many levels simultaneously

All these methodologies are about involving the whole system in the change conversation. They construct change as a social process that can occur dynamically and simultaneously across the organization. Change does not have to be a top-down linear process. Change effected from this perspective is messier, yet has the potential to be faster and more coordinated.

6. *They connect to values to gain commitment*

These methodologies call not just on the power of logical argument but also on the power of emotional motivation. By involving people in ways that allow them to discover and share some of their deepest values and motivations, and to join with others in discovering how these can be expressed in the unfolding future, these methodologies can create a powerful and resilient motivation to action and change. This is particularly important for, as Cheung-Judge and Holbeche write, "The deep changes – in how people think, what they believe, how they see the world – are difficult, if not impossible, to achieve through compliance" (2011, p. 265). Discussing this further they note that there are two types of employee engagement: emotional commitment and rational commitment. They argue that emotional commitment is four times as strong as rational commitment in driving employee effort (p. 291). These co-creative methodologies help create this emotional commitment.

7. *They create hope and other positive emotions*

A key effect of these approaches, because of their emphasis on involvement, participation, and seeking out the positive, is that they create hope. The more I work with organizations going through change the more I understand the importance and power of this particular emotion. The more people start to feel helpless (unable to affect what is happening to them, in their world) the more likely they are to start feeling hopeless. Appreciative Inquiry explicitly works to create positive emotions. However, the other methodologies mentioned here also have this capacity, which can be further encouraged by positive framing of the topic or the questions used.

8. *They encourage high-quality connections and the formation of high-energy networks*

These are two concepts from positive psychology, and I wrote about them earlier (Lewis, 2011). High quality connections are characterized by trust and respect. They are intimate and meaningful. They are a foundation of connectivity and resilience. The experience of them is life-enhancing.

The probability of experiencing a high-quality connection with a colleague is heightened in these co-creative encounters compared to a standard "board meeting" discussion of change. Positive energy networks are a related phenomenon. The term describes a network of people that has a high proportion of these kinds of connections. Quite often the network is focused around one particular person, but either way it is generative, responsive, breeds positivity, and generates possibility, hope, and commitment of discretionary time to activities. It is easy to see how helpful these organizational features are during times of change.

9. They allow people to feel heard

A key point of these co-creative methodologies is the exchange of voices or perspectives. The voice of everyone present is valued. Everyone gets to talk about what they think is really important. They may even get to make decisions, depending on the decision-making status of the event. I can't stress enough how important this is during organizational change. As we mentioned earlier, during imposed, top-down, programmatic planned change people can feel voiceless, reduced to inert components of a machine or a chess game, moved about at the behest or whim of others. Forced, perhaps, in the apparent interests of fairness, to, as they see it, "reapply for their own jobs" they feel their confidence and power dribble away. By the time management thinks to ask for their "suggestions" about the change via a suggestion box, they have lost the belief in their power to influence, or the goodwill towards management to contribute. And so a vicious circle of "they don't contribute: they don't listen" is re-enforced.

Co-creative methodologies are a powerful antidote. Ideally, of course, a system-wide co-creative event would be held at the beginning of the process. However, such processes can create a space where people can have influence over what is happening in their work environment at any point in the process. Be warned though, some preparatory work may be necessary in the organization to create or release the belief or hope that this event might actually "make a difference." Those who are resigned to their fate can find the invitation to contribute to, or to experience, hope as unsettling as it is exciting. Their re-engagement with hope can be very tentative. Assuming the event is of a voluntary nature, a minimal level of hope needs to be engendered beforehand if people are going to risk even engaging in your event.

To ensure that your event or process maximizes the positive features and benefits of co-creative events as outlined above, it is useful to understand a few key principles of practice.

Principles of Practice for Achieving Change in Living Human Systems

1. Seek to discover strengths and resources in people

Developing an appreciative eye or ear, and the ability to affirm the good that you see, acts to magnify and grow the best of what is around you. It also creates a different conversational or interactional dynamic. I am currently engaged in a coaching assignment for the first time in a while. Much of each session involves me eliciting and amplifying the coachee's successes, and affirming how they are an appropriate expression of his strengths in action. In this way I am very consciously looking for the positive, and I thoroughly believe in the value to be gained from learning from success and in "strengths-spotting" as a coaching practice. Even so, I am mildly astonished by how useful and informative the coachee finds this process. Not only does he always declare that the sessions have been so but he also talks about how energizing he finds the sessions. The effectiveness of this approach is supported by the fact that the positive change in his management style and his growth as a leader have been noticed and commented on by those above and below him in the organization, as well as by others with whom he interacts in the organization. He credits much of this to our sessions, which is highly flattering and affirming of course; however, I credit it to the power of a positive approach to elicit growth and change.

Whitney and colleagues, discussing the characteristics of appreciative leaders, talk about the strength of strengths-spotting. Strengths-spotters are "able to hear positive potential through the haze of problems, dilemmas, issues and troubles" (2010, p. 68). As they note, appreciative leaders find strengths in people and situations because they look for them. Meanwhile, O'Hanlon and Beadle (1997) remind us to inquire about resources beyond the person, to recognize that everyone is plugged into a bigger network that contains resources that might be useful. The key question to access these is "Who or what else can help?" In this way we are working with the theory of the world as a network and as an economy of strengths. By helping people tap into the resources around them we quite literally increase their resourcefulness.

2. Create accounts of possibility that motivate

Positive approaches to change are predicated on drawing motivation out of people rather than on the more traditional method of trying to push it in. Attractive images of the future – images that people have helped to create and of which they can see themselves as being a part – draw people towards them. In so many situations, asking people about how things *could be*, rather than how they currently are, acts to switch their focus away from the current stuck situation. The shift in motivation from wanting to get away from something (i.e., the unrewarding present) to wanting to move towards something else (i.e., the potentially rewarding future) creates hope, which in turn releases new resources of energy and cognition.

3. Ask, don't tell

Key to producing change in people is asking questions rather than telling answers. Asking questions usually stimulates thought and engagement. Telling answers often produces push-back, resulting in the familiar "Why don't you? – Yes, but" conversation. As mentioned earlier, Whitney and colleagues note that, "Inquiry requires daily practice: to ask more and tell less" (2010, p. 29). It also requires a shift in our understanding of what leadership looks like. When we move to ask more and tell less it can induce a strange sense of dereliction of duty. Essentially we ask ourselves, "Aren't I supposed to have answers? Isn't that why I'm paid more?" So the guidance here is all predicated on that shift in mindset from "I am here to *direct* change" to "I am here to *create the conditions* that enable change to happen." Asking questions is a key skill in enabling change to happen. I find the potential of questions to produce effects endlessly fascinating. Here are a few examples of different kinds of questions and their potential effects. There is more about different kinds of questions and their effects in Lewis, Passmore, and Cantore (2007).

a) Expanding questions
Cooperrider refers to the "exponential inquiry effect" (2015). As we inquire into the good and the positive from an appreciative mindset, so we "establish the new and eclipse the old" (2015). This is another way of expressing the power of focusing people's attention on what they want rather than on what they don't want, what they can do rather than what they can't, and what excites them rather than what depresses them; this

refocusing of attention establishes these as the important topics to which we must attend. The new topics, the new energy, the new motivation eclipses the old attention grabbers. It's not so much that these approaches resolve the "old" problems as that they dissolve them. What loomed so large in the mind, the imagination, and the world is now diminished, its power much reduced; without the oxygen of constant attention it no longer fills our vision.

Appreciative questions expand our dialogue about what works, increase our appreciation of the possible and expand our awareness of our resources and resourcefulness even as they build them. Appreciative questions are growth questions, and growth is at the heart of change. Appreciative leaders use questions to access both their own potential and that of other people.

b) Energy questions

Hoogendijk classifies some specific questions such as "What are you most proud of?" and "Can you remember a person who highly inspired you?" as energy questions, noting, "The act of remembering positive emotions boosts one's energy" (2015, p. 32). He recommends them as great starters to a constructive conversation. He identifies the positive virtuous circle that can stem from these simple questions. "Asking these questions puts you in an appreciative mode. Being in an appreciative mode helps you find more energy questions. It's generative!" (p. 32). Having energy is essentially a state of being motivated.

c) Positive questions

Whitney and colleagues suggest that "All you have to do is ask, and a wealth of information, ideas and knowledge unfolds" (2010, p. 28). Positive questions, that is, questions focused on the best of experiences, reveal "treasure troves" of best practices, success stories, and creativity (2010). Positive questions produce the positive emotions that are at the heart of high performance. Emotions such as pride, courage, confidence, and generosity encourage initiative-taking and high performance; they also encourage learning and innovation. We consider how to create positive and appreciative questions in Chapter 6 (see Box 6.3). A typical positive question focuses on a highlight moment such as "When have you felt at your best at work?" or "What has been your proudest moment in the last few months?"

d) Focusing questions

Questions focus our attention. They are not neutral data-gathering tools; they have an impact on what we see in the world, what we consider to be important. So ask questions about the things you want people to be focusing on. Very typically, this is what you want more of, so instead of asking, "What went wrong in that last project?" you might ask, "What did we do really well in the project and what can we do even better next time?" Alternatively, you might want people to focus on the small things that make a difference, so you might ask "Thinking about the best meeting you have ever been part of, and one almost but not quite as good, what made the difference?" Or you can ask people at loggerheads to identify each other's best qualities. We learn about what we ask about, so we should think carefully about what we inquire into.

e) Magic questions

These are great. These transport people out of their enmeshment with the current world into another world. Classics include: "Imagine a miracle whereby this problem/issue/bad thing was solved/disappeared/wasn't affecting your life any more. How would things be? How would you know the miracle had occurred? What would be different? Talk me through your day without this problem"; "If you had three wishes of how things could be different, what would they be?"; "Imagine I have a magic wand and I make it possible for you to give a great presentation/get that sale/have a great conversation with that difficult person, what would be happening?"; and "What if your wildest dreams came true?" These questions can produce great moments of insight and energy for change.

4. Motivate through stories not lists

Appreciative questions are designed to provoke stories rather than lists. Sharing stories is a great way to stimulate growth and creativity that doesn't provoke resistance. When we hear inspiring stories that resonate with us in some way we start to imagine ourselves in different scenarios and futures; we are inspired and motivated. Our brains are particularly geared to respond to storytelling. Stories may soothe, excite, frighten, or even bore us (especially if we are hearing them for the nth time!), but in general they engage us. Hearing other people's success stories can inspire us to try new things or adopt new practices. They can inspire us through a competitive edge – "Well if they can learn that new thing I'm damn sure I can" – or through reassurance – "Well if this person I trust got good results from it then maybe I will give it a go." They enrich our sense of possibility and build our confidence to face uncertainty. We can become hopeful. We begin to dream big and be more willing to take risks. They also inspire us to raise our game (Fredrickson, 2003).

5. Be alert to the holy trio

Inspiration, hope, and creativity are at the root of personal and collective transformation. We are always working to create these in situations where something needs to change.

6. Aim beyond engagement for flourishing

Flourishing is a term increasingly used to describe a state of positive well-being, emotionally, mentally, and physically. Given that we spend more time engaged with our work organizations than we do with our families, friends, or other institutions (Hochschild, 1997), work could be a major source of flourishing for people. Since flourishing is not traditionally a primary concern of organizations, we could ask, why should organizations take an interest in people's levels of flourishing? Increasingly, research demonstrates that "happiness," which we might accept as a proxy for flourishing, is positively related to engagement, energy, motivation, confidence, goal achievement, and contribution (Pryce-Jones, 2010, p. 3). How then can we create flourishing at work?

A positive work identity is a key source of flourishing. Work identities can be positive in four different ways. First, the work identity can be a function of the content of the work and the extent to which it allows people to exercise their "best self" in terms of character strengths and virtues. Second, there is the effect of someone's subjective evaluation of their role, that is, the person feels good about their work identity as a fireman or doctor, for example. Third, our identity can be enhanced through our sense of self as the job enables us to mature and adapt, to grow and learn; and fourth, identity is enhanced when the job allows for integration of other important identities with the work identity – for instance, when someone can integrate other identities, such as being gay, or a single mum, or an enthusiastic trainspotter, into their work identity, rather than having to split them off in separate compartments (Dutton, Roberts, & Bednar, 2011, p. 156).

Ibarra suggests that positive work identities promote flourishing at work in three ways. First, people who explore new possible selves at work, to adapt to demands of changing work, experience more coherence between who they are and what they do (e.g., enhanced psychological functioning). Second, positive work identities also foster positive emotions, which, as is now well accepted, are positively related to the likelihood of succeeding (Achor, 2011). And third, positive work identities also promote more prosocial behaviour (Ibarra, 2003). In addition, research shows that positive self-evaluations of work-related identity are an important predictor of work engagement (Mauno, Kinnunen, & Ruokolainen, 2007), and that work engagement is associated with adaptive behaviours such as using initiative, which in turn affect the bottom line (Harter, Schmidt, & Keyes, 2003). All this means that people with positive work identities are more able to deal with current challenges and to take advantage of opportunities (Dutton *et al.*, 2011, p. 157). Flourishing at work is also enhanced by the five factors identified by Seligman as key to individual flourishing (positive emotions, engagement, meaningfulness, positive relationships, and accomplishment) (2011), and Cameron's factors for flourishing organizations (positive deviance, affirmation, and virtuous practices) (2003).

7. Pay special attention to leaders

Working in this way can be very hard for leaders. Asking questions rather than giving answers, calling on the collective wisdom of the organization rather than being the individual hero, being authentic rather than playing a part, all of these can be unusual or alien behaviours. They need to understand what they are getting into and what is required of them to make it work.

These events are predicated on relationship and trust as the source of leader power rather than command and control status. For leaders in many organizations this is unexplored territory. In addition, "We are biased toward telling instead of asking because we live in a pragmatic, problem-solving culture in which knowing things and telling others what we know is valued. We also live in a structured society in which building relationships is not as important as task accomplishment ..." (Schein, 2013, p. 4), while at the same time, "... the art of questioning becomes more difficult as status increases" (p. xii). This is because in hierarchical systems "having to ask is a sign of weakness or ignorance, so we avoid it as much as possible" (p. 5). So it is wise to be aware of how much we are asking of leaders when we suggest working this way, and to give them time to understand these differences and what they mean. We also need to help them understand that they are part of the change, not just the commissioners of the change.

I have learnt from experience to be wary of the lip service agreement managers and leaders offer, the "yes, yes" of compliance that means "Just do it, it won't affect me anyway, it's their problem." Inevitably, it isn't just "their problem," and, assuming the event is successful, it will affect the managers and leaders. Once or twice I've gone along with the "top and tailing" approach, where a leader suggests that they will come in at the beginning and return at the end to see what has been achieved. Big mistake. They need to be present (and I mean present, not in a corner working on their laptop), involved in and influencing discussions and decisions as they happen. Nothing kills an event dead quicker that an energized group presenting their ideas to a leader who has missed all the background to and investment in these ideas or decisions and who then proceeds to critically evaluate (pick holes) in them all. The group will visibly deflate before your eyes and not much will happen after the event.

8. Pay attention to the decision-making status of the event

This leads us to the important point of deciding beforehand the decision-making power of the event. Ideally, the event can make decisions there and then. Try to avoid the need to present the outcome of the event to some other decision-making body. Again, I have fallen foul of this with strategic-oriented large group events where the output has been ideas to go to "the strategic planning group." This stops everything in its tracks and the energy to make the changes drains away.

9. Prepare for afterwards

Again, a lesson learnt the hard way is the importance of planning what is going to happen after the event. At one time I naively assumed it was obvious: the embryonic projects and project groups that emerge from a good event need to be supported; managers need to take an interest; a process needs to be put in place to encourage, coordinate, and celebrate the groups and what they are achieving. Turns out it was only obvious to me, and I wasn't there to make it happen. Help those who are there understand the importance of tracking and fanning the small beginnings of change (Bushe, 2010). In his research into the effectiveness of Appreciative Inquiry interventions Stellnberger (2011) noted that the organization that had a clear follow-up structure of weekly Appreciative Inquiry branch meetings was still reaping the benefits of their big event some two to three years later, much more so than the two other organizations who hadn't put such things into effect.

10. Aim for volunteerism

With all these methodologies the volunteer principle is important. This alone makes them counter-cultural in many organizations. Organizational realities mean it may not be possible to negotiate that attendance at the event is voluntary, although I would fight pretty hard for this for all sorts of reasons – one clear benefit being that the organization has to start experimenting with different behaviour just to get the event to happen. They have to entice people rather than order them, and that demands a different understanding of the relationship at play, which acts to recast the understanding of the organization from a power-based hierarchy to a relational-based system.

However, not all battles can be won. It is not uncommon to end up with the organizational fudge where attendance is "voluntary" yet people know they are expected to be there. So be it. Once they are at the event you are in charge. Creating choice creates choosing. So make it clear at the beginning to any that protest about being here that, while you are pleased they are there and hope since they are they will choose to take part, as far as you are concerned they are grown adults with many pressures and priorities to balance and it's for them to decide where they need to be. If you give permission for them to leave if they feel there is somewhere more important they need to be, then you create choice for them. And given choice, they may choose to "hang around and see how it goes." Key to facilitating this shift is doing everything to help them maintain face whatever choices they make, and making staying an attractive option. The organization may be treating them like a wayward child, but you are treating them respectfully as an autonomous adult daily facing the challenge of making choices among competing priorities. They must choose as they see fit. Given the choice, freed from the constraint of having to be there, usually people do choose to stay.

Conclusion

In this chapter we have considered some of the common characteristics of co-creative events and some of the key principles of practice that enhance the likelihood of creating successful, engaging, positive, and impactful change processes or events. We have described some further positive psychology research that supports these approaches and have identified, in passing, some of the challenges they can produce for organizations, leaders, and participants. Next I want to consider how to work with positive psychology at an individual and at a team level.

5

Using Positive Psychology to Achieve Change at the Team and Individual Level

Introduction

Much of this book is devoted to exploring large group transformational collaborative approaches. However, many of the principles can be applied to help achieve individual and team development. We will discuss applications at the organization or large group level in the next few chapters; here I want to give some guidance on how to apply this thinking at the individual, team, or small group level, and to introduce some of the many particular techniques that have been developed in this area. Unlike opportunities at the larger system or organizational level, which usually have to be negotiated, opportunities to create change at an individual or team level occur all the time. Understanding a few key principles will help you to make the most of opportunities as they occur. We will then go on to look at ways of putting these principles into action.

Principles

1. Use micro-moments well

Life is a series of micro-moments. At a recent conference, Rath quoted a figure of 19,200 moments in a day (2015), all of which have the potential to change what happens next. Change is so often thought of as a big bang event in organizations, yet it can equally well be seen as the culmination of lots of small shifts in behaviour, lots of micro-moments where something different happens. Recognizing micro-moments as opportunities either to reinforce the status quo or to create change by saying or doing something different increases the opportunities available for achieving change. Making use of these moments greatly magnifies the resources being utilized to create change. In other words, the interaction doesn't have to be labelled "coaching" or "workshop" to have the potential to contribute to change. At a very basic level, deciding to ask a question rather than state an opinion at a contentious point in a meeting can transform the conversation.

A key micro-moment occurred during a recent piece of work. The group I was working with were facing an ethical dilemma. It was clear that the product was declining and it was likely that the unit would close. Redundancy loomed. Human Resources were encouraging everyone to apply for other jobs in the organization as they arose, including the management. As I walked into the room of managers I knew that one of them had already secured another job. This wasn't yet common knowledge among the group. I knew he was feeling very conflicted about this because he had told me so in a pre-conversation. Not long after the meeting started, another manager stated how he couldn't leave his unit until the bitter end, that he was obliged, he felt, to go down with the ship. As a leader he felt this to be the only honourable course of behaviour. As he was saying this he looked terrible, very stressed. It was clear there was the potential for a very hostile and accusing conversation in the room.

Later in the session we began to address this as I asked them all to answer the questions "How can I be a good person in this difficult situation?" and "How can we support each other?" People began to speak about the issue and how they felt about it. Unhelpful metaphors such as "rats deserting a sinking ship" were beginning to feature in the conversation. The conversation was intense and heartfelt. I was attempting to open up options, trying to create an understanding of honourable behaviour that had more than one interpretation. We created enough space that the manager who had another job was able to share that information, and also that he felt very bad about it but felt he had no option, given his family needs and so on. So it emerged we had a group where pretty much everyone was feeling bad about the decisions they were making, feeling trapped, and feeling a strong need to justify their decision as the "correct" way to behave. It was a very classic example of the downward spiral of negative emotions, dualistic thinking, and so irresolvable issues.

The leader had been listening and contributing to the discussion. He could have said that one or other course of action was the more honourable. He could have told them that as managers they shouldn't think of themselves, only of others. He could have suggested that their concern should be to ensure that their staff didn't find other jobs and leave the unit in the lurch. Instead he said, "Do I want to leave? No. If a suitable job was on offer would I apply? Probably." There was an audible wobble in the room. With this comment everything changed. The unthinkable became thinkable. If the leader wasn't going to sacrifice himself on the altar of doing "the right thing" why would anyone else? The discussion opened up and we created a much more flexible account of "right things" and "honourable behaviour," recognizing different people's needs and priorities. Once the group was able to accept that different people would make different choices and that those choices didn't make them bad people, it also became possible to recognize that everyone still wanted the unit to do as well as possible and that everyone would do what they could to achieve that, whatever their decisions about moving on or staying until the bitter end. To plan to leave was not the same as to abandon. From here they were able to move to what they could do to support each other as a group through this very difficult time. That was a leader using a micro-moment to make a huge change.

2. Kick-start self-renewing virtuous circles

Positive images, actions, and emotions can form virtuous circles of connection that then become self-reinforcing. "Through their words, actions and relationships, appreciative leaders start waves of positive change rippling outwards" (Whitney *et al.*, 2010). Positive ripples keep magnifying and multiplying through relationships. When we are done well by we are more likely to do well by. When we experience positive emotional states we are more likely to help create them in others (and vice versa, note!). When we see others doing or being good, we are inspired to emulate them (Fredrickson, 2003). As the leader you may need to regularly kick-start these virtuous circles, but once started they will continue to have effect for an unpredictable amount of time in unpredictable ways.

3. Constantly renew positive psychology processes

Robert Quinn says, "Organization is always breaking down" (2015). In other words, organization is as subject to the process of entropy as any other phenomenon. The point of leadership, he suggests, is to counteract this process; in other words, to coordinate, connect, and generally help create coherence in a system. Importantly, this isn't achieved by "knowing and doing" so much as by the leader's "state of being … [or] … moral condition" (2015). As we mentioned in Chapter 2, a leader has influence through words and deeds. The important organizational processes that promote flourishing at all organizational levels are affirmation, virtuous practices, and positive deviance (Cameron, 2008a). Leaders need to constantly renew these processes by: noticing and connoting the positive (encouraging individuals, teams, and organizations to move in the direction of the positive); creating positivity (in the many ways described in this book, for instance); modelling virtuous behaviour (essentially being their best self in their interactions with people); creating hope and optimism (which will build the organizational psychological capital and contribute to resilience); and, by supplying support, encouragement, and positive feedback. Ideally, these ways of behaving become the organizational culture and everyone is able to create these psychological states and features with everyone else. Even so, organization is subject to breakdown, so the job is never finished. As the leader you need to devote time and energy to supporting, creating, and introducing ways to create and renew these positive psychological processes. A client quote from Whitney and colleagues' research echoes this, recognizing that it takes work to keep up the positive because of a societal bias towards negativity; the client says, "If you don't pump positivity into the system, negativity will set in on its own" (2010, p. 21).

4. Be the centre of a positive energy network

People want to be around people who are positive, who have a positive energy. Whitney and colleagues' research identified different ways this positive energy is expressed; for instance, positive people make the best of situations and draw on what is positive in any situation. They use positive reinforcement. They find the positive in others. They let people make their own decisions. They exert a magnetic pull that makes others want to be part of what they are doing (2010).

5. Be appreciative

Recognition lets people know they are on the right track. Appreciation communicates and reinforces your values. Compliments foster a positive work environment. Gratitude is a verbal immunity boost; it is good for your health. Praise is good for the health of those you honour. Acknowledgement creates a sense of safety. Gratitude encourages risk taking and experimentation (Whitney *et al.*, 2010, p. 137). It's possible to reap these benefits for yourself as well as bestowing them on others. "Going fishing" for appreciation is when you let others know that you need a positivity or appreciation boost and ask them if they have any positive feedback they can share with you, and is a recognized mood self-management process (Pryce-Jones, 2010, p. 54).

6. Use language with care

Words are important. "The habitual language of business renders the creative spirit invisible" (Whitney *et al.*, 2010, p. 151). People are stimulated, inspired, and excited by elevated language that speaks to the whole person. Use language, words, and stories that resonate with the heart and open the mind. The careful use of words helps meaning-making, can stimulate the collective wisdom, and can raise the awareness of everyone about the aspirations and ambitions for the future. O'Hanlon and Beadle identify a use of language they name "escalator language" (1997, p. 18). It is a way of projecting the best of the present into the future, so moving people forward. It can help move people out of problem talk. It involves listening appreciatively for the positive (which may essentially be the reverse image of the problem being described) and amplifying it as a possibility. He gives an example.

Someone says: I feel hopeless and lost and I don't know what to do.
To which one responds: So you'd really like to get a sense of hope back in your life.

There are three steps to using escalator language: reflect back their concerns as preferred goals rather than as problems to be got rid of; use words that convey an expectancy that the desired future will come about; and, use phrases like "yet" or "so far" to suggest that at some time in the future the problem will end or things will be better.

7. Stay optimistic

Moods and behaviours have ripple effects. Pryce-Jones quotes Barsade's 2002 research on emotional contagion and asserts that negative behaviour has a ripple effect to two degrees, but that a positive ripple spreads even further up to three degrees (2010, p. 49). We also know that managers' generalized optimism is related to positive organizational outcomes; for example, higher future success expectancy, better coping with stress, and enhanced job performance and job satisfaction during and after downsizing (Armstrong-Stassen & Schlosser, 2008, cited in Ko & Donaldson, 2011, p. 146). As mentioned elsewhere in this book, this advice comes with a health warning that unrealistic or obsessive optimism can be counter-productive if not downright dangerous, but as a general principle being optimistic is good place to start from when working with people or teams.

8. Seek out the positive in people and situations

Look at people with appreciative eyes. Be aware that all their potential may not be readily available to the naked eye; instead one needs to uncover or discover the hidden positive potential, that is, the strengths, resources, passions, and abilities not yet being fully accessed. There are many ways to learn about the positive potential in people; for example, looking out for their strengths and capabilities, revealing patterns of behaviour behind high performance by asking about past successes, or listening for or inquiring into the dream behind the cynicism. Receiving affirmation for the best of themselves encourages people to become more expansive in their thinking.

With groups, you are looking to stimulate new connections in relationship or ideas. New connections can be generative, and in turn generativity is a feature of high-quality relations. When working with groups, help people of different views reach for "both/and" ways forward that combine the best on offer. Try new ways of doing things, ways of asking the question, or even new venues to stimulate new thinking. The brain wakes up when faced with something new, while the familiar tends to encourage lazy "following the existing tramlines" thought.

9. Challenge the unspoken assumptions

When people are locked in present difficulties they tend to become very demoralized and stuck, unable to imagine better times or to be creative in the present. When people are at a low ebb they often see the world through the unspoken assumptions that this is how it is, how it has always been, and how it always will be. However, it is unlikely that the issue has always existed, or indeed that it is fully present all the time right now. By forming questions predicated on these two assumptions, that things have been different at other times, and that the intensity of the challenge varies even in the present, you are likely to be able to shift mood and increase the ability of the person to gain access to their own resources and creativity.

To do this you can ask directly, saying for instance, "Tell me about times when you aren't dealing with this problem? What are you doing?" or "When was the last time you didn't have this problem?" Or you can ask comparator questions such as, "When is it least worse?" Further, you can inquire into the exceptions; for example, "Can you tell me about the times you don't argue, when you can see the good in her." You can expand this with compare and contrast questions, comparing when the difficulty exists, "I don't feel motivated at work," to when it doesn't, "Tell me about when, in your life, you do feel motivated? Let's explore the differences."

10. Resurrect old patterns

As Quinn says, organization atrophies (2015). It is not uncommon for good strategies to become overwhelmed by time pressure, a change in personnel, or procedure and to fall, accidentally, into disuse. Only yesterday I noticed myself that my "ideal day" pattern, which involves two short breaks for exercise, including a brisk afternoon walk, had fallen into disuse due to the disruptive effect of being away for the best part of three weeks and coming back to a pile of work. As I write I am suffering a flare-up of my repetitive strain injury, a sure sign for me of being over-stressed. Typically, my response to feeling I have too much to do is to want to "bang on through it" and "just get it done," which I attempted to do late one Friday evening, and here I am a week later still suffering the after-effects. It took me until yesterday to recognize that I had allowed a very good pattern to fall into disuse even though I know that, perversely, it allows me to manage my workload better and to avoid stress symptoms. Today I shall be taking breaks! So, help people find helpful patterns of behaviour from the past that might be useful now.

Positive and Appreciative Practices

While it is great to have an idea of general principles, it is also useful to be aware of some of the specific positive psychology-based approaches that have been created to help those interested in redesigning their human resource or organizational development processes to create highly affirmative experiences for organizational members. I introduced some of these in my previous book (Lewis, 2011), such as best self-feedback as an alternative to 360-degree feedback and various strengths-based psychometrics. In the interim I pulled some of the strengths-identifying resources together into a short article (Lewis, 2012). Meanwhile, this is still an emerging area as practitioners and leaders work out how to put theory into practice in the work place. Some of those I am aware of are outlined below.

1. *Appreciative Coaching*

Appreciative Coaching is a specific coaching approach based on the 5D model of Appreciative Inquiry (Orem, Blinkert, & Clancy, 2007). Working to their model, the commissioning or *define* phase works to shape the coaching objective as an appreciative topic or aspiration. During this period some time is spent reviewing the highlights of the coachee's life so far and identifying what these highlights reveal about the person's values and aspirations, both for life and for the coaching experience. The *discovery* phase is focused on helping coachees develop an appreciative view of themselves and developing their understanding of what "gives life" to them. "Peak experience" questions help to reveal people's strengths and values, while inquiring into flow experiences will further enhance their understanding of the skills and challenges that engage them. Essentially, this phase is focused on discovering when they flourish at work and what makes that possible. The *dream* phase focuses on exploring and creating motivating visions of possibility, which are then worked into more concrete desires for the future. The *design* phase focuses attention on how they are using their attention, energy, and activity in the present to increase the probability of the futures they desire coming to pass, while in the *destiny* phase people focus on incorporating their dreams and achievements into a coherent and appreciative sense of self.

2. Performance appraisals

Few organizations find the process of appraising individual performance easy, or indeed effective. It is supposed to be a motivating, energizing, supportive process yet all too frequently becomes a disliked bureaucratic process focused on face-saving at best and scapegoating at worst, frequently producing the exact opposite effect to that intended as people become disheartened, demoralized, and demotivated. One of the many reasons for the poor performance of many performance appraisal processes is that they don't acknowledge or allow for the socially constructed nature of the engagement, by which I mean there is a fiction afoot that "appraising" someone's performance is an objective process, based on facts alone. There is also the fiction that we are highly autonomous agents completely in charge of our own destiny, meaning therefore any failure in performance is entirely down to us alone. This roughly translates as "if things go wrong that *I'm* doing it's because of those other idiots, if things go wrong that *you're* doing it's because you are an idiot." Technically known as the attribution fallacy (Jones & Harris, 1967), it is something from which we all suffer.

If we can take it as read that appraisal processes can't be "neutral, factual, and objective" then we can give up the hopeless quest to make them so (that usually results in ever more paper work), and can concentrate instead on enabling them to perform their original purpose of re-energizing and enthusing people and giving them the opportunity to dream and shape how to grow in their work role: to produce positive change, in other words. A couple of new practices have been developed that approach the appraisal process in this different way. I would like to share these with you.

a) The enthusiasm story

This simple process is directed at the appraiser before any formal appraisal meeting (Bouskila-Yam & Kluger, 2011, p. 141). It invites them to recall a specific event in which they were enthusiastic about the employee in ques-tion, and then to recall that incident in as much detail as possible, asking: What happened? What specifically were you impressed by?

This exercise in itself can be a revelation to the appraiser, who is often to be found focusing on what isn't happening that they feel they will need to talk about, rather than what is. I had a highly illuminating experience of this recently. It was a one-off coaching session as part of a development event. The young man, fairly new to management, was very concerned about one of the staff members he had inherited who wasn't doing something the way he thought it should be done, and who didn't seem to be making changes, despite his considerable efforts to direct her. We went around in circles for a while until I asked something like, "When has she most impressed you?" The answer was very quick to his lips. Shortly after he'd taken over she had achieved a very impressive sale. So my next question was, "How did she do that?" With a look of stunned wonder on his face he said, "I don't know." Hanging in parenthesis was, "and I never thought to ask." It was a pivotal moment. You could almost see the mental readjustment as his view of this woman expanded from "trouble, failure" to include "astonishing salesperson." He had a slightly stunned look on his face for the rest of the session.

Having accessed the story, the appraiser then opens the appraisal process by telling the story, saying something like, "I am going to tell you about an event where I was especially enthusiastic about you/your work. I would like you to listen to the event and to allow yourself to enjoy it without playing down your contribution." Having done this, the appraiser then goes on to ask, "What else can you tell me about what was going on at that event for you? How was it motivating or enthusing? What about it seemed to bring out the best in you?" The conversation then moves into a discovery about this person at their best and what needs to be in place to help that happen. In brief the question is, "What does this tell us about when you perform at your best?" (Bouskila-Yam & Kluger, 2011, p. 141).

b) Feed-forward interview
This preparation enthusiasm story can be linked to the feed-forward interview. This is an Appreciative Inquiry interview process that is shown to yield new insights for the appraising manager and to reduce resistance to performance appraisals. It increases positive mood and perception of learning (relative to a control group) and increases ideas regarding possible actions an interviewee can perform to achieve a personal goal. It increases self-efficacy. The interview is focused on planning for future performance and development and is concerned only with positive experiences. Negative experiences, or corrective feedback, are dealt with in a separate meeting (Kluger & Nir, 2010).

The meeting opens with the appraiser or manager saying something like,

"I am sure that during your work here you have had both negative experiences and positive experiences. Today, I would like to focus only on your positive experiences.

Could you please tell me a story that happened at your work, during which you felt full of life (happy, energized), even before the results of your actions became known?" (Kluger & Nir, 2010). This last condition may seem a little odd but it is important to separate the motivating effect of the nature of the work from the rewarding effect of success. The question is designed to illuminate what is innately motivating and rewarding to the person. This is likely, in itself, to be a reflection of his or her innate strengths and it means strengths exploration can be incorporated as part of this process.

Staying focused for the moment on the idea of the feed-forward interview, the next part of the process is designed to explore in more detail what is happening when the person is really at their best and feeling great, by asking, "What was the peak moment of this story? What did you think at the peak moment? How did you feel at that moment (including your physiological reactions)?" The conversation then goes on to explore what the conditions were that produced this exceptional experience: "What were the conditions, in you, others, and the organization (physical, temporal) that allowed this story to happen?" And finally, the interview arrives at the feed-forward questions: "Recall the conditions that allowed you to feel alive at work. Consider these conditions as road signs or a beacon that shows you how to flourish at work. To what extent are your current behaviours at work or your plans for the immediate future taking you closer to, or further away from, the conditions that allowed you to feel full of life at work?" (Kluger & Nir, 2010, p. 237).

c) Empowering principled performance

Whitney and colleagues introduce the idea of principled performance to describe what is necessary for people to be self-motivated to work to a high standard, consistently (2010). They suggest that knowing and being able to use your strengths, combined with an understanding of your own performance principles, will result in consistently great performance. When people are working with their strengths and allowed to do their best they are self-motivated to produce great performance, indeed it almost becomes impossible not to. By the same token, asking someone in this situation to do less than their best is a great way to introduce dissatisfaction. For instance, I eventually came to understand that I hated writing "development reports" because, although it was a writing task, which I usually love, the nature of the task (data reporting) and the strict time constraints for each report meant I couldn't exercise my creativity: I couldn't write while thinking deeply; instead I had to just get the data down in one sentence after another. In other words, I couldn't express my values in this work. As a lecturer, the speed marking of assessed work produced a similar intense sense of dissatisfaction with the standard of the work I was doing. To understand your principles, think about such things as what you believe creates high performance and what your standards of excellence are. You can help others achieve principled performance by helping them understand the principles that underpin their best work. Being able to exercise our principles as well as our strengths is what helps us be able to take pride in our work.

For an organization or group, principles are the overt expression of the beliefs that underlie the high performance culture. These need to be developed from the people present, not imposed from on high. Appreciative Inquiry discovery questions can help people and groups to discover the principles that inform their understanding and execution of excellence. This is known as revealing the positive core, sometimes expressed as "what gives life" to the organization. These principles, once discovered, can be written up as an articulation of "the best of the present," known as "provocative propositions." "A provocative proposition is a statement that bridges 'the best of what is' with your own speculation or articulation of 'what might be'. It stretches the status quo, challenges common assumptions or routines, and helps suggest real possibilities that represent a desired image for the organization and its people" (Watkins & Mohr, 2001, p. 141).

When people feel they can work to their own high standards they are more able to take a pride in their work. This idea relates to Seligman's recognition of achievement as one of the factors that enables people to flourish (2011). Asking people to reflect on and articulate their own standards of excellence fosters self-respect and accountability for quality and success. Asking people to articulate and work to principles liberates energy, creates dedication for success, and fosters integrity at work. On the other hand, telling people what to do breeds fear of failure. You empower principled performance across whole organizations by facilitating the discovery and articulation of shared principles. Without shared principles people do not hold together or work collaboratively (Whitney *et al.*, 2010).

3. Appreciative check-in

Kline suggests that people discuss difficult issues better if they are in a good state of mind before they start (1999). Given what we know about the effect of positive mood states on cognitive and social processes, this makes perfect sense. Kline calls on this with her "time to think" methodology where she recommends that proceedings start with a structured round of good news (1999). Whitney and colleagues also suggest starting meetings with what they call an "appreciative check-in" (2010, p. 63). Asking people cold, who have never been asked before, to think of some good news to share before tackling the "work" agenda can be a little challenging the first time. Counselling a friend of mine who wanted to introduce such a round with her team before a difficult meeting but was a bit at a loss as to how to do so, I suggested she frame the exercise as it was, that is, an experiment that she would really like them to all try out with her and then they could see what they thought afterwards. We considered that maybe she might "confess" that she had never tried anything quite like this before but thought it sounded interesting. She was effectively calling on "trust and participation" persuasion to get people to engage. She was also being brave enough to do something different and to exercise her leadership role in a slightly different way from normal. She reported back that it had gone very well. Given how she had introduced it, she felt free from responsibility to "do it well" or indeed to ensure that it "was successful." In the event, people had responded very well, and she, and they, had learnt new and interesting things about each other and lifted the mood. It had become one of their best ever meetings. People who have been using this practice for longer note the need to keep it alive as a process, retaining a sense of interest and novelty, so it doesn't just become another "mindless" routine.

This exercise may not sound like much but it can be very powerful in switching mood and behaviour. I had a very salutary reminder of this not so long ago when I turned up for a meeting, my attendance at which I hadn't negotiated very well and, if truth be told, about which I was feeling a little resentful. Unusually for me these days, my general mood was low. Not a great way to turn up anywhere and definitely not recommended as good practice! However, we started the meeting using the three successes exercise, in which I participated. Within 15 minutes I found myself a woman transformed. I was also consumed by remorse for the less than charitable thoughts I had been harbouring as I had endured the pleasure of the London tube on the way there: it was a salutary lesson indeed. The point I want to emphasize is that even though I am highly familiar with, and frequently use, the exercise as a workshop leader, I am rarely just a "regular participant" like this, nor am I usually engaging from such a low point, and the experience was highly illuminating. It is a very powerful mood shifter, is all I can say!

4. The flip

There is an Appreciative Inquiry process known as "the flip" that works to shift a push motivation to a pull motivation. Essentially, once someone has outlined what is wrong, you then say something like, "Ok, I understand what you don't want/what the problem is/what isn't working/what is frustrating" (being sure to demonstrate that you truly do understand by reflecting your understanding back to them, i.e., ensuring that you have actually heard their pain, frustration, hopelessness, etc.), and then say something like, "So tell me something about what you do want?" or "Describe to me how things would be if this problem didn't exist," or "If you woke up tomorrow and by some miracle the problem/issue/frustration had disappeared, how would you know? What would be different?" All of these and many others are ways of encouraging the person to talk about the dream instead of the problem. And talking about the dream is motivating, energizing, and induces positive emotional states.

Of course, judgement has to be applied as to when it is appropriate to attempt to "flip" the conversation. At the 2015 World Appreciative Inquiry Conference there was some concern expressed that sometimes it seemed that people didn't want to even hear about the problem before moving onto encouraging people to describe the dream. It was pointed out that the problem story has value and meaning and must be honoured. I thoroughly agree, and I explored this conundrum in my earlier book on Appreciative Inquiry (Lewis, Passmore, & Cantore, 2007). Barbara Fredrickson puts it very well and, I believe, successfully squared this circle when she emphasized that "Positive Emotions act as a reset button for negative emotions that have *outgrown their usefulness*" (2015). Deciding when to introduce a flip question is a situated, context-sensitive judgement.

5. Prosocial organizational practices

Organizational practices are the "distinctive set of recurrent, patterned activities that characterize an organization" (Orlikowski, 2002, cited in Dutton, Roberts, & Bednar, 2011, p. 158). They shape how the organization's knowledge is organized, how resources are created, and how organizational learning and organizational change occur. Dutton and colleagues make the point that organizational practices are linked to employee *doing* which is linked to employee *becoming*. What we want is to be promoting organizational practices that are conducive to the development of positive organizational or work-related identities, that is, for people to feel identified and aligned with the organization rather than alienated and oppositional to the organization. Prosocial practices, those designed to protect or promote the welfare of other people, provide a conduit for employees to participate in routine helping and giving at work. Helping others and contributing to a cause bigger than ourselves promotes flourishing. They report that engaging in prosocial practices at work often increases psychological and social functioning as indicated by greater persistence, performance, and citizenship behaviour on the job.

These prosocial behaviours are integral to how work is performed and make a huge difference to, for example, the generosity or otherwise extended to new members needing help, or the willingness of colleagues to cover for each other to accommodate life crises and so on. Prosocial behaviour can also be more institutionalized through schemes that encourage members to donate time or money to help others in the organization and the community, such as insurance schemes or donating free leave days to volunteer work. Effectively, these schemes create opportunities for people to experience themselves as good people and to feel good about themselves, both of which bolster mental health and are a source of resilience.

It should be noted that a slight backlash is emerging against these practices on the basis that they are a hijacking of the wellbeing agenda by the capitalist profit agenda (Davies, 2015). The warning is well sounded and I am wary of the clarion call that what is good for the business is good for the people in it. So whether you regard the phenomenon of people devoting some of their leave to do "good work" in the community with the support of the organization as the spreading of general good where everyone wins, or as the exploitation of the willing for more nefarious ends, is a personal and ethical dilemma. However, the evidence that helping others creates a rich reward in wellbeing for most of us seems fairly clear.

6. Seeking out the root cause of success

There are many established processes to lead us to the root causes of failure; somewhat fewer to lead us to the root causes of success. Working to establish root causes of success is linked to the idea of positive deviance, that is,

Box 5.1   Root Causes of Success Analysis

Whitney and colleagues outline a general root cause of success analysis process. They suggest there are two key questions around which the process is built. First:

Tell me about a time when you experienced us at our best.

One then probes to learn more about who, what, when, and how:

What caused us to be our best in this situation?

Following up with "Why did it work so well?" and "How did we do it?" to identify strengths, capacities, and enablers.

Adapted from Whitney *et al.* (2010, p. 80)

a deviation from the norm in a positive direction. Taking an interest in positive deviation is one of the defining characteristics of a flourishing organization (Cameron, 2008a). It encourages us to expand our organizational learning orientation from "Why did that go wrong?" to include "Why did that go right?" Positive deviance is seen as the growing tip of organizational behaviour. At the growing tip lies the greatest potential for future learning and growth (Ben-Shahar, 2015). The key point is that the causes of success are not only, or necessarily, the polar opposites of the root cause of failure (see Box 5.1).

One well-recorded root cause of success analysis is of the Hudson River forced landing of a passenger jet in 2009. The investigation of US Airways Flight 1549 included both why the aircraft ditched in the river and why all on board, passengers and crew, survived. In general terms, root cause analysis is an approach for identifying the underlying causes of why an incident occurred. Ordinarily, root cause analysis investigations of plane crashes only address the causes of what went wrong, such as the bird strikes, the loss of the engines, and ditching in the river. The root cause analysis below, for US Airways Flight 1549, also investigated what went well regarding the smooth ditching, and the successful evacuation and rescue of all on board.

On January 15, 2009, US Airways Flight 1549 "ditched" (landed in water) in the Hudson River without losing a single passenger. The most important, and frankly amazing, aspect of this incident is that nobody died.

None of the 150 passengers, three flight attendants, and two pilots lost their life due to the crash. There were no fatalities from the crash itself, from hypothermia, or from drowning, which are all certainly possible outcomes for a water landing in New York City in January. So, although the plane did crash, due to the loss of altitude caused by the loss of both engines (likely due to being simultaneously struck by geese, though this has also not been confirmed), the Captain landed in the river, rather than a populated area. His co-pilot has said that another consideration in choosing the river was to ensure that passengers would be rescued quickly thanks to the proximity of many ferry boats. Passengers avoided hypothermia by being rescued quickly, thanks to the quick response of the ferry boats, whose captains are trained in water rescue. Passengers were also aided by other passengers, thanks to clear instructions from the crew. No passengers drowned. The plane was evacuated extremely quickly, thanks to passengers who used their last minutes of air time to review the safety card instructions, and to the performance of the flight attendants, who are trained to evacuate a plane in 90 seconds. That the evacuation was complete was ensured by the captain and police divers, who checked and double-checked that everyone had made it out safely. The article from which I have taken this account has a fully annotated Cause Map (Think Reliability, 2014).

The article pulls out the lessons learnt from what went right in this incident and suggests that the concepts are applicable within any organization interested in improving their reliability. I have chosen to quote the following section pretty much whole as I think it makes the points, draws the analogy, and asks the pertinent questions very well. The article highlights the particular behaviour of high-reliability organizations, and the actions that distinguish them from less safety conscious organizations. The emphasis is mine, showing the points relevant to any organization.

> *"Cross-check and verify"*
>
> This incident provides a valuable reminder that little tasks can have a big impact on reliability. When you hear flight attendants say "cross-check and verify," they are double checking the exit doors and emergency slides. A girt bar, attached to the exit door, must be manually engaged before take-off and then disengaged after landing. This ensures the slide will deploy when the door is opened "in the event of an emergency." Photos from Flight 1549 show passengers climbing onto the floating slides on either side of the forward

exits to be picked up by boat. The forward slides on Flight 1549 had been armed and functioned properly when needed.

What are the girt bars in your organization?

Some tasks may seem insignificant, because "nothing ever happens," but in certain situations those minor tasks can mean the difference between life and death. The girt bar is moved into and out of position on every single commercial flight. *In some organizations, tasks that appear unnecessary may eventually be skipped.* In high risk operations it's important to maintain a disciplined approach. Within healthcare, checking the girt bar is analogous to verifying the medication that's about to be administered to a patient. Within industrial companies, its verifying energy sources in a lock-out, tag-out procedure. *When someone asks, "Do we really need to do this every time? Nothing has ever happened," the response in high reliability organizations is "Yes … every time."* The proper position of the girt bar is a cause of zero passenger fatalities. (Think Reliability, 2014)

The lessons learnt from this particular success root cause analysis include: the benefit of over-training pilots (and cabin crew) so that they can continue to make good decisions under stressful conditions; give passengers a task that will both keep them occupied (helps with rising panic) and enable them to play their part in ensuring the safe evacuation; and make sure everyone understands that the routine, boring tasks may only pay off once in a blue moon, but when they do, the pay-off is huge. At least, that's my reading of it. I think the question about what are the little things your organization does all the time that seem unimportant and have little consequence at the time of doing them but may have huge consequence at a later date, is very interesting and well worth pondering. Examples I can think of include getting contracts signed even when there is a hurry to get going, or following safety procedures in dangerous environments like building sites and manufacturing even when there is a rush on. Not so long ago I was in a hurry and so took a short cut across an industrial site, failing to stay "within the yellow lines" designated for pedestrians. My justification to myself was there was no traffic around. A worker, who was hanging around a hanger entrance in anticipation of a goods arrival, noticed this and was on to me like a shot, patiently explaining why this system existed and how important it was that everyone followed the rules at all times. He was absolutely right; I was suitably chastened. Now *there* is an organization with a strong safety culture.

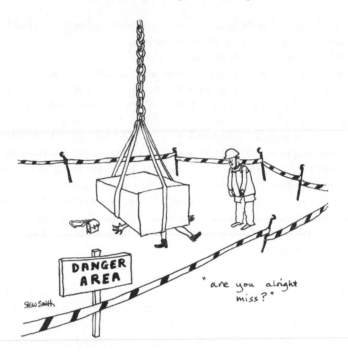

7. Positive psychology tools

Various tools are available to support positive personal or organizational development. A number of organizations have produced sets of strengths cards and I have produced a set of positive organizational development cards (www.acukltd.com). These various tools and resources can be used by executive teams as part of their strategy development to identify current and future cultural patterns, for example. Team leaders and consultants can use them as a preparation aid, as a direct question crib, as a source of inspiration, and directly with groups. Coaches can use them with individuals, particularly the strengths cards, which really help people articulate their strengths and the strengths of others. I have little doubt that more resources like these will be available soon to help organizations bring positive psychology to life in organizations and to help people makes changes in organizations at all levels and in all domains.

8. Organizational memory, legacy, and elders

Whitney and colleagues have some very nice points to make about the importance of proactively engaging with, and making best use of, the accumulated wisdom and experience of the organization's older members. With the general emphasis found in many organizations on youth it's easy to overlook this organizational resource. I frequently use the length of service exercise at the beginning of a workshop. The benefits of this exercise can play out in many ways, not least that of making the history of the company become a living, breathing thing to those who have joined more recently. It often also offers them an insight into why things are the way they are and a different sense of the company they joined. The newer members also get to hear about some of the great things that happened in the past and start to see "the old guard" in a different light, especially if the earlier stories are of the pioneer days with tales of autonomy and audacious risk-taking and derring-do.

Another idea is to create an elder's advisory council that can be called upon to bring their accumulated wisdom to bear on ideas or key issues. Alternatively, long-serving staff members can be invited onto strategy teams to the same end. A very nice idea is actively including them in the induction programme so that new employees can quickly come up to speed on the history and culture of the organization while also having an internal mentor. In a similar way, staff with long-term knowledge can be asked to act as teachers to the rest of the organization. All of these ideas will also help build intergenerational relationships. Of course, all of these suggestions are predicated on an atmosphere of trust and mutuality and a culture of collaboration. More can be found on these ideas in Whitney and colleagues (2010, p. 105–106).

Conclusion

There is an emerging expertise on how to apply positive psychology principles, theory, and research to everyday workplace activity and challenges such as performance development, team development, and strategy development. Specific tools such as card sets and games are also appearing to support these processes. In the next four chapters we shall be looking at specific co-creative, large group, or whole system transformational methodologies that can be seen as positive psychology in action.

6

Appreciative Inquiry

Recently I was invited to help an organization undergoing change. I was asked to come in and work with the front line staff, who were seen as being in need of some support. By the time I got to meet them they were at that difficult point in the change programme where they had put in their applications for a job in the new structure (or alternatively for voluntary redundancy) but didn't yet know the outcome.

It was agreed that I would run a three-hour session focused on "making sense of the changes." Attendance would be voluntary. It attracted about eight people the first time it ran, one of whom appeared close to tears when we started the session. It was clear that it was an emotional time for people. After some scene-setting and so on, I structured the session around three questions: "What will be different?" "How will it impact our work?" and "How can I positively affect my own experience and that of those around me?"

The initial discussions provoked a lot of expressions of dissatisfaction and blame. It became apparent that the work environment was being experienced as highly negative. As is not uncommon in these situations, the managers were being held to account for a lot of the difficulties staff were suffering. The general story was that the managers "aren't telling us anything," and "are too busy," and "aren't doing this change well." There wasn't a lot of respect evident for their managers in the initial conversations. While I was fielding the morass of negative experiences unleashed by the first question, and wondering if I would be able to move the group on to a more productive conversation in the time available, I asked something like, "Has the whole change experience been like this, or is this a more recent situation that you are describing?" Questions

Positive Psychology and Change: How Leadership, Collaboration, and Appreciative Inquiry Create Transformational Results, First Edition. Sarah Lewis.
© 2016 John Wiley & Sons, Ltd. Published 2016 by John Wiley & Sons, Ltd.

like this are designed to produce an awareness of the variation in the experience. Once we have established that there has been a variation, we can focus on exploring the "better" experience to see what that tells us about the best of the past. From there we can move on to consider how things, from experience, could potentially be in the future. At the point that I asked this question it had little impact, and the conversation continued to be directed at people who weren't present, and focused on discussing things the people present couldn't change. I highlighted this, and suggested that they had choices about how we spent our time together and what we spent the time doing. I was attempting to shift their focus from who wasn't there and what they couldn't change (what had happened in the past) to who was there and what they could influence (in the present and the future). I also suggested that they had choices about the sense they chose to make of what was happening.

At some later point in our conversation one of the participants said something like, "It wasn't like this when it (the change process) started." This comment may have been elicited by my earlier question, or it may have arisen quite independently. Either way, "it wasn't like this when it started" was the comment I'd been listening for. It was an invitation to explore a positive difference. So I asked, "What was it like when it started?" which elicited the information that it had originally been very consultative. My next question was, "So what's changed recently?" Part of the answer was that a project manager had been appointed and there seemed to be more activity directed exclusively at the management group.

Considering this, we were able to construct some alternative accounts of what was going on, such as: the managers were bound by some confidentiality edict; they were out of their depth themselves with this change and were floundering; they didn't know how people were feeling because no one had told them; they were assuming that if they couldn't give good news, they had nothing to share; or they were very upwardly focused at present, perhaps worried about their own futures. As people began to engage with these alternative ways of making sense of what was going on, so different possibilities for action emerged.

The focus of the discussion started to move away from creating accounts of the bad behaviour of individual managers into creating a story of the changing context. In doing this they were able to gain some perspective on what might have been going on for the managers recently. Remembering that it hasn't always been like this also creates hope that it can get better. Once a group starts to feel a bit hopeful, things can start to move along. We started to move from a stuck position of it's awful because these people are awful and there's is *nothing we can do about that, to it's awful because we are all caught up in this difficult situation which is affecting our relationships and our behaviour. Moving from personality attributions of behaviour to circumstantial attributions of behaviour creates more room for choice and change. It allows for different emotional relationships to surface, making room perhaps for sympathy and empathy that act to displace blame and anger. The stories we tell about people affects how we feel towards them, which in turn affects our behaviour around them. Feeling differently about other people allows us to make different attributions about them and to behave differently towards them.*

The mood in the room shifted, people started to believe that they could proactively affect the situation. They could move from being helpless victims of the behaviour of others to being proactive members of the organization who had a responsibility to help make this change as good an experience as possible, even in these difficult circumstances. A quick reflective round at the end revealed that, compared to when they walked in, they were now feeling more positive, more accepting, more assertive, more proactive, and braver. They also felt they had more choice about what they could do.

And these feelings were translating into action intentions; they were motivated to do different things when they left. One had decided that he was going to set up a meeting with his manager to attempt to explain the situation from the team's point of view. He wanted to do this in a way that was careful not to accuse the manager of any wrongdoing; rather he wanted to see if they could negotiate a different way of communicating going forward. Another had decided that she wasn't going to amplify other people's tales of woe, leading to a downward spiral of helplessness; rather she was going to challenge them about what they could do to make things better.

By acknowledging people's current reality while redirecting their attention away from the things they couldn't change (but could companionably grumble about together) towards those that they could directly influence, we were able to effect helpful change through the power of question and consistent attention redirection.

Introduction

Appreciative Inquiry has many technical descriptions: it is a dialogic organizational development change process (Bushe & Marshak, 2015a), or a collaborative transformation methodology (Sanchez, 2010), or a large group process, but however you describe it, it was one of the first of the co-creative change methodologies to be fully articulated. A deceptively simple process in my experience, it is highly adaptable, flexible, and robust in its application and effects. However, like the three other methodologies explained in later chapters, it needs to be conducted from a co-creative rather than a top-down mindset to be most effective (Bushe & Marshak, 2015a). Indeed, Bushe and Marshak argue that only when applied from a co-creative, or dialogic, mindset can it be transformational in its effect (2015a).

Process

The first articulation of Appreciative Inquiry was as a 5D model (Cooperrider & Whitney, 2001) (see Figure 6.1). The 5D model invites participants first to define an appreciative topic, then to discover the best examples of that topic in present and past experience, then to dream the best of what *can be* based on the discovery of the best of what *has been*, then to design the organization in the light of the future possibilities, and finally to experience their destiny as the future unfolds. This unfolding is based both on their internal reorientation experienced as being part of the process, and on active plans made as the result of the process.

In its original form, Appreciative Inquiry is experienced as a workshop event following the sequence above, but it is very versatile and the process can be experienced over time, in parallel process groups, or indeed as a coaching or team intervention. Appreciative Inquiry is an approach to, and a philosophy of, change as much as it is a defined process. There is much free information on the web, and there are many books now available about Appreciative Inquiry. While I recommend my own, *Appreciative Inquiry for Change Management* (Lewis, Passmore, & Cantore, 2007),

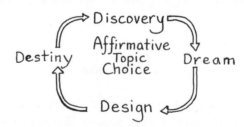

Figure 6.1   The 5D model. Source: Derived from Cooperrider and Whitney (2001, p.9)

I also recommend *The Thin Book of Appreciative Inquiry* (Hammond, 1996) and *Appreciative Inquiry: Change at the Speed of Imagination* (Watkins & Mohr, 2001), as well as, of course, David Cooperrider's books.

Purpose

The purpose of Appreciative Inquiry is to allow the organizational members to co-create a way forward for themselves and their organization that springs from a deep knowledge of the heart of their success and their resourcefulness; and to co-create contextualized aspirations for future success.

Recommended Use

Appreciative Inquiry is very scalable and can be used with individuals and teams as well as whole organizations. It is particularly recommended when there is a need to inject some positivity and hope into a situation. Like the other methodologies mentioned here, it is helpful when the challenge or opportunity is a system-wide issue; when the collective intelligence of the whole organization is needed to address the challenge or opportunity; when the way forward is unclear and needs to be created; when the system needs to boost its confidence about its ability to engage with the challenge; and finally, it is particularly valuable when there is no obvious push for change or, as organizational members may put it, when there is no burning platform. Rather than trying to create one, Appreciative Inquiry works instead to create a compelling future.

Key Ideas

1. Focusing on what is working will solve the problem

Appreciative Inquiry isn't about ignoring the problem, it's about approaching it from a different direction, or it's about talking about the same thing in a different way. "Every problem is the expression of a frustrated dream" strongly illuminates the idea that when we say we have a problem we are in some way comparing the current state to some other, better state, and we are aware of a shortfall. The idea of the other state is present in our expression of dissatisfaction with the current state. Equally, in talking about the other state, the "could be" state, we are also talking about our dissatisfaction with the present state. So to talk about the desired state *is* to talk about the problem, just in a way that is different from usual.

We can come at the apparent paradox central to Appreciative Inquiry, that it is possible to affect what isn't working by focusing on what is, from another direction by seeing it as using pull factors rather than push factors to achieve change. All the things that are wrong in our current situation act as push factors for change. We are pushed into action to relieve ourselves of unpleasant emotions, situations, results, relationships, and so on. Once we obtain sufficient relief from the unpleasantness, we may well stop attending to the issue. Thus resolution is a state of minimal non-dissatisfaction. This is unlikely to be the maximal satisfaction state; rather it is the minimal tolerable state. Desirable future states act as pull factors for change. The motivation excited by them is of a different order. Accessing this motivation requires a different process. There is no limit on what can be aspired to except our ability to imagine. There isn't the self-limiting stop signal that there is with push change.

2. The motivating power of the positive core

The concept of the positive core is that at the heart of any organization, team, or individual is a set of positive values and beliefs that are key to enabling the person, group, or organization to achieve goals, do things, and generally make a difference. The positive core is that aspect of our lives that can make us feel good about ourselves, our organization, our ambition, and our daily behaviour.

The difficulty is that the positive core becomes obscured from view by the requirements of daily life. So for individuals, the busyness, the "must do" lists, the anxiety and stress can layer over the positive core of motivation and ambition to the extent that life becomes a round of endless drudgery of lists, tasks, and duties. Similarly, in organizations and teams the requirements of production, the effects of organizational hierarchies, and the functional divisions can obscure the positive core of the organization from immediate view.

One of the aims of an appreciative approach is to reveal this positive core. If you just ask people, "What's at the heart of this organization?" they can't always access an answer just like that. Appreciative Inquiry processes bring answers into the light in a less direct way by asking appreciative questions and generating stories. The stories people tell in response to appreciative questions about highlight moments or sources of pride are laden with information about what is important to them, and about what they value about themselves, their work, or their colleagues. Listening to the passion in the stories, it becomes very easy to understand what makes up the positive core of the individual, group, or organization.

3. The transformational power of generativity

We have Gervase Bushe to thank for alerting us to the key importance of generativity to the effectiveness of Appreciative Inquiry (2007). Generativity refers to the phenomenon of something new occurring during the Appreciative Inquiry intervention. "A generative image is a combination of words, pictures, or other symbolic media that provide new ways of thinking about social and organizational reality" (Bushe & Marshak, 2015a, p. 23). Bushe is particularly keen on the role of metaphors. When the group comes up with a metaphor that encapsulates how they understand themselves or how they see their future selves, this can be a sign of something generative taking place.

For myself, I notice it as a qualitative shift in the group dynamic. Very often this shift is signalled by the fact that the group members are now talking directly to each other rather than through me. But sometimes it's a subtler shift; an awareness that people are saying new things to each other, or maybe a change in the feel and atmosphere of the group. Appreciative Inquiry is all about creating newness in the moment, creating change in the moment. We are very much socialized to think of change as occurring after an event, but actually significant change can occur as a group comes to understand itself differently. Appreciative Inquiry is a form of organizational learning. Gervase's definition suggests that "organizational learning ... revolves around two or more people inquiring into their experience and generating new knowledge that leads to a change in their patterns of organizing" (Bushe, 2010, p. 49).

4. The principles underpinning Appreciative Inquiry

Ten principles underpin Appreciative Inquiry theory and practice (see Box 6.1). They are an expression of the social constructionist philosophical base and the dialogic organizational development practice base. In addition, they bring an emphasis to the importance of intervening at a system level to achieve sustainable change.

**Box 6.1   The Five Original Principles of Appreciative Inquiry
and the Five Emergent Principles of Appreciative Inquiry**

The Five Original Principles of Appreciative Inquiry

The Constructionist Principle

Reality and identity are co-created.
Truth is local. There is no absolute truth.
We see things as we are.
We are deeply interconnected.
Words create worlds. Reality is constructed through language.

The Poetic Principle

Life experience is rich.
We have habits of seeing.
Whatever we focus on grows.
Find what we want more of, not less of.
Develop an appreciate eye.

The Simultaneity Principle

We live in the world our questions create.
Change begins the moment we question.
The unconditional positive question is transformational.
Develop your sense of wonder.

The Anticipatory Principle

Positive images create positive futures.
Vision is fateful.
Create vision before decisions.
What we believe, we conceive.
Big change begins small.

The Positive Principle

Positive emotions broaden thinking and build.
The positive core expands as it is affirmed and appreciated.
Identify and leverage strengths.

The Five Emergent Principles of Appreciative Inquiry

The Wholeness Principle

Wholeness provides more expansive thinking than reductionism.
Learn to be present to the emerging whole.
Whole systems bring a variety of stories and more possibilities stretching us beyond our system's perceived potential.
Honour the multitude of opinions, perceptions, knowledge, and experiences that exist within organizations.
Each and every one of us is a whole human being bringing a whole life story and endless resourcefulness that go beyond job titles, formal education, or our position in the organizational chart.

The Enactment Principle

Embody what you want.
Just try something.

The Free Choice Principle

Freedom from internal and external forces is one type of freedom.
The freedom of inner clarity allows us to pursue life freely.

The Awareness Principle

Awareness is understanding and integrating the Appreciative Inquiry principles.
Surfacing assumptions is important in good relationships.
Practise cycles of action and reflection, where we act, reflect, and act with awareness.

The Narrative Principle

We construct stories about our lives.
Stories are transformative.

With thanks to Jackie Kelm (2005)

Critical Success Factors

1. Event preparation

Over the years working with organizations using these collaborative transformational methodologies, I have come to realize that preparation is key to producing an impactful, effective, and sustainable change, especially if you only have a one-day event opportunity with the group.

a) A planning group

As with any development event, preparatory work is necessary. It is best, if possible, to work with a small group that is representative of the system that will be present at the event. This group, while working with you to create the event, becomes versed in the philosophy of Appreciative Inquiry and understands how the event will run. This means that on the day there are some people embedded in the group to help support the event. They can also act as ambassadors beforehand as they become excited about the possibilities of the event. Make no mistake, working with the planning group is part of the intervention. How you work with them needs to be in concordance with the event philosophy and approach, that is, you need to be working with them in accordance with the appreciative principles.

For instance, sometimes it proves impossible to negotiate as much time for working with the planning group as you think desirable, or you can't get exactly the people you would like, or people have to miss some of the meetings, or they arrive late and leave early. As frustrating as this can be, always bear in mind the key principles. For instance, focus on what you can do, not what you can't; be appreciative of the people who are there, not focused on those who aren't; and remember that change is an iterative rather than a linear process.

b) Topic choice

One of the most important tasks of this group is to determine the topic of inquiry. Essentially, this will be what they want more of rather than what they want less of. And the one isn't necessarily the opposite of the other. Work with the planning group to inquire into what they want to grow more of in their team or organization (e.g., more effective team work, more innovation, or better interdepartmental connections). Help them think about the discovery questions that will help people access the best of the past experience in the organization in this area. It's helpful to "trial" these questions with the planning team, both for their experience, and to get a sense of what organizational experiences or memories these questions might access.

c) Addressing the "what ifs"

Another thing the planning team is useful for is running "what if" scenarios. As you explain the Appreciative Inquiry process this is likely to happen anyway as people inquire into the process and begin to explore how it might play out. Typical questions in my experience include variations on: "What if people don't have any good experiences?"; "Our people are very intellectual, I'm not sure they are going to take well to the idea of 'dreaming' or playing with Lego ..."; or "What if no one volunteers to do anything at the end?"

I addressed a number of these challenges to negotiating to work in an Appreciative Inquiry way in an earlier book (Lewis, Passmore, & Cantore, 2007). At one time I considered these "what ifs" and "yes buts" to be expressions of concern, doubt, or anxiety. I have since developed a more appreciative frame and see them as questions that offer an excellent "road testing" service to the ideas we, as the planning group, are developing of how to proceed. People's questions of this nature are based on a concern that the event should be successful, that their credibility should be enhanced rather than harmed, and that their colleagues should not be embarrassed. These are good motivations. Seeing such questions as gifts that create the opportunity to acknowledge that there is a risk inherent in proceeding in this way allows me to engage with them in a more authentic and positive way. While I will offer the reassurance of my experience in running these events, I can also say, "Yes, that is a risk we run. We'll do everything we can, in planning the design and in how we invite people, to militate against such disasters, but in the end people are free to choose whether to engage fully or not. One of our jobs is to create an event that is inviting, enticing, and exciting, that also looks as if it might actually make a difference and will be psychologically safe enough that people feel they can take risks of contribution, but there are no guarantees." I have a short video about working with sceptics on my YouTube channel (Lewis, 2015).

2. Who to invite

The invitees to the event need to be the people who make up the system. Deciding who is part of the system tends to be an iterative process that unfolds as you increasingly refine what the intervention hopes to achieve.

Box 6.2   ARE IN

Event organizers need to invite people with:

Authority to Act – i.e., people with decision-making power
Resources – people with contacts, time, money
Expertise – people with knowledge pertinent to the issue under
   consideration
Information – people with information about the topic that no one
   else present has
Need – people who need to be involved as they will be affected by the
   outcome and can speak to the consequences

Weisbord and Janoff (2007, p. 17)

It is remarkable how many people hope to resolve issues or improve working patterns or relationships with other groups but see no need to include them in the event. As Bushe so succinctly puts it, "Partnership with the problem people can't be rebuilt if they are not part of the conversation" (Bushe, 2010, p. 55). I have had a university request to work on the student experience without including any students; a finance department who wanted to work differently with other parts of the organization without including them in the process redesign event; and an IT team who wanted to improve relationships with outside contract project managers without including them. This experience is not uncommon. Sometimes it is possible to negotiate to include the excluded. The next best thing is to find some way to bring their voice into the proceedings. These experiences just emphasize that a key part of the pre-event negotiation is deciding who is the system defined by the topic, and the success criteria, and therefore who should be invited. An early opportunity to influence these factors is to be treasured. Weisbord and Janoff came up with an acronym to help us decide who the system is in any particular context, ARE IN (see Box 6.2) (2007).

3. Voluntarism

It really helps to negotiate voluntary attendance at Appreciative Inquiry events, and indeed all the co-creative events. It is not always possible but the voluntary principle adds to the potential power of Appreciative Inquiry events in a number of ways.

a) Voluntary attendance

Ideally, people are invited to attend the Appreciative Inquiry event. The event topic, the nature of the event, and the invitation have to be sufficiently compelling that people prioritize being there of their own volition. When people make an active choice to invest their time in the event, they are keen to get a good return on that investment. When they are compelled to be there by management diktat, it can be a recipe for frustration, and even sabotage of the process. The necessity of securing voluntary attendance immediately focuses organizational attention on making the event relevant and compelling to all.

The necessity of securing voluntary attendance.
Stew Smith

b) Voluntary participation

The voluntarism principle needs to extend to participation in any and every particular activity or discussion that is planned for the day. We never know what may be going on in people's lives to make some topic of discussion unbearable. They may need, during the day, to prioritize their own need for some quiet time, or to make a timely phone call. It is my experience that when people are treated as adults, constantly juggling competing priorities, trying to make good moment-to-moment decisions in complex contexts, they manage it very well, and with minimum disruption to the process.

c) Voluntary contribution

Calling on collective intelligence is a key feature of large group processes. However, people are free to choose whether and what to contribute; so the event needs to create an atmosphere where people feel safe and trusting, and so desire to share information and dreams and to build connection and intimacy.

With most Appreciative Inquiry-based events there is a shift at some point from a focus on the *process* in the day to a focus on *actions* in the future. Often this involves forming project or work groups to progress activity. And the groups need members. Again, group membership needs to be voluntary. The desire to contribute to changing things for the future needs to stem from the motivation and community built during the day. Forcing everyone to sign up to a post-event group activity regardless of their energy, time, or passion for the topic or project just creates drag, and sometimes derails the whole process.

The ideal outcome of an Appreciative Inquiry event is that everyone is so affected by the event process, discussions, and aspirations that they are motivated to make small changes in their own behaviour on a day-to-day basis that will aggregate to a bigger shift, and even transformation within the organization as a whole. In addition, they may volunteer to be part of specific groups working on specific projects. By definition, these personal shifts in behaviour and the group project activity are above and beyond their job description: it is voluntary, discretionary behaviour. Bushe expresses this well when he says, "few arrive wanting more work, few leave without having volunteered for co-operative action" (Bushe & Fry, 2012).

Key Skills

Appreciative Inquiry's effectiveness is predicated on a few key skills. These skills in themselves are familiar facilitator skills, but with a different twist.

1. Crafting appreciative questions

Questions are used by facilitators, and people in general, to different ends. Schein, in his recent book *Humble Inquiry* (2013), for example, notes diagnostic inquiry, confrontational inquiry, and process-oriented inquiry. Diagnostic inquiry is focused on finding out, while confrontational inquiry covers assertions disguised as questions, and process inquiry inquires into process. These questioning approaches are all based broadly on the belief that there is a reality to be uncovered by careful questioning. In this sense they are part of the diagnostic organizational development practice (Bushe & Marshak, 2015a).

Appreciative Inquiry questions, on the other hand, are designed not so much to encourage articulation of known accounts or beliefs as to create previously unheard accounts or beliefs. Appreciative questioning works to bring new accounts into the present conversation. Each time we ask an appreciative question we are hoping to hear something that hasn't been articulated before. In addition to creating new possibilities through the creation of new accounts, appreciative questioning is very focused on creating positive energy for change, and positive possibilities for the future. At which point it is necessary to reiterate that Appreciative Inquiry is not an approach that "doesn't allow us to talk about the negative things, or to express negative feelings"; on the contrary, as explained above, it is very focused on making things better, it just goes about it in a different way. Appreciative questioning is the social constructionist principle in action. How we talk about the world creates the world. Box 6.3 illuminates the characteristics of good Appreciative Inquiry questions.

Box 6.3   Creating Good Appreciative Inquiry Questions

A good Appreciative Inquiry question:

directs attention towards the positive
unleashes new accounts – generative stories
focuses attention on what you want more of
brings different aspects of organizational life into focus
identifies strengths
identifies the positive core of the organization
is context specific, resonating with language meaningful to the
    organization.

A few starting points for Appreciative Inquiry questions.

Tell me about a time when … who, how, what, when, where …
If you had three wishes for this organization/system, what would they be?
If by a miracle we woke up tomorrow and the system was running as
    we dream, how would we know? What would we notice?
Tell me about how we got from there to here, what was the first thing
    that changed?
What is the smallest thing we could change that would make a
    difference?
What is the unimaginable thing we could do?
If we could do absolutely what needs doing, what would we do?
How will our customer know things are changing here?
If our success were completely guaranteed, what bold steps might
    we choose?

---

2. Listening and looking for the positive

One skill an appreciative practitioner needs is an ability to hear the positive, or potential positive, in talk, discussion, and conversation, and indeed an ability to turn the conversation in a more positive direction if needed. The importance and the impact of doing this is illustrated in the case study that opened this chapter, where the remark "it wasn't always this bad" created the opportunity to move the group from talking about what was wrong now (a deficit conversation to which the group was initially very strongly wedded) to what was right in the past (a discovery conversation). From here the conversation could move on to what could be better in the future (a dream conversation), and then on to what people needed to be doing differently to make something different happen (a design conversation), and finally they could resolve to take specific actions to positively affect the future (destiny).

3. Using stories to make sense

Appreciative Inquiry is a social constructionist-based approach; it recognizes that together people co-create their social realities. They do this through their patterns of talk and interaction. This means that to change people's perceptions of themselves or their situation, or their colleagues, is to change reality. The stories we tell about our reality create our reality. Story creation is an aspect of sense-making. Sense-making is the human endeavour to make sense of what is going on around us, particularly what is affecting us. In the absence of information, we form our own hypothesis of what is going on and then find the confirming evidence. Bushe says that the sense-making process "is endemic to human relations. It cannot be stopped," (Bushe, 2010, p. 22) so better to work with it than either to ignore it or to squash it.

In the case study that opened this chapter we first identified the stories people were constructing to make sense of the situation in which they found themselves, and then created other possible accounts of what was happening that could also explain the situation. Working like this to increase the pool of sense-making stories from which people could choose, we also expanded the pool of possible reactions they could have to the situation. Making sense of a situation differently allows us to engage with it differently. In other words, it creates the potential for change.

4. Noticing shifts

One of the arts of being an appreciative practitioner is noticing when significant shifts occur in a group's dynamic, and then being able to capitalize on that for the benefit of the group. Such shifts can be indicated by a small positive comment. For example, maybe the group is working itself down into a negative spiral and your efforts to flip or switch the conversation to positive talk don't seem to be taking, but then unexpectedly one of the members echoes something you said earlier, or answers a question you asked a while ago, and the possibility of creating a conversational shift presents itself, as in our case study example.

A shift can also be indicated by a change in the quality of the interaction. One that I notice frequently with teams is the point at which they stop talking "through me," as it were, and start really talking to each other. At this point we have shifted from "report talk," reporting to me, to something more generative. As this progresses and the group talks to itself more, the group heart or identity begins to form in the middle of the circle of chairs. It is a fantastic shift to observe. It was articulated by one leader who, at the end of a team development day in response to the "what's changed today?" question, said, "I no longer feel alone." She had arrived feeling she carried all the burden of leadership. Her senior team was more a coordinating group than a team. Facing the challenge of leading significant change she needed to move her senior managers towards being her leadership team. Over the course of the day, as connections were made, relationships strengthened, and joint aspirations created, the feel of the room shifted. The only way I can describe it is to say that where there had once been an empty space between people, there was now a connected space buzzing with life. For the team leader, as she expressed it above, the feeling was of now being *one of* many rather than just *one in charge of* many.

Other shifts are things like growing excitement, the emergence of hope or optimism, and the emergence of good possible futures. One of the arts of being an appreciative practitioner is being sufficiently connected to the group and "of the moment" to experience and notice these moments, while simultaneously having a sufficiently detached sense of what achievement, growth, and forward movement look like to be able to help the group work with such shift moments to achieve further growth.

Origins of the Methodology

As a postgraduate, David Cooperrider (Cooperrider & Srivastva, 1987) experimented with focusing his organizational development activities on what was working in an organization as well as, or indeed instead of, what wasn't. He discovered that by just focusing people's attention on what was working he could induce positive change in an organization. In other words, he realized that organizational growth and development could be stimulated by an inquiry into things other than "the problem." Indeed, change could be induced by specifically focusing on things that very definitely weren't the problem.

It is hard to appreciate now just how counter-intuitive this must have seemed at the time. It was obvious that if you had an organizational problem then to solve it you would need to focus on "the problem." It stood to reason. It still does. It is still sounds counter-intuitive when you say to people, "In order to address this problem, challenge, or issue, we are going to focus on something else; we are going to enquire into things that are not the problem." For many people, their willingness to engage with Appreciative Inquiry as an approach runs onto the sands right there. For guidance on how to avoid this and other such sandbanks of counter-intuitiveness when introducing Appreciative Inquiry into an organization, see Chapter 10, "How to introduce Appreciative Inquiry and related approaches to your organization," of my book *Appreciative Inquiry for Change Management* (Lewis *et al.*, 2007).

When to Use and Counter-indications

1. Leaders wedded to command and control

There can be many reasons why a leader might not be ready for this kind of intervention. The most obvious is that the leader is wedded to the command and control model of leadership and feels it incumbent upon them to come up with all the answers. While these beliefs can of course be worked with, it may not be possible to create enough of a shift in time for the event. If the leader is not ready or able to effectively call on, activate, and work with the skills, strengths, and energy of the group then you are probably wasting everyone's time by going ahead with the event. There is also a danger that you will queer the pitch for those who come after you hoping to work in this way.

2. The timing isn't right

To get the best from an Appreciative Inquiry process there needs to be an investment of time and energy into the process, including after the event. Ideally, an organization is ready for the energy unleashed by an Appreciative Inquiry and has the space to really work with the outcomes to get the benefit. Reviewing some research on the effectiveness of Appreciative Inquiry summits, Stellnberger concludes that, "An organization needs to be ready for the summit and ready for what comes afterwards" (2011, p. 98).

3. Change is seen as event not process

What happens after the event in terms of supporting the unfolding of activity is as important as what happens at the event; organizational change is a process, Appreciative Inquiry is a process. Both regularly get recast as one-off events. Organizations get most benefit from Appreciative Inquiry when they understand it as an iterative process, as a cultural way of being. At the very least they need to understand that the summit or group event is not the total Appreciative Inquiry experience, it is only the most visible part. What happens before and what happens afterwards are equally important parts of the change process.

4. Wrong topic

Be wary of being asked to focus on a smokescreen topic. I can possibly best illustrate this with an example. I was asked by an organization to come and do some "Appreciative Inquiry training." I've learnt from experience that the best way to introduce Appreciative Inquiry to an organization is to do an Appreciative Inquiry. In this way one can explain the theory as the event unfolds, as if revealing the software, or offering a meta-level of theory to complement the practice level of experience. They agreed that sounded like a good way to proceed, so we sought for a topic.

A voluntary, charitable, mission-based organization, they decided they wanted to work on fundraising. Essentially, they wanted the organization to make the shift from *just* having a specialized team of fundraisers, to having a specialized team of fundraisers *and* a staff group who recognized the importance of fundraising and embraced it as a key part of their role. At present the slightly unpleasant task of asking for money was hived off to a special team and everyone else carried on with their daily work untainted by such pecuniary considerations. I exaggerate for clarity; however, it was clear that this difficult yet key task was split off from much of the organizational consciousness.

This sounded like an interesting topic. I could see that the story held by many in the organization about the unpleasantness of the necessity of asking for money needed to shift. Rather than "doing good" and "asking for money" being two oppositional aspects of the work, they needed to become much more clearly connected as part of the larger ambition of achieving the organization's mission. I thought we could possibly achieve this through the co-creation of new stories where raising money was, in itself, doing good. It seemed an interesting challenge for an Appreciative Inquiry event.

As the planning group worked together, some of the recent history of the organization emerged, particularly that there had been a round of redundancies a short while before, and that it was possible there would be more. This experience had created some strong feelings, as for some such behaviour was in contradiction of the organization's mission. Others objected to how it was done. Some of the people in the planning group were working out very long notice periods. It also seemed there was another split in the organization, between the public conversation of "one big family" and a reality of people being treated differently. As we proceeded to try to plan this event, more organizational splits emerged until it became apparent, to me, that what the organization really needed to be focusing on was some internal healing, before it tried to address this operational issue. It seemed to me it needed to create some coherence about the past. It needed to co-create an account of how the organization could both be a good organization and have to do these difficult things.

In due course it became apparent that there was a key (unacknowledged) split in the leadership team. It was impossible to talk about this split because that involved acknowledging negative emotions about each other, and to acknowledge such realities would mean that as people they fell short of their ideals. However, it also became very apparent that if this leadership split wasn't addressed before the event, there was a clear danger that it would explode in the middle of the event, with an audience of the whole staff team. I didn't think it responsible to let this happen. From an ethical perspective one of my roles is to try to create and promote psychologically safe places for people to work together. Therefore I requested that I be granted a session with just the leadership team, together, before we ran this event. Although agreed in principle, the mere idea of having to be in the same room together (it transpired that they hadn't actually worked together for some time) focusing on themselves was enough to produce change in the system, with two members becoming proactive about leaving the organization.

In the end, neither of these planned events happened: I didn't get to run a session with the leadership team; neither did I get to run an event, either a healing-focused event or a fundraising-focused event, with the whole organization. It was a very challenging engagement. However, I offer it here as an example of the potential danger of focusing on a less central topic rather than the one that is actually affecting the whole system.

No warplan survives first contact with the enemy

Conclusion

Appreciative Inquiry is a highly effective, well road tested, and highly versatile process for achieving change at individual, team, and organizational levels. While, with its emphasis on the importance of positivity, it is probably most obviously the "operational arm" of organizational positive psychology, the other methodologies explored in the next few chapters can all be delivered from a positive and appreciative perspective.

7

World Café

Some time ago I was asked to act as chair for a debate within the counselling community. This was at the time when, in the UK, all health professionals were being asked to register with the Health Professions Council (HPC). Some groups of counsellors or therapists weren't entirely convinced that this body would understand their unique and particular perspective or approach. The idea was that a representative of each of the main UK counselling bodies, plus a representative from the HPC, would hold a debate on a raised dais in front of an audience of counsellors and therapists. I was effectively being invited to referee a bun fight on stage and then field audience questions. The image the organizer had in mind was the kind of adversarial debate newscasters like to conduct.

This invitation was not attractive; however, the idea of being able to work with a large group of people always is. I held some conversations with the people who would be on the dais and read some background literature. It was evident that feelings were running very high about this. The questions the organizers wanted to ask suggested they were a bit caught up in the counselling culture of digging deeper into difficult feelings. The language of many of the questions as originally written was freighted with strong negative feelings. It seemed to me the HPC spokesperson was in danger of being publicly lynched, figuratively speaking. I wanted to help them construct a more constructive way of proceeding that also allowed the audience, who were in effect the system being affected

Positive Psychology and Change: How Leadership, Collaboration, and Appreciative Inquiry Create Transformational Results, First Edition. Sarah Lewis.
© 2016 John Wiley & Sons, Ltd. Published 2016 by John Wiley & Sons, Ltd.

by this proposal, a much wider say in the matter. I also wanted to create sufficient safety for all the panellists.

After a lot of negotiation, we agreed on a design that delivered a tightly controlled panel session and then an afternoon World Café. The point of the panel session was to create a shared awareness in the room of the degree of commonality or difference that existed between the different organizations. It was also an attempt to separate truth from rumour, fact from fear, and the negotiable from the non-negotiable. To this end each panellist was asked the same questions, which they had been given in advance, and were allowed up to five minutes to respond. Panellists indicated in advance which questions they were interested in addressing, so no one had to speak for the sake of it. I negotiated to make these questions as positive and appreciative as I could. They may not look particularly so, but they are considerably more so than those originally proposed. They included questions such as: "What structures exist for further negotiations by members of the professional community with the Health Professions Council on areas that continue to be contested?"; "What capacity does the HPC have to address the ongoing concerns expressed by the professional community?"; "What would the consequences be of not joining the HPC register? Will the practitioners have their membership of their current umbrella organization withdrawn?"; "The HPC Standards of Proficiency are raising concerns because they are formulaic. How would the HPC ensure that these do not restrict good practice that is process-based and that will take into account ruptures in the practitioner–patient relation-ship that are often part of the therapeutic process?"; "What would be the role of independent training organizations in a post-regulation culture?" Then, after a break where people could consider not only what they wanted to ask but also how, we had an audience-to-panel question session so they could engage with what had been said so far.

In the afternoon we were able to move to a World Café structure for a whole group discussion. The question we constructed for this was, "How might we continue to work towards a regulatory structure that robustly protects the needs of the customer, patient, or client, while preserving the vibrant creativity and intellectual vigour of these professions?" We held two rounds of conversation focused on this question and then spent a final period pulling the discussions together. It was evident that the group mem-bership was not really interested in the divisions between their professional organizations, but was much more focused on finding constructive ways forward that would enable them to continue practising their particular school of therapy or counselling with confidence. While people might not like being brought in under this particular regulatory umbrella it was clearly going to happen and the key thing was to negotiate the best possible ways forward. In other words, attention was switching from fighting a rear-guard action against things they couldn't influence to focusing on a forward orientation to focusing on things they could influence. It was a tough day but, from my point of view anyway, constructive and conducted without the need for bloodletting!

Introduction

In the example above, ideally I would have liked to negotiate the whole day for a co-creative process, but in this instance it was not possible. However, I was able to incorporate a World Café (Brown, Isaacs, & The World Café Community, 2005) into the design, which is another co-creative methodology. World Café is a dialogue-based methodology particularly suited to connecting and combining people's knowledge and expertise to create new awareness and insights about particular opportunities or concerns. The process brings together everyone connected to the issue, with all their particular localized knowledge and personal experiences, to address specific questions. These questions are designed to move group thinking forward on an issue. People talk together in small groups about a specific question, challenge, topic, or opportunity. A clear process, refined through trial and error, offers guidance on how to ensure the conversations are productive, generative, and connected.

The Process

The World Café process was designed as, "a simple yet powerful conversational *process* for fostering constructive dialogue, accessing collective intelligence, and creating innovative possibilities for action, particularly in groups that are larger than most traditional dialogue approaches are designed to accommodate" (Brown, Isaacs, & The World Café Community, 2005, p. 3). The conversations facilitated by the World Café process allow those present to "notice a deeper living *pattern* of connections" (p. 3).

Stew Smith

The process of World Café is very straightforward. To open the event the host or facilitator introduces the session, sets the context, explains the process, and introduces "café etiquette" (see Box 7.1). Following the introduction there are a number of rounds of discussion at small tables or in small groups. Each round is focused on a question or questions. That is, sometimes all tables are working on the same question, as in our example, and sometimes on different questions. Rounds can last any length of time, usually about 40 minutes to an hour. The process itself can extend over a couple of hours or a couple of days.

Box 7.1   Café Etiquette

Focus on what matters
Contribute your thinking and experience
Listen to understand
Connect ideas
Listen together for patterns, insights, and deeper questions
Play, doodle, and draw (on the paper tablecloths!)
                    Brown, Isaacs, and The World Café (2005, p. 167)

At each table is a designated host whose job it is to make sure people introduce themselves and to encourage the recording of key conversational discoveries and insights. This is often done informally. Famously, this typically means on the paper tablecloths that ideally are provided at the café tables for precisely this purpose. Hosts are not charged with facilitating the conversation in any way, only with effecting introductions and encouraging recording.

At the end of each round, a brief discussion is held to connect the table conversations and to illuminate the value of the conversations so far. This is to ensure that the collective knowledge that emerges becomes visible to the whole group. After each round, participants are asked to redistribute themselves for the next round of conversation. The host stays put and everyone else disperses to different tables. The next round starts with the host connecting the new group with each other (introductions) and with "the story so far" at that table. In more or less formal ways, the new group will bring their experience of their previous conversations into the discussion. In this way it is likely that the collective knowledge, insight, and group wisdom around the issue under discussion will grow.

After the final round, the event host will conduct a final inter-table conversation to illuminate and connect the various insights and discoveries that have emerged at each table and to bring the proceedings to a close. They may well inquire after any ideas for action. They close by clarifying what, if anything, will happen with the data that has been generated, and by recording any forthcoming plans of action.

Purpose

The purpose of the process is to generate collective knowledge-sharing, to create or support webs of personal relationships, and to generate new possibilities for action. It is specifically or purposefully "designed to avoid predetermined outcomes" (Brown, Isaacs, & The World Café Community, 2005, p. 52).

Recommended Use

The World Café process is designed to help people talk together, exchange ideas, and develop their thinking about an issue in a relaxed, informal, yet purposive way. In small café groupings of no more than six people, groups discuss particular questions or topics with the aim of expanding their understanding of their own and others' views, and of the possibilities for the future. World Café is useful in many contexts, and excels when the main object is to connect knowledge and explore ideas around a particular topic. At its best it produces conversation that connects, has energy, is emergent, and is valuable.

World Café works to create new insights or new possibilities for action by combining and recombining the knowledge and experience in the room in different ways. Like all these co-creative methodologies, it is usually a highly dynamic and motivating experience. Generally, people come away changed by their conversations in terms of: their mental maps of the situation; their understanding of their colleagues; their energy for engaging with the issue; and their willingness to work with others to make things happen. It is a methodology that trusts participants to be able to hold conversations around things that are important to them in a committed, thoughtful, and adult way. It doesn't require a professional facilitator at each table, instead different roles are assigned to participants to help them hold and connect the various conversations. Senior people present become part of the community, one voice among many.

As ever for larger events, good planning is needed beforehand to ensure that the event is clearly located in the bigger context, and to ensure that there is clarity about the decision-making and action-taking processes connected to the event. Sometimes there is no expectation that decisions will be needed or actions taken, in which case the café is run as a very open-ended discursive exercise to raise awareness of the importance or impact of a topic and to get people to engage with the topic. It can be run with the sole purpose of connecting people around an organization-wide topic that can't easily be addressed through the normal managerial processes.

In this way it is particularly suitable for conversations about organizational culture. Culture, being a process, is very difficult to manage from the top. It is a product of individual thoughts and actions created within an intangible but very real understanding of the affordances and constraints of the existing culture (see S. Lewis, 2011). In other words, culture is perpetuated by the daily words and deeds of organizational members. In order to change culture, everyone needs to feel the need to, and believe they have permission to, behave differently. They also need the skills and the personal contacts to do so. World Café, with its combination of individual influence and group conversation, and its output of personal impact and organizational learning, can be very helpful in facilitating organizational culture shifts.

World Café is also particularly suited to counteracting the challenge of "a silo mentality," the bane of much organizational life. The development of a "silo mentality" is a recurring challenge to organizations that becomes particularly problematic in times of change. For reasons of efficiency, most organizations are functionally split into different departments. These activity-based splits are often further reinforced by more concrete divisions such as walls or physical distance. Often, different functions are located in different offices or workshops, on different floors, on different sites, or in different countries. Few organizations put the same degree of energy into keeping these separate units connected as they do into fostering connections within each unit. Over time, each unit can become more and more self-contained and less and less connected to the wider system. The World Café process sets out to help people gain a more system-based understanding of how their organization works. They begin to understand the deeper patterns of the organization, not just those of their own space.

Key Ideas

1. Calling on the collective wisdom of the system

In 2004, Surowiecki published *The Wisdom of Crowds: Why the Many are Smarter than the Few*. In it he cites many examples of when the crowd is smarter than the individual. For example, he tells a story of Galton, a scientist and psychologist of the late nineteenth and early twentieth century, who was a pioneer in using statistics to measure human variability. He is particularly known for his early work on intelligence and other hereditary traits. Galton found himself at a fair with a "guess the weight of an ox" competition. After the event he collected all the tickets and averaged out the crowd guess. As Surowiecki reports it,

> Galton undoubtedly thought that the average guess of the group would be way off the mark. After all, mix a few smart people with some mediocre people and a lot of dumb people [sic], and it seems likely you'd end up

with a dumb answer. But Galton was wrong. The crowd had guessed that the ox, after it had been slaughtered and dressed, would weigh 1,197 pounds. After it had been slaughtered and dressed, the ox weighed 1,198 pounds. In other words, the crowd's judgement was essentially perfect. (2004, p. xiii)

Stew Smith

The wisdom of crowds

Surowiecki quotes many other examples, arguing that "under the right circumstances, groups are remarkably intelligent, and are often smarter than the smartest people in them" (2004, p. xiii). These right circumstances refer to the nature of the challenge and the nature of the group. The wisdom of crowds doesn't hold for all challenges. However, its potential to create greater wisdom than any individual seems quite remarkable, as the story below illustrates.

Surowiecki finishes his introduction with another story about the location of a lost submarine. In essence, this lost submarine could have been anywhere in a 20-mile-wide circle. Working with a group of people's best guesses as to the most likely scenario of what had happened, and the effect of that on calculable things like speed of descent, he pinpointed a spot on the ocean floor (which was not one any individual had guessed). The submarine was found 220 yards away. He says, "What's astonishing about this story is that the evidence that the group was relying on in this case amounted to almost nothing. It was really just tiny scraps of data. No one knew why the submarine sank, no one had any idea how fast it was travelling or how steeply it fell to the ocean floor. And yet, even though no one in the group knew any of these things, the group as a whole knew them all" (2004, p. xxi).

Stew Smith

At the time, the wisdom of crowds was a fairly new concept and the book was very popular. The title is still quoted by people at opportune moments. World Café, and the other co-creation approaches, call on this collective wisdom that is available to us as a group and unavailable to us as individuals. World Café works with the "assumption that people already have within them the wisdom and creativity to confront even the most difficult challenges" (Brown, Isaacs, & The World Café Community, 2005, p. 4), and that the process can "evoke and make visible the collective intelligence of any group" (Brown, Homer, & Isaacs, 2007, p. 180).

2. *The social nature of learning*

In tandem with the growing understanding of the collective intelligence of the organization, we are becoming more aware of the social nature of learning. Senge was alert to this in his work *The Fifth Discipline* (1990), where he identified the team as the learning unit of the organization (rather than the individual). Sharing knowledge and insights, debating and discussing, groups create new knowledge. Brown and Isaacs note that the World Café process, "Allows people to drill through the formal layers of their professional titles and bring more of their whole person to the conversation" (Brown, Isaacs, & The World Café Community, 2005, p. 31). This encourages the development of human relations, which in turn encourages good listening and conversation.

3. The motivating power of conversation about things that matter

We take conversation for granted: it is such an everyday phenomenon that we become inured to its transformational power. Yet it is our primary tool for collectively "discovering what we care about, sharing knowledge, imaging the future, and acting together to both survive and thrive" (Brown, Isaacs, & The World Café Community, 2005, p. 18). It is "the core process by which we humans think and coordinate our actions together" (p. 19).

While there are many different kinds of conversation for different purposes, World Café is interested in creating conditions for collaborative conversation, particularly conversation that helps people co-create stories and images of the future. In World Café, people move from ordinary conversations, "which keep us stuck in the past, are often divisive, and are generally superficial" (Brown, Isaacs, & The World Café Community, 2005, p. 4), towards conversations that matter (e.g., those that generate deeper collective understanding or forward movement in relation to a situation people really care about). Brown and Isaacs see World Café as a conversational greenhouse, "nurturing the conditions for the rapid propagation of actionable knowledge" (p. 4). Conversation is understood as a living force, with the World Café process allowing organizations to engage its power. Conversations can be how we discover what we know and how we discover what we don't know.

4. Process over personality

World Café, in common with the other co-creative approaches, privileges process over personality. To some extent this can be seen as the further embodiment of the wisdom of crowds philosophy: in a large group the idiosyncrasies of personality are likely to have less influence. But it is mostly that we are more interested in influencing the system, and the patterns of the system, than in influencing any particular individual. We are more interested in connections and patterns than in bits of data or individual contributions. By moving people around the groups, the process also regularly breaks up any unhealthy dynamics (such as dominance by one member) that might have emerged in any one conversation. It is my experience that when people are feeling good and engaged in an important task they cope remarkably well with some of the less socially skilled, less emotionally intelligent, or more insensitive members of the group. The regular movement of people around the tables means that any difficult dynamics are only temporary and don't become entrenched in the event. In this way, the ability of the system to access and utilize the knowledge of some of the more difficult characters, without being distracted by an emotional reaction to their "personality," is enhanced. In a carefully structured situation like World Café it becomes more possible to draw on all the resources in the room.

5. Actionable knowledge

In the World Café environment, we are interested in developing, or creating, actionable knowledge. We want "whatever emerges from a Café to be some-thing that can be put into practice" (Brown, Isaacs, & The World Café Community, 2005, p. 29). In other words, the café is not just a theoretical thinking exercise. This desire guides the design of the café topic, the questions, the invitees, and of course the process as a whole. As with all these co-creative methodologies, a World Café benefits from careful context-sensitive and context-specific design. So although the principles laid out below are general, their application in each case is tailored to the specific event.

Critical Success Factors

There are eight design principles that "improve people's collective capacity to share knowledge and shape the future together" (Brown, Isaacs, & The World Café Community, 2005, p. 3). These can be regarded as the critical success factors.

1. Introducing the event and setting the context

The context is "the situation, frame of reference and surrounding factors that, in combination, help shape the ways we make meaning of our experiences" (Brown, Isaacs, & The World Café Community, 2005, p. 48). Context is affected by the opening introductory welcome as well as by the people present, and by the focus of the event. The context is also set by the venue, the tables, the layout, and the materials, such as the paper tablecloths, flowers, and vases. In addition, it is influenced by the post-event activities and how the event is documented. All of these need attention to ensure the creation of a relaxed, café atmosphere. The event host can begin to create a shared context for the ensuing discussions by addressing questions such as, "Why this conversation now?" "What is our purpose?" and "What do we hope to achieve?" Addressing questions such as these should illuminate the social, economic, organizational, and community factors that make this an important conversation.

The opening comments should also clarify the broad parameters of the conversation. They might suggest what it is not likely to be helpful to spend time talking about, as well as giving some pointers for potentially more fruitful ground. So for instance, they might note that although the current IT system causes problems and people might imagine that a complete upgrade would solve all the problems, this is outside the scope of the conversation. However, it is hoped that what can be achieved is a pulling together of all the wisdom people have acquired in their own sections about how to get the best out of the existing system. This might include such things as how to get it to do what is required and the workarounds and hidden features they have discovered. Shared knowledge of these should help to improve the productivity of the group or of the whole organization with this less-than-ideal current system.

The event host, in his or her opening remarks, may also cover the expected possible tangible outcomes and the success criteria. These might include, for example, discovering new strategic direction, considering innovative programme or policy options, or illuminating new business opportunities for a specific product. But equally often, as in our example, World Café is not focused on finding an immediate answer or solution, it is more about discovering the right questions to ask, and creating an opportunity to think and explore the situation together. It's about building relationships, sharing knowledge, and providing opportunities for contribution.

It is often useful in the welcome speech to talk about how the event is a learning event, just one that is different from the kind of learning events the participants may have attended before (e.g., those involving extensive use of PowerPoint and speeches). World Café, like the other co-creative approaches to learning and change, is a many-to-many conversational design. This can be something of a novelty to people in organizations that more usually use a one-to-many model. The naming of the event can be important. Calling it a World Café may not be the most appropriate or resonant in any particular organization.

2. Accommodating the experts

If the topic under discussion is one in which there are organizational experts, for instance in the example above the IT team, it is important to talk to them beforehand to help them be clear that the conversation is not intended to be a scrutiny or critique of their work. It is also useful to help them think about how they can best feed in their expertise in a way that will be helpful to the group at large. For example, one might discuss how they can minimize their use of jargon, or how they can manage their reaction to the many bizarre mental models people may have of how the IT system (or indeed computers in general) actually work and what they are or aren't capable of. Helping them understand that this isn't about them demonstrating what they know (that is taken as read), but that it is about helping to increase the IT literacy of the whole organization, should increase the value of their contribution to the process. This will involve much listening on their part so they can select what bits of specialized knowledge or information to share, and when, in the conversation. A similar pre-conversation is often very useful with leaders, who may also be concerned about how to contribute effectively.

In both these situations I find that helping people think of themselves as part of the organizational community and, for this conversation, privileging their community hat over their many other organizational hats, for instance leader or expert, leads to more effective participation. Of course, they can access the knowledge they hold because of their position in the organization, and indeed it is important that they do, yet they need to speak from the position of a community member. This is often a useful point to emphasize for everyone in the welcoming speech.

3. *Creating hospitable space*

"Miss Phelps, are you still there?"

It is important to create a hospitable space. This is defined by Brown and Isaacs as an environment that nurtures "authentic conversation" (Brown, Isaacs, & The World Café Community, 2005, p. 61). However, creating a nurturing, welcoming, hospitable space in a corporate environment isn't easy. For example, many offices I visit make valiant efforts to incorporate some elements of "home" into the office. These include providing spaces to make your own coffee, and comfortable sofas for less formal chats. Yet one rarely sees, for example, mirrors anywhere except in toilets. The artwork on the walls is usually corporate and rigidly arranged, not in the higgledy-piggledy style that emerges in most people's homes. The ideas of a corporate environment and a hospitable environment don't necessarily mesh together that well. So the deliberate creation of a more welcoming, more hospitable environment for the World Café has to be a very conscious act; and it can feel uncomfortable at first. It is easy to think that a lack of flowers, or tea and biscuits, or tablecloths doesn't really matter; after all, we are at work and we are here to work. But this is to miss the whole point, which is that by changing the environment we heighten the possibility of changing the interactions and the conversational pattern. From this, something new is more likely to emerge.

In a similar way of thinking, it is easy to "settle" for the larger tables that the organization already has rather than holding out for appropriately sized tables. But big tables are a barrier to small group conversation. Add in the fact that these tables are often arranged in a confined space, and you will find that large tables, where people have to strain to hear the people opposite them over the people behind them, quickly diminish people's engagement.

4. Exploring questions that matter

Questions are key to the World Café process, as they are to the other co-creative methodologies presented here. Questions don't just uncover existing knowledge (e.g., "Do you know where the toilets are?"), they also create knowledge by promoting new thought (e.g., "How might things be different if …?"). Thoughts are brought into being by language. Once in spoken or written form, they are accessible to others, and the ideas contained within them become more likely to be actioned as they capture the imagination, and gain the commitment, of others.

The World Café process is ideally based around a series of carefully constructed questions, designed to facilitate collaborative inquiry. Brown, Homer, and Isaacs (2007) suggest that some characteristics of effective

World Café questions are that: they are appreciative; they evoke a sense of possibility; they are clear; they are connected to purpose; and they are meaningful to participants in practical ways.

5. *Encouraging everyone's contribution*

World Café is based on an understanding of organizations as living human systems. This suggests that the organization and its environment cannot be known or understood by any one person; rather, all the agents or elements of the system (the people) understand something of what is going on. By bringing different voices together into one conversation in a structured way one is building on the knowledge of each individual to create a greater intelligence. When two previously unconnected "bits" of information are brought together into the same space, they can combine to create new knowledge in a manner more similar to multiplication than to simple addition. As we bring our individual knowledge together our collective knowledge can expand exponentially.

The World Café process, with its small group conversations, relaxed and informal environment, and meaningful questions, creates the potential for this. The way the invitation is issued, and other work before the event, helps encourage people to feel that their contribution is important. How the host sets the context and invites contributions helps to maximize this potential.

6. *Cross-pollinating and connecting diverse perspectives*

The World Café process is designed to connect the emerging ideas as people move around between the tables. At the same time, the host works to keep the conversation connected between discussion rounds by asking for updates from tables of how their thinking is going. In addition, the paper tablecloths allow a highly visible record to emerge of the conversation at each table. Through the "small, intimate conversations [that] link and build on each other as people move between groups" (Brown, Isaacs, & The World Café Community, 2005, p. 4), ideas are cross-pollinated and new insights emerge into questions or issues that really matter in their life, work, or community. The participants access "dynamic networks of conversation and knowledge-sharing around an organization's real work and critical questions" (p. 4). Through these conversational processes the organization begins to see and experience itself as a living system and the collective wisdom of the group becomes more accessible.

7. Listening together for patterns, insights, and deeper questions

Conversation by its nature consists of talking and listening. In World Café events, participants are asked to listen on a deep level for the insights and knowledge that emerge in the conversation. They can be encouraged to ask the unasked questions that hover close to consciousness and that would, if asked, move the conversation on to a deeper level of understanding. Brown, Homer, and Isaacs talk about how, as people make new connections, "sparks of insight" begin to emerge that no one would have had on their own (2007, p. 182).

8. Collecting and sharing collective discoveries

Somehow the process must make collective knowledge and insight visible and actionable. This is achieved through the recording process. It is also achieved by the event host, who helps to create links and to articulate discoveries. The host can also be active in encouraging much scribbling on tablecloths. A summary of critical success factors is outlined in Box 7.2.

Box 7.2   Critical Success Factors

1. Create diversity
2. Focus on the invitation and on hospitality
    The invitation should make people feel wanted and needed
    Give people time to get to know others
    Cultivate an atmosphere of friendliness
    Create space for great conversations
    Valuing everyone
3. Be aware of the acoustics of the space, for example the presence of noisy chairs
4. Ensure the ability to move around
5. Encourage and share insights
6. Encourage committed action
7. Create questions that matter
                    Brown, Isaacs, & The World Café Community (2005)

Key Skills

1. Including diversity well

For a World Café to work well it needs to be able to access a diversity of thought and experience. However, high levels of diversity can cause conflict if people fail to understand the perspective, context, and constraints of the situation of others whose experience, professional emphasis, or personal ambitions differ from their own. World Café creates an emphasis on exploring and understanding over deciding and acting. Without the pressure to reach decisions, people have more time and ability to seek to understand different points of view. The event host needs to emphasize this, encouraging people to ask questions of each other in their quest to better understand and honour all contributions. Everyone sees something different, and each of these perspectives has value. As we have seen, World Café encourages many different perspectives to come together to generate enough information to create good understanding of situations and, if appropriate, good decisions.

2. Devising good questions

The questions are key to the process. They need to be relevant, engaging, and capable of creating new insights or knowledge.

3. Effective facilitation

While the process is based on principles of self-organization and the attraction of critical questions, it still needs facilitating. However, the focus of the facilitator is less on guiding the conversation and more on guiding people through the process. The way the process encourages "intimate exchange, disciplined inquiry, cross pollination of ideas, and possibility thinking tends to create psychological safety" (Brown, Isaacs, & The World Café Community, 2005, p. 7), and to lessen inappropriate grandstanding or over-attachment by people to their own ideas.

4. Encouraging the strength of humility in leaders

World Café asks leaders to exercise the strength of humility, to recognize that they can't do it all on their own, and to be humble enough to ask for the help and assistance of all in the organization. Café conversations are "an act of respect for our people and their capacity to contribute" (Brown, Isaacs, & The World Café Community, 2005, p. 33).

Origins of the Methodology

This process was originally devised by Juanita Brown and David Isaacs, who very kindly brought all their experience together into the definitive book on the topic in 2005. Experienced community workers, they noticed that as people shared time and space together focused on particular challenges their conversations often took a particular turn. Initially there would be an expression of the impossible dreams of difference (i.e., "if-only" conversations). Sometimes these progressed into dreams of possibility (i.e., "what-if" conversations). These could be, "What would happen if …" or maybe, "What would be the worst that could happen if …" or perhaps, "If that were possible, how would things be different?" One can see immediately the similarity with the Appreciative Inquiry methodology and the importance of ideas of possibility and dreaming. Often, as ideas of possibility took hold, the conversation would advance to a more determined, hopeful "why-not" state, as in "Why not give it a go?" "Why not at least ask?" or "Why not involve them in our conversation?" In this way, impossibility changes to possibilities, the stuck situation changes to the fluid situation, and the hopeless outlook changes to the hopeful outlook. All of these changes create and support the energy for action to make things different.

They noticed that a lot of these truly transformational and energizing conversations happened outside the formal conference or community event sessions they ran, and they began to wonder how they could increase the likelihood of these valuable conversations. In seeking to do so, they identified two key questions that their process needed to address, namely, "How can we enhance our capacity to talk and think more deeply together about the critical issues facing our communities, our organizations, our nations, our planet?" and "How can we access the mutual intelligence and wisdom we need to create innovative paths forward?" (Brown, Isaacs, & The World Café Community, 2005, p. 3).

In their book, Brown and Isaacs tell the tale of how they first stumbled into the methodology that is at the core of the World Café process. While they tell it as a response to the constraints of a particular rainy day, it is also, of course, an expression of their conversation wisdom gleaned over many years. In particular, one can see their sensitivity as facilitators to what is actually happening in front of their eyes rather than what they had in mind before the day began. To cut a longer story short, on the second day of a process people arrived into a very welcoming room with small tables set out and, "while waiting for the others," just began to have conversations at the table related to the topic of the event. It seemed unhelpful to interrupt these energized and on-topic conversations. When someone expressed an interest in knowing what was being discussed at other tables, the idea of moving between tables was born. When more time had passed and more curiosity about what was happening at the other tables emerged, the idea of rounds was born. And the improvised paper tablecloths were just conveniently there as part of the early morning effort to create an impromptu working space when the anticipated outside space was unusable. When people wanted to record what they were discussing they just used what was to hand, and so the paper tablecloths recording process was born. After some time had passed, they collected their sheets of recordings together, arranged them around another, as yet blank, piece of paper and walked around to see what they had created. The story is a lovely example of making it up as we go along. It is a systemically situated response to changing and emerging conditions with a clear focus on the key purpose of the event.

What they noticed was that this emerging café process somehow "enabled the group to access a form of collaborative intelligence that grew more potent as both ideas and people travelled from table to table, making new connections and cross-pollinating their diverse insights" (Brown, Isaacs, & The World Café Community, 2005, p. 15). This idea of the value of informal, less directed, more discursive conversation has precursors such as the French salon movement that gave birth to the French Revolution. And of course many have noticed the "water cooler" phenomenon, where the most important conversations happen in the less clearly work-orientated space.

What emerged from this early discovery is a process that "consistently connects intellect and emotion to a business frame of reference" (Brown, Isaacs, & The World Café Community, 2005, p. 32). That is, as a process World Café calls on both our rational data-analysis or problem-solving skills and our psychological group processes. The rational data processes allow us to become more knowledgeable about the issues and options, while the psychological processes help generate innovative thinking, motivation, energy, and coordination. It is the ability of the World Café process to access both these important facets of human life that Brown and Isaacs note as "a key strategic business advantage" (Brown, Isaacs, & The World Café Community, 2005, p. 32).

Conclusion

World Café is a wonderful group conversation process. It can easily be incorporated as part of a larger group process, such as an Appreciative Inquiry event, as well as being an event in its own right.

8

Open Space

We want to run a rehearsal process for our EQUIS assessment, and a strategy development day for about 180 people simultaneously. Are we being too ambitious? Can you help us?

I had run the annual "team day" for this business school community of academics and administrators for the past two years. The first year we introduced Appreciative Inquiry to help bolster their creativity and innovation, the second year was focused on the student experience. This was the most ambitious objective yet. Throughout the day, teams of people would be disappearing to table discussions in a simulation of a forthcoming, very important, assessment process. At the same time, the body as a whole was to engage with three strands of strategic thinking around: the student experience, the balance of teaching and learning and research, and the integration of services.

The challenge was to create a design for the event that would facilitate the people involved in the simulation to leave and rejoin at specified times, and one that also allowed three themes of discussion. Working with the planning team, I designed a day based on Open Space Technology that would allow the rehearsal assessment panels to run concurrently with a strategy development conversation. In addition, we worked with the technology department to create "video tweets" of the different discussions, and a "voting" process at the close of the day to help identify the most important ideas and suggestions from the various discussions.

Positive Psychology and Change: How Leadership, Collaboration, and Appreciative Inquiry Create Transformational Results, First Edition. Sarah Lewis.
© 2016 John Wiley & Sons, Ltd. Published 2016 by John Wiley & Sons, Ltd.

Around 180 people attended the event. I was supported by a small team who helped ensure people got to the conversations they wanted to attend. During the day, there were 24 discussions around strategic questions identified by the group, such as "How can we improve our relationship with alumni?" and "How to improve the experience for international students and stop them feeling isolated?" All discussions produced a record of strengths, opportunities, aspirations, and potential results in the area under discussion. At the same time, the assessment rehearsal process ran smoothly in a nearby room. Most people who weren't involved in it weren't even aware it was also going on. The built-in flexibility of the Open Space process allowed people to move between the conversations, and to move between taking part in the Open Space and in the assessment process, in a relatively seamless way.

During the day, short videos were produced that summarized each conversation, and these were shown briefly after lunch before the generation of the final round of conversations. The electronic voting process at the end of the day was exciting and energizing, and the day ended on a buzz of a sense of achievement.

The day was deemed a great success. We had worked with the complexity of the system in a way that generated productive and useful conversation while supporting the primary purpose of assessment rehearsal and preparation. The senior team came away with a clear idea of the co-identified priorities for the school moving forward in these difficult times for academia, and with some concrete suggestions for next steps. In addition, the individuals present forged new relationships, discovered shared areas of aspiration, and were energized to help the school adapt to the changing context and environment. The assessment participants also got extensive feedback about their performance in the simulated assessment.

Introduction

Open Space Technology (OST), to give it its full name, is a methodology originally formalized by Harrison Owen (1997), although he is quick to acknowledge that "the creation of OST has been a collaborative project involving perhaps thousands of people on four continents over a period of twelve years" (Owen, 1997, p. xi). Put simply, it is a way of running meetings that makes them much more productive and engaging. The Open Space process allows people who have gathered together in order to discuss something, first to set their own agenda and then to attend the discussions where they have the most to offer or gain. The process is highly responsive to rapidly changing situations as people set the agenda in the process of the meeting, rather than three weeks beforehand. It also allows agenda items to take many different forms. For instance, when it is used at the Appreciative Inquiry practitioner networking events that I attend, it can produce: requests for help with a particular piece of work; a more general request for the sharing of resources about something; or the dissemination or sharing of an interesting or innovation piece of work, as well as questions about practice, or more general questions about theory. By making it possible for people to attend conversations of their choice, and to switch between them at will, it maximizes people's ability to invest their time most profitably, for themselves and for others. I find it a highly versatile, flexible, and useful methodology that I regularly incorporate into my workshop designs.

Essentially, OST is a process that should allow you to "do incredible things without a planning committee, without facilitators, and without a conference management team" (Owen, 1997, p. 7). All of which is true. However, in my experience, there is a considerable investment needed initially to persuade the various powers that be to contemplate such a free-for-all (as they hear it) structure. I will address some of these concerns, and how to answer them, in our discussion below. While this process can be used for very large groups over three-day events, I am only going to address that in passing since such opportunities arise fairly rarely. I am much more interested in exploring how we can use this methodology on a more ad hoc basis as part of our working lives. Should you be lucky enough, or powerful enough, to be able to negotiate a larger, more complex event, then I thoroughly recommend Owen's book and some expert facilitation. You might like to read his book anyway to see the level of skill that can be applied and the depth to which the process can be taken. If you are in the position, explored throughout this book, of needing to work in conjunction with a more traditional approach to change, then you should find much of use here.

Purpose

The purpose of Open Space is to facilitate a diversity of people coming together to discuss things that are important to them in a way that is effective, productive, engaging, and enjoyable.

The Process

The Open Space process allows people to come together to create their own agenda. For this to work effectively, people need to recognize that they have both the right and the responsibility to raise the important issues that need discussion. In addition, Owen devised some specific principles and a law that, if adhered to, allow people to make the most of the opportunity presented by this particular design (1997).

1. Introducing the principles and law

Open Space is run on four key principles and one law (see Box 8.1). The principles, as below, are designed to stop people fretting about what isn't happening (who didn't come, what didn't get said, etc.) and to focus instead on what is happening. They also serve to remind us that a group of people who have gathered together with a specific purpose in mind are quite capable of organizing themselves to have a conversation; and that they may choose to ease themselves into conversation with a little social preamble or catch-up chitchat. Without needing to be directed, the group will sooner or later get focused on the topic in hand. The last principle helps us recognize that when a conversation reaches some sort of conclusion, the conversation is over and there is no need to carry on extending the discussion to fill the

---

Box 8.1   Open Space – Four Key Principles and One Law

Four Principles

Whoever comes is the right people.
Whatever happens is the only thing that could have happened.
Whenever it starts is the right time.
When it's over, it's over (and when it's not, it's not).

The Law of Two Feet

If during the course of the gathering, any person finds him- or herself in a situation where they are neither learning nor contributing, they must use their two feet and go to some more productive place.

Owen (1997, pp. 95, 98)

allocated time. Personally, I love those moments of "finish." Sometimes they are indicated by a thoughtful silence that follows a pithy comment or summing-up. Sometimes it's a question that captures the whole nub of the discussion. Sometimes it's an explosion of delighted laughter as people realize they have cracked it, whatever it was. Either way, people know when a good conclusion to this discussion right now has been reached.

The law of two feet is key. It mandates people to leave boring or unproductive discussions and head off elsewhere. It has three key effects. It greatly reduces, if not eliminates, the likelihood of soapboxing, hobby-horsing, barracking, badmouthing, and general conversation domination by those with big egos, loud mouths, or strong opinions. It makes each person responsible for the quality of their own learning or contribution. And it creates bumblebees and butterflies. Butterflies are the quiet centres of non-action. These are the people who choose not to join a session. Others may periodically join them to share and enjoy their silence or to engage in some new, unexplored topic of conversation. Bumblebees buzz from conversation to conversation, spreading ideas.

Stew Smith

2. Creating the agenda

This part of the process is based on two fundamentals, passion and responsibility.

Each person who cares to is invited to identify any issue related to the central task for which they have some real passion, to write it down on a piece of paper, and to stick it on the wall. By doing this they also accept responsibility for convening a session on their topic and making a written report of the results. It is useful to emphasize that "Everybody has the right and responsibility to place items on the agenda." It is this "which allows the unspeakable to be spoken" (Owen, 1997, p. 8). Once the agenda is in place, we are ready to start our conversations.

3. Opening the village market

With smaller groups, once the topics are assigned a space in the agenda then people can be left to choose where to go. With larger groups, and time permitting, it is an idea to get people to sign up for topics which can then be allocated to rooms of different sizes, depending on the interest they seem to have generated. This can be done while everyone has a coffee break. Either way, you are going to end up with an agenda that clearly indicates what topic is being discussed where and when, and at least one person they should expect to find in the space at that time: their host.

4. Capturing outcomes

When people respond to the call of responsibility then every issue of interest, concern, or excitement to anybody will have been raised, and all issues will have received full discussion, to the extent desired. Other possible outcomes include a full report of issues and discussions in the hands of all participants and the establishment of priorities and action plans. One of the fantastic outcomes of these volunteer-based events is that work is assigned to those who care to do it. The value of this, in terms of energy, motivation, speed of action, and so on, can't be underestimated. The old adage that one volunteer is worth 10 pressed men continues to hold good.

The outcomes achievable depend to some extent on the length of the event. Owen suggests that a one-day event is great for intense discussion but little recording. This has been my experience. People get great value out of the discussions, but the recording doesn't extend beyond the flips produced in the groups. He suggests that two-day events are similar in nature but differently paced, with much better recording, while three-day events produce a qualitatively different experience that allows for the prioritization of all issues, the convergence of related issues, and effective action planning. Events usually result in one of three outcomes

a) Actions to be taken are so clear that it remains only to do them
I have found this to be a frequent outcome of using this methodology. However, this can be the result only if relevant decision-makers are in the room. If everyone is ready to roll and yet somehow the organization reverts to form and decides that the group outcomes are "recommendations" rather than action plans, and that therefore they need to be deferred to some other decision-making forum for ratification, there is a grave danger of an instant loss of energy, motivation, and time. When running one-day events, I usually aim for action groups to have identified who is in the group, what they aim to achieve, and the first step (which is often a first meeting) by the time they leave.

b) Actions to be taken are pretty clear, but more information
or consultation is required
In this case it is important to set a time by which these tasks will be sorted.

c) The issue remains as clear as mud
This might be the situation when there has been much useful exploration of the issue but no resolutions or forward actions are suggesting themselves. This is not necessarily problematic. Sometimes the purpose of the session is precisely that airing of a topic, the formation of an organization-wide conversation to create engagement and connection and to stimulate thinking about an important issue. However, if more definite action outcomes were anticipated, then it may be an indication that the topic as framed was too big, loose, or ill-defined. At any rate, some learning about the nature of the topic and the way people relate to it, or engage with it, will have been discovered. From this, next steps can be considered, which may or may not include a more focused Open Space!

Recommended Use

The Complete Guide to Facilitation lists five particular situations where Open Space might be your approach of choice (Justice & Jamieson, 1998).

1. When the issues at hand are complex and potentially conflicting

It may seem strange to suggest that such a flexible process be recommended in difficult situations. In fact, three key things contribute to its suitability in such a situation. First, people aren't locked in the room together; the process gives explicit instruction that people should move on from any discussion that gets, shall we say, "stuck." This allows people to manage their own emotional reactions better, giving them scope for walking away when they need to. Second, there isn't any inbuilt assumption of arriving at conclusions or making decisions, therefore people can keep talking until they get the breakthrough from "either/or" to "both/and" thinking. And finally, as the people present set the agenda, the minority interest that always gets pushed off the agenda can get an airing.

2. When a diverse group of people must deal with an issue

Again, the flexibility of the process makes it easier for a diverse range of topics, of particular interest to particular parties, to be discussed. In addition, the relaxed conversational nature of the sessions means that no one is disadvantaged or silenced by being unfamiliar with that organization's formal meeting protocol, or, where the meeting is of an international nature, that country's formal meeting protocol. And since no one knows what the agenda will actually be until the day, there is likely to be much less lobbying and politicking beforehand to secure agreement to particular perspectives or decisions.

3. When nobody knows the answer

This is where these co-creative processes in general come into their own as they work to call on the "collective intelligence" of the system. Frequently, although no one person seems to know the answer, the system working together can discover, create, unearth, or generate answers. However, it isn't easy for leaders and others to admit that maybe no one knows the answer. For example, this approach is excellent for culture change work, particularly when it reaches that stage in the change process where, despite all the brouhaha and planning, no one seems to really know what this change looks like and very little seems to be happening: the point of all heat and no light. Open Space can work to bring together all the questions and the unknowns.

Working in this open way has a number of benefits. First, people are often relieved to discover they aren't the only ones who are puzzled. Second, they begin to realize that there is scope to influence the question of what all these change-related communications actually mean. Third, they start to feel more empowered, motivated, and engaged as they begin to develop potential answers to their own questions.

4. When upper-level decision-makers are willing to listen to unpopular points of view that they have previously discounted

As we have established, planned change approaches often produce resistance to change. Often the first instinctive reaction to any resistance to change by those in charge is to ignore it, discount it, or attempt to discredit it. It is at this point that you will hear expressions such as "people need to get on the bus or get out." At some point they may be persuaded that there is some validity in the questions or objections being raised. Assuming people can be persuaded that the change process owners are now genuinely interested in listening, Open Space can offer, for the reasons outlined here, a low-risk environment for engagement. Once again, the emphasis is on exploration rather than, necessarily, decision-making.

5. Conflict management

Someone much wiser than me once said, "If it's too simple make it complex, if it's too complex make it simple." Wise words. They were referring to the organizational story about whatever was under discussion. Conflict arises in, and contributes to, situations where the story has got "too simple." People take a limited number of positions, only one of which they believe can be right.

There are, of course, a number of conflict management and mediation methodologies that engage directly with conflicts. Open Space creates room for conflict reduction in a different way. By facilitating multitudinous discussions on multiple issues it opens up the complexity of the situation. This in itself can create room for more nuanced opinions and voices to be heard. It also allows people to break out of their established oppositional patterns as they hear their antagonist saying something unexpected in a different context, perhaps something they can relate to. It allows people to hear, see, and understand each other differently. As with the other co-creative methodologies, conflict isn't so much "re-solved" as "dis-solved." Somehow the focus and the heat move on to different topics as people find new and maybe unexpected areas of commonality.

This isn't to say that Open Space is a panacea for conflict. It isn't. But getting more voices into a binary conversation that are able to open up areas for discussion and help move conversations away from "either /or" into "what if" and "both/and," or in other ways reframe the topic away from the binary choice, is frequently very helpful in finding ways forward from a "stuck" situation.

6. *Geographically dispersed groups*

Computer and internet technology have made it possible for Open Space events to extend across time and space. Various computer conferencing options can help with multi-site simultaneous Open Space events as each site can have access to the other discussions. Discussions can also continue online after the face-to-face events, and others not even present initially can join in.

Key Ideas

1. *The process is based on self-management and self-organization*

Open Space is probably the most obviously self-managed and self-organized of all the co-creative methodologies covered here. The facilitator provides only process. The group create the agenda, facilitate, lead, or host the discussions, and if they want recordings of the proceedings, they have to make them.

When working with people who feel disempowered and "done to" by the ongoing change process, or with an organization that wants to create a "more empowered" culture where people "take responsibility and are accountable," Open Space offers a great opportunity to give people that sense of agency, proactivity, and empowerment. As long as the issue under discussion is of crucial importance to those present, the process will work.

However, commissioners do sometimes find it hard to believe that the process will work and during the planning stage suggest ideas for ensuring that the "right" discussions are promoted and the "right" people attend them. To help allay the fears behind these suggestions and to keep things moving along, I have occasionally accommodated the idea of pre-designed questions to be posted on the walls of the room as "prompts" to those present, in case they are stuck. By the time we get to the event, such fears have often subsided anyway and the idea becomes moot. On the rare occasion when "ideas" for discussion have been posted in the room beforehand, they don't seem to harm the process, although equally they add little. One just has to watch out for one of the commissioners "suggesting" that someone else might like to promote one of these ideas. The principle is crystal clear: if no one feels passionately that they want to have this discussion, it doesn't happen, whether someone thinks it "ought to" or not. I also, of course, make it clear to the commissioners that they are free to suggest all these ideas when the agenda is designed in the meeting.

2. It's supposed to be a creative process

This is a creative process. The content is unknown, the outcome is unknown, and the conversations are unknown prior to the event. It could hardly be a more creative process. This is both the power of the process and, in the eyes of some, the risk. It is also creative in that it "creates" new patterns in the moment: different people talk in different ways about different things with different conversational companions. This in itself shifts the ratio of rehearsed to generative talk. New ideas, knowledge, and perspectives come together in the same space and create something new. And since everyone present has chosen to be in that conversation – all volunteers, no pressed men – so the quality of the contribution, whether speaking or listening, is better than an "average" meeting where attentiveness waxes and wanes as people dip in and out of the bits of the conversation that interest them. In short, the conversations stand a higher chance of being generative, that is, producing something new, than do most "normal" business meetings.

3. The recording and sharing of discussions is instantaneous

If people want proceedings then they get to create them. This is not a situation where someone else is expected to take it all away and type it up. Owen has some clear recommendations for how this can be done for a large event. He suggests you need five computers per 100 people and a printer. They need to be arranged to allow space for the flipchart paper from which people will be transcribing. If you are likely to be managing this type of logistic for a large event, Owen's book (1997) is excellent on this sort of detail: a wealth of tips gleaned from experience one suspects!

Smaller events

For smaller events I find getting groups to post their outcomes on the walls is a good first step. Often there is time to give brief feed-outs. Often this is as good as it gets and is sufficient. However, they can be encouraged to take away their own flipcharts to type up and distribute to each other, or to give to someone who volunteers to act as the coordination point.

In the case study that opened this chapter we had the facility to use flip-cams to record 60-second feed-outs from each discussion. This process was different; it helped with time management and produced useful material for the organizational website later. The output was very rough and ready, and speaking readily into a camera summarizing 40–50 minutes of discussion in 60 seconds isn't a skill possessed by everyone. However, I think the principle was good and I'd happily try it again. There were also written notes. The video helped to pull things together in the middle of the one-day event, as well as providing some web-friendly material for later use.

4. It's quick and cost-effective

In theory an Open Space doesn't take long to set up; and once a group of people are familiar with the process, indeed it doesn't. For example, I belong to a couple of professional support groups who use this methodology as the backbone of their events. It works really well and makes for a lively variety of sessions. In practice, with organizations that are not familiar with this approach, I have found a certain amount of preparatory work with commissioners is necessary!

The process only really needs one facilitator, although having more helps, if only in helping people with the process. There is a lot to think about to run a good event, especially if you add in things like video recording. I have found having other people around to help with the sheer detail of the preparation logistics very helpful for larger events. Of course, these can be people internal to the organizations or volunteer colleagues keen for the experience.

5. It works with people's energy

The people present discuss what they want to discuss. In selecting which discussions to attend, people follow their own energy, choosing to engage with what they have energy for. They don't discuss what other people want discussed, and they certainly don't discuss what those not present want discussed! As the agenda is being created, one of the things you are listening out for is someone who is carrying someone else's issue (probably that of someone not present). There is absolutely no point in this issue being on the agenda unless someone in the room "owns it." Usually, people will say something like, "I've got one. J, who can't be here because ...," asked me to make sure we discussed ...," to which one responds, "Is this something you feel passionately about?" They may say, "No, not really, but J ...," to which you reply, "It's unfortunate that J isn't here, but that doesn't mean we are obliged to discuss his agenda item that he can't be here to host. Does anyone else feel the need to host this item?" If no one does, it doesn't go up.

The other time when you have to watch out for the dilution of energy is if the event ends in a move towards forming "work groups" to carry some ideas forward. This in itself is fine; however, there may be a move by some present to insist either that everyone present signs up for something, or that each group have an equal number of people in it. Both of these pressures are to be resisted. The volunteer principle holds to the very end of the event.

Critical Success Factors

1. An appropriate space

How much space you will need will, obviously, depend on the size of the group. Regardless, you will need one main room for the whole group together in a large circle and, for larger groups, some breakout rooms. As a rough guide, a room that can accommodate 200 in a theatre style will accommodate 100 in the Open Space circle style. You'll need approximately five breakout rooms per 100 people, and a variety of other spaces, including possibly outdoors. Many conference centres or hotels also have public spaces that are useful. You want the main room to have one long wall where you can stick things (and they will stay stuck). You might also want room for the coffee stand and somewhere for the computers if you are using any. Keeping these in the main room can help keep it an "active" space while people are in the meeting sessions. Try to have food and drink on tap or readily accessible so that accessing it doesn't interrupt the process. It is a good idea to make sure the wider team, for instance the venue staff, broadly understand what you are up to and what the pattern of movement is likely to be.

2. Kit

You are likely to need: masking tape, flipchart pens, flipchart paper, and sticky notes (postcard size). Computers are optional. A microphone may be helpful for a group of 70 people or more.

3. Site preparation

All of this is fairly straightforward. Just ensure that:

- the chairs are in a circle, with gaps for entry and leaving; beware fire exits
- the wall is accessible
- paper, pens, and masking tape are available in the middle of the room
- the signage to rooms or conversational spaces is in place
- the four key principles and the law of Open Space are on posters on the wall in the main room
- on the long wall there is the "blank" schedule (also known as the time–space matrix) with start, finish, and break times, and then slots called session 1, 2, etc.

4. Welcome and getting started

The welcome needs to be made by the official sponsor. It is very important that the event is seen as belonging to the organization, not the external facilitator. Encourage them to keep it short and snappy and then to hand over to you. Start by helping the group to settle and focus. State the theme of the session. Giving this talk while walking around the "space" achieves a number of things that doing it sitting in the circle does not. It allows you to catch everyone's attention through movement. It allows you to get a good look at everyone, and them at you. And most importantly, it brings life to this important "between us" space.

Describe the process, attempting to excite passion and interest. By running through what is going to happen in this way, you can plant the idea that you will be asking them for contributions before you come to do so. This should help get their brains working. State any intended outcome, such as a good debate, or a record of ideas, or a vote of interest. It is important to be clear about the decision-making status of the event beforehand. This is all part of managing people's expectations. As you are explaining the process, keep an eye out for when the group looks like it might be ready to offer ideas. You might see people making notes or a sudden "light bulb" in their eyes. It's a judgement call deciding when to move on to calling for contributions.

5. Volunteer basis

Try to ensure that attendance at the event and in the groups, and participation in further action, is voluntary. This can be quite hard for organizations to accept. Even if attendance at the events becomes mandated, you can still use "the butterflies and bees" principles to make it clear that people are only expected to attend conversations that interest them. As Owen puts it, "Being a volunteer is the prime prerequisite for the full expression of passion and responsibility" (1997, p. 19).

6. Make the invitation attractive, and widely offered

As a general principle it is helpful to issue personal invitations, although in practice this is not always possible. The invitation should emphasize how much the invitee's presence is valued and ensure that the implications of their absence (i.e., not being part of an important discussion) are clear to them. Even so, in terms of attendees, the emphasis is on quality not quantity. This raises the question of how many people you need for a successful event. Owen suggests groups of five can find it useful. Even if they all decide they want to attend all the sessions, the process of designing their own agenda is valuable, and, of course, it is quite possible even in a group this small to have two parallel streams. I have used it in training workshops of about eight people, as a live example of how it works, usually with two streams. With organizations, I have used it with small groups of 15–20 people very successfully, as well as with larger groups such as in the case-study example at the beginning of the chapter.

7. Politely decline to answer questions during set-up

Some people's anxiety may start to express itself as a desire to be verbally convinced of the efficacy of the process before they engage with it. Try not to get drawn into extensive explanations. Enough people will get it. It only slows things down, dissipates the energy, or frustrates those ready to roll.

Key Skills

1. Framing the topic and the invitation

Before the event, identify what you want to focus on and then spend some time defining what you want to accomplish. This needs to be something people care about, a "real business issue that is of passionate concern to those who will be involved" (Owen, 1997, p. 20). This is often best stated as a question. As mentioned before, questions are more likely to engage and incite curiosity than statements. So working with, "How can we stay competitive in a changing world?" might create more engagement than, "Staying competitive in a changing world." Similarly, you might use, "What are our inspiring future aspirations?" rather than, "Designing an inspiring future" as your event heading.

A big part of the preparatory work for large events in general is framing the invitation. Almost inevitably there will be a written version of the invitation. The temptation is often to give lots of information, including explaining the process in detail. This desire tends to stem from the anxiety of the organizer and is of little benefit to the invitation recipient. The job of the invitation is solely to get the person to come to the event. Therefore, the most important criteria for the invitation are that it is attractive, it arouses some curiosity, and it stimulates the imagination. Try to make it brief and interesting, emphasizing, if anything, the opportunity it presents for potential attendees to have a real voice in, and influence on, the question under discussion. Include some of the sub-questions the event is likely to address; for example, "What should our priorities for growth be over the next two years?" or "What opportunities are we in danger of missing?" or "How can we reconcile the need for *this* and *that*?" Try to find questions that people are likely to have strong views about, to which they may have given thought but not yet found an appropriate forum for expression. In the invitation, don't be overly fussy about the methodology, instead point to the desired outcomes.

However, in this day and age written invitations are rarely sufficient. They get lost in the general noise of work and excessive emails. It is really important that the event is demonstrated to be important by leadership action and behaviour. The more leaders and managers emphasize their interest, excitement, and expectations about the event in person, and the more they issue very personal invitations to attend, the more likely it is that people will raise their heads from the daily grind to notice, and decided to seize, this opportunity to have real influence in their work environment. This is another good reason for having a pre-event planning group whose members can act as ambassadors in their own work areas throughout the preparation time.

2. *Calling for conversations*

After the set-up comes the point where you will need to call for session topics. Owen suggests that the request be formed like this: "I am going to ask each of you who cares – and nobody has to – to identify some issue or opportunity related to our theme for which you have genuine passion and for which you will take real responsibility. ... powerful ideas that really grab you to the point that you will take personal responsibility to make sure that something gets done" (1997, p. 88). While people are thinking or gathering the courage to name a topic, remind them of the very limited nature of the responsibility they are signing up to if they volunteer a topic or session: just to be in a certain space at a certain time; to convene, not facilitate, the discussion; and to ensure it gets recorded.

Make it clear what they need to do (i.e., write their topic on one of the pieces of paper, announce it to the room, and put their name on it). For small groups, these can just accumulate until you are ready to create the agenda. For larger groups, you may want to encourage people to stick them on the wall (not yet in the matrix) so that people can keep track of what has already been raised.

As the facilitator, this is probably the most challenging or nerve-wracking part of the process; will people generate enough ideas? The key is to be able to encourage people to come forward, and to allow a group to be silent. Ideas often come forth in fits and starts rather than as a steady stream. One idea may prompt a few others and then that stream of thought may dry up. There may be a pause before a fresh topic is identified. It can take people time to name an issue for all sorts of reasons: it takes a long time to percolate through from their semi-consciousness into something they can state; they dislike speaking up in a group; they worry people will think the topic they want to raise is stupid, irrelevant, or too dangerous; or maybe they are paralysed by anxiety when it is quiet and their brain seizes up. Often people are weighing up whether they want to take the risk of raising something or not. The longer you are able to hold this space the more potential you create for the emotion behind the issue to build up to create the motivation to speak up.

Stew Smith

Along with being able to hold a silence, you need to be able to manage the anxiety of group members who find the silence very difficult, or those who get worried that the group is "failing" whenever there is a pause in the flow of contributions and who want to rescue it by cutting the process short. It's a balancing act between those slowly contemplating whether to put their idea into the mix and those squirming in their seats or locked solid with their eyes to the floor who are just praying for this bit to be over. Every group is different; it is a judgement call when to move on. As a rule of thumb, you want at least twice as many conversations as session times so that there is always an element of choice for people.

And yes, any individual can offer more than one topic. Best at this stage to get as many as possible and to sort them out so that no one is required to be in two places at once through a "horse-trading" discussion once all topics are in. In other words, you are looking to generate a wealth to choose from, an embarrassment of riches. For organizations of a very efficient mindset this is counter-cultural. You may well find people in your group who assume that once there are enough topics to fill the spaces in the time–space matrix then the job is done. To generate extra is, on their default thinking mode, just wasteful. So you may need to explain that "filling the gaps" isn't the purpose of the exercise, rather it is to ensure that all topics that are important to everyone here get raised.

3. Working with time and space

Owen identifies the two key facilitator skills as creating time and space and holding time and space, which essentially means that "Under the best of circumstances, the facilitator will be totally present and absolutely invisible" (Owen, 1997, p. 57). This is achieved by doing less rather than more. The ability to do this allows Owen, at least, to conduct Open Space sessions for groups using a language he doesn't understand. As the facilitator you are working to create a time and space in which the group can reach their potential; a place where the group feel safe to explore new options and to be discursive.

The two principles "when it starts, it starts" and "when it's over, it's over" help people to throw off their usual meeting behaviour of diving straight into the topic, sans introductions, and finishing because the big hand reaches 12. The two principles give the group permission both to "chat" while they assemble until it "feels" right to get to the topic in hand, and to stop when they have reached a stop point. There is no need to "fill the time" with more discussion.

4. Being authentically present

How you show up is really important. It really helps if, as the facilitator, you are fit, healthy, well rested, and focused on the day. Holding space and time is interesting work and it requires a high degree of non-intrusive attentiveness. It is a very particular kind of attentiveness. You want to be present as "your best self," able with ease to be helpful, forgiving, accepting, interested, and generous. You need to be all there, not distracted, not trying to "do something else" while the sessions are running. Have no attachment to fixed outcomes. This is very important: you are there to provide the best opportunity for something great to happen, not to make it happen. It is not your responsibility how people choose to use that opportunity. This is possible when you understand that as the facilitator your concern is process not content.

5. *Addressing common concerns*

a) "What if no one comes to a particular session?"
I always say in this case there are two options. First, that you can use the time to think on your own about this topic, and write up your thoughts; and second, that you can, after waiting long enough to be sure no one else is coming, go to another session.

b) "What if the people I think should be there don't come to the right sessions or, indeed, at all?"
In general terms, the answer is that the right people for an OST event are those who want to come, and that the focus is on the quality and quantity of the interaction rather than on specific individuals. The second answer is that there are two likely outcomes. One is that until they care to come the job won't get done, in which case let's focus on what we can achieve with the people who are here. The other is that perhaps we can still get things done as it turns out they weren't as essential as we originally thought (Owen, 1997, p. 21).

c) "What if people don't use the session time well?"
They will use the time well because they were drawn to this item and so will find it very engaging. If for some reason they find they aren't engaged, they are not only free to leave but positively encouraged to do so. If the conversation takes a moment to get going, remember the point is about creativity and spirit, not rules and timetables. As long as the volunteer principle is adhered to, this concern tends to be a real red herring.

d) "What if people suggest stupid items?"
I would say, honour the process and the person and put it up anyway. The process is self-correcting. Essentially, people are voting with their feet and they have an opt-out vote. If the item is that irrelevant or stupid, the host will find themselves sitting on their own. This is another reason it is important to allow for butterflies: better they are out of a session than creating mischief because they had to go to something.

e) "What if no one offers any agenda items?"
This is the biggest facilitator fear. Remember, and remind them, there is no agenda, there is no plan B waiting in the wings. Owen says, "I'm quite prepared to stand here until something happens." Note the phrasing: not "until we get some items" but "until something happens." Theoretically, that could be the group deciding that actually they have nothing to talk about and disbanding: choice is all. More likely, someone will break the silence with a first suggestion, or there might be a suggestion of a break to give people time to form their thoughts. I see no harm in that, although I would keep it fairly short. Allowing people to briefly walk and talk can get the juices flowing. Either way, the responsibility for producing an agenda, at this point, is theirs, not yours. Good preparation of people for what they are coming to helps with this.

f) "What if people don't attend any sessions?"
As we have said regarding butterflies and bees, there are many ways of adding value in these events.

Origins of the Methodology

The birth of Open Space Technology began with Owen's frustration in 1983 when it took him a year, with others, to organize an international conference for 250 people. Although the conference was deemed a great success, the balance of effort to effect, input to output, not to mention the emotional wear and tear, left him feeling "never again." This decision was reinforced by the general post-event view that, while the event had indeed been outstanding, the most valuable part had been the coffee breaks! (Owen, 1997, p. 3). Reflecting on it all afterwards, he realized that what he wanted to know was: was it possible to combine the level of synergy and excitement present in a good coffee break with the substantive activity and results characteristic of a good meeting? And could it all be done a bit quicker?!

Pondering these questions, he took inspiration from an event attended long ago in West Africa around an initiation ceremony for young men. During this event he had observed 500 people organize themselves over four days without any visible planning committee! He noted how the layout of the village, a circle of huts around an open space, helped. His account of the village shape puts me in mind of the long-lost "village green" pattern of English villages: a higgledy-piggledy collection of various abodes around a commonly owned space where all the important village events, from the market to the maypole dancing, took place. The human circle, suggests Owen, is the "fundamental geometry" of open human communication (Owen, 1997, p. 5). No head, no foot, no high or low, just people with each other, face to face, equidistant from "the centre."

He noticed how during the ceremony groups moved from the perimeters of the circle (behind the huts) into the centre of the circle, creating a really alive centre. There was a rhythm as groups swirled in and out of this space of energized peaks and lower energy times. At the end, the energy ebbed as people flowed back to their homes. He compares this to the rhythm of breathing. So while this might be appropriate to village ceremonies, how was it helpful to the different rhythm of organizational life? How could this process, in effect, be applied to organizational challenges? What would the content of the event be? To help with the generation and organization of content, he drew on further aspects of village life: the community bulletin board and the marketplace. In particular, he sees the marketplace as "a way of bringing interests together in an orderly way" (Owen, 1997, p. 6).

From these observations of how life can be self-organized – in a village, with its marketplace and bulletin board, or in ceremonial circles, or in breathing – he identified key processes, and the pattern and rhythm to use as the basis for a meeting that was all coffee break! Except that, of course, it has the potential to be much more consistently the best of the coffee break experience: connective, energized and energizing, creative and passionate. By drawing on these aspects of human life, he created a process that is both new and familiar. While doing these things in a workplace setting may seem odd or unusual, the elements that inform the design are not. Essentially, we know how to do this. This belief is borne out, in my experience, by the speed with which people "get" Open Space when it is introduced into an event.

Conclusion

Open Space Technology is a highly participative and engaging process that is extraordinarily responsive to the needs of the moment. Its use is highly recommended in complex, fast-changing situations. It is relatively easy to incorporate into other events and usually people find it an exceptionally valuable way of working. There is no reason for it not to be an organization's default mode for managing meetings. It won't have escaped your notice that I have drawn heavily on the work of Harrison Owen and I thoroughly recommend that you do too!

9

Simu-Real

"We are bringing in a new ERP system across the whole manufacturing process; it will affect everyone. It will be much more sensitive to accurate data than the old system. People will need to be much more disciplined in the way they record and enter data. Can you help us make everyone enter data properly?" This was the work invitation.

The organization was a manufacturer of about 250 people, most of whom were based on one large site. The people involved in each part of the manufacturing process were separated from each other by distance and by physical barriers: it was a typical silo organization. Historically, the site had managed the many inadequacies of its "grown like Topsy" legacy IT systems by workarounds, off-system excel spreadsheet accounting, and the like. Good, clean, accurate data could be hard to come by. While the implementation of a new IT system was to be welcomed in theory, in practice it meant a lot of work. And it was clear the investment would be pointless unless there was a real change in work habits.

First we reframed the challenge as "making work work better." This better reflected the idea that the investment and involvement being asked of the workforce to ensure the successful implementation of this new IT system could help make their working life better, and wasn't just for management benefit. We entitled the particular event, "Every count counts."

Working with a cross-hierarchical, cross-functional planning team, we decided to use the Simu-Real process, whereby the whole manufacturing process is recreated in a large space. Working with this group in preparation for running the Simu-Real was in itself a great learning experience for the organization. The planning group were astonished at the complexity of the organization. It became very clear that no one brain was big enough to truly understand how the system

Positive Psychology and Change: How Leadership, Collaboration, and Appreciative Inquiry Create Transformational Results, First Edition. Sarah Lewis.
© 2016 John Wiley & Sons, Ltd. Published 2016 by John Wiley & Sons, Ltd.

functioned at present, never mind how it could be improved. It also became very clear that by and large the present data problems in production were the result of good intentions meeting inadequate systems. Our list of people who needed to be present to represent the "whole system" expanded through our discussions and explorations as it became clear how this truly was a "system-wide" issue.

On the day, everyone assembled in the Simu-Real space, a huge hotel ballroom now adorned with chairs grouped to represent the different functions, meeting spaces, a decision-making table, and various "artefacts" from the workplace, including bits of "kit."

We framed the task as:

To improve the accuracy of counting and recording across the whole production process while keeping the processes as simple as possible. Specifically to:

- *reduce counting and data recording to a minimum*
- *ensure that counts and data recorded are accurate*
- *bring the record and the reality closer together.*

After introductions, we asked the system during the "action" sessions to address three issues in turn. Round one was: What happens now? Round two was: How could work work better? Round three was: Testing out our decisions.

In round one we asked each "home group" that made up the system to engage with questions such as:

- *How does what you do link to what other people do?*
- *How are the figures you produce used by others?*
- *What difference does it make how accurate they are?*
- *What actions of others impact on you and how do your actions impact on others?*
- *The data you work with, where does it come from?*
- *What does it take for someone to get you that data?*
- *How well do they understand why you need it and what you use it for?*
- *What data do you need that you don't get, or don't get in a timely fashion?*

In between the "action" sessions were the reflective sessions where people could share what they had learnt from the "action period." Here we asked people to consider such questions and issues as:

- *What observations do you have that you can share about the process that we just went through?*
- *What did you notice about your own feelings of trust as you went through the action period?*
- *What information did you find yourself lacking that was needed in order to reach an intelligent decision?*
- *What helped you get the data or what held you back from getting that information?*
- *Given what you have learnt during this analysis session, think about what you might do to help the organization work more effectively on the tasks or issues during the next action period?*

Throughout the day there was an action table where decisions could be made regarding the process. As these decisions were made they held for the duration of the exercise. At the end of the day there was a collective discussion about what needed to happen and who would do what.

The energy and engagement on the day was tremendous. Learning happened in the moment as people realized the difficulties caused to others by their actions and where time and effort was wasted or duplicated. People came together to design process changes and to decide on ways to improve the situation. Specific decisions were taken and work groups were set up to implement them. Some of the ambitions and outcomes were:

1. *Implementing a system for accurate counting of scrap in a particular function (individual scrap counters provided at each station).*
2. *Weighting individual items, pipes, and gutters as appropriate rather than taking gross "guesstimates" from weighbridge data.*
3. *Bringing the intranet into the plant (which was done by installing a new PC in that area almost immediately).*
4. *Introducing an electronic maintenance system.*
5. *The accurate setting and use of scales (again scales were quickly all calibrated, repaired as necessary, instructions for use laminated and secured to a surface, a procedure produced; this ensured that the weight of the box accurately reflected the number of items in the box).*
6. *The design of a new "easy to read, and secure" label for the booking-out system.*

This self-organized, active follow-up relied on minimum push or drive from management. Instead it was built on the energy and enthusiasm of those whose working lives would benefit by these changes, and the experience of being supported by management to make them. This event proved to be the beginning of a series of events that resulted in clean data and good and widespread understanding of the dependencies of the physical and virtual system; and facilitated the on-time implementation of the new system.

Introduction

Simu-Real as a process was first formulated by Klein (1992). It is a large group method that allows people to do work in real time. They do the work, examine how they do it, and then adapt how they do it in real time. This means it is not a role-play. All that is simulated is the organizational structure, which is recreated within the one room. Within the exercises, people are working from their normal work role perspective. It can be seen as a form of action learning on a large scale. As Klein, the originator of this methodology, says, "Simu-Real is a method that uses simulation to help an organization become more visible to itself" (1992, p. 566). It can be seen as a way of holding a mirror up to a system or organization. Simu-Real allows organizations to address critical issues while at the same time helping the people involved understand, and so improve, the dynamics of how they are working together.

It is particularly effective at illuminating the lack of effective feedback loops in the organization. In other words, it is quite possible that in the normal run of events Department A does something that either particularly benefits or disadvantages Department F; however, they never get to hear about it because there is just no process to support that "backward" flow of information across a system. Instead, the system is geared to a "throughput" model of getting the product or the people in, processed, and out the door. As Department A and F are geographically separated and have no reason for direct communication with each other, the opportunity doesn't arise by accident either; hence Department A have no way of knowing of the impact of their actions on Department F, so they just keep doing things that are unhelpful, or make a unilateral decision to stop doing things that were very helpful. Equally, Department F may well not be aware that this action originated in Department A as they receive input only from Department E and, occasionally, D. I'm sure you get the general picture.

Simu-Real disrupts this "normal" pattern by using a simulation "to represent a current, complex real-world situation. It creates a simplified and, to some extent, stylized operation model that abstracts and accentuates certain aspects of an actual organization' (Klein, 1992, p. 568). Although the organization is a simulation of the complex reality, "All participants in Simu-Real take their own roles in the organization that is being simulated" (p. 568) as the exercise is run.

Purpose

To help people grasp the whole system in its complexity, to see the simultaneous activity, and to collectively and co-creatively determine what needs to change.

The Process

Simu-Real is often conducted in one day. It involves three action periods each followed by an analysis period. During the action periods the group members work on the task for which the event was organized. During the analysis periods they look at how they worked during the action period and what this says about the dynamics of the organization. They also consider how group members can work better together. The Simu-Real needs to be conducted in one large space. A key point of Simu-Real is that organizational members are able to literally "see" their whole organization in a way that they are normally quite unable to do: by having the whole organization in the room the whole system relationship becomes much more visible.

A planning group works beforehand to decide the central task for the event. They also work out how to create a "simulation" of the organization in the space available for the event. Within the simulation space, people are grouped as they are in the organization (e.g., into marketing, finance, customer service, etc.) The idea is to recreate the spatial-geographic reality of the organization as much as possible. It is possible for any individual to have membership of more than one group, as is often the case in organizational life. It is for them to negotiate with colleagues how they enact multiple memberships. The simulated organization should also reflect the psychological reality of organizational life. Two departments may exist in close physical proximity but have a very distant psychological relationship with each other. The planning group have to decide how best to represent the situation.

During the action sessions the "organization" is asked to complete a task. Organizational members are free to arrange conversations and meetings with other parts of the organization during this time, and meeting spaces should be provided in the action space to facilitate this. They can propose action in relation to any other group and they are free to try out new activities or ways of doing things. They do this as real organizational members with real roles and responsibilities. The facilitator acts as an applied anthropologist "unobtrusively observing events, eavesdropping on conversations, and occasionally conducting brief 'curbside' interviews to determine how people are perceiving and feeling about events in the organization" (Klein, 1992, p. 575). The facilitator also acts as a conductor of the simulation during the action periods. They ensure that the ground rules are being followed, make procedural judgements, and keep time.

During the analysis periods, members move out of the action space into a reflective space where the groups are arranged to be cross-organizational, allowing the learning by different groups during the action phase to be brought together. Participants are seated in a large circle or a series of smaller circles. It is very helpful if the analysis space is a separate space. Other techniques may also be needed to help people "move" from the one space to the other; for example, commencing the analysis session with a short period of reflective silence or encouraging everyone to start by sharing one positive thing they learnt from the action session. Alternatively, some physical activity may be needed to release any adrenalin-fuelled tension before considered conversation can begin. Encouraging people to take a few moments to frame the questions they want to ask, or observations they want to make, in ways that are designed move things forward can help best use be made of the available time for learning. In other words, for this time to be used to most value, people may need some help in transforming emotions aroused by the action period into useful questions and observations that will enable to the group to explore the future possibilities rather than the past blame. Of course, sometimes a reconstruction of a narrative about the past can be incredibility helpful in terms of opening up future possibilities. As ever, life as a facilitator is a series of judgement calls. As a facilitator you may choose to ask questions and/or offer tentative hypotheses to aid the group to move forward ready to do something different in the next round.

Generally, the goal is to help the organization learn from each action period and to determine what to change for the next action period. The suggested ideal group size, since this is related to organizational dynamics, is between 25 and 50. However, the upper limit is open to exploration!

Recommended Use

Klein (1992) and Bunker and Alban (1997) suggest this process is recommended when there is a need to:

- involve the whole organization in meeting the challenge, or solving the problem
- develop the organization's learning ability, moving towards a "learning organization"
- reveal the organizational dynamics

- make speedy, informed decisions on real issues involving everyone
- do some silo-busting on a system-wide issue
- reduce implementation time
- test drive a restructuring plan before it is implemented
- make a decision about a complex, concrete problem or issue
- uncover the structural or procedural blocks to solving a problem effectively
- solve complex problems
- work on the redesign of some parts of the organization
- determine goals and priorities
- engage in future planning.

Key Ideas

1. Simulating the whole reality of the situation

While essentially the emphasis is on simulating the formal organizational structure, it is important to also include the "psychological" structure. So if decisions tend to get made informally in other environments (like the local pub, the golf course, or the smoking area) then you might want to include them in your simulation but maybe partly screened off to reflect their particular "important to but not official part of the organization" status. In this way they are included as a behind-the-scenes group of which other organizational members are aware but to whom they don't have access. Containing the whole simulation within one large space is necessary to ensure that people can see what is going on but can only hear another group discussion by moving out of their own space. In other words, the groups are more or less out of earshot of each other, as they would be in the organization.

2. Testing hypotheses

As well as simulating the present reality, you might want to simulate an alternative future structure and see how things work out in your simulation. In effect you can design a "prototype" of the new organizational structure and test it out in the safety of a simulation space before launching it into the organization. Simu-Real allows an organization to test the impact of plans and to study the consequences of hypothetical situations. It is a safe space for "seeing what happens when" and "what might happen if."

3. Simplifying complexity

Configuring the organization in a simplified way and arranging for its component parts to function within the confines of a single, large space reduces complexity. This makes it much easier to see what is going on around a particular topic or system, and to gather data and temporarily "reconfigure" the organization, than it would working directly in the organization.

4. Focused attention, high quality connections

The process gives participants permission to focus solely on the task in hand. The work-focused simulation set-up means that every conversation people need to have is purposeful. The rules of the game mean that people can get straight to the point about things that matter to them. This means that people can engage together in meaningful and impactful conversation very quickly. Relationships are formed very quickly around a joint ambition.

5. Making the invisible visible

By bringing the whole system into the room and watching it work on a task, hidden behaviours, presumptions, assumptions, beliefs, conflicts, misalignment of purpose, misunderstandings, or misinterpretations of the actions of others all become much more visible, to everyone. Once they are visible they are much easier to consciously challenge or change. Similarly, it becomes much easier to notice how feedback loops are, or more usually aren't, working in a complex system. The relationships between actions and consequences, usually obscured by factors of time and space, are suddenly evident in a very powerful way.

6. Slowing things down to speed things up

Simu-Real not only simplifies organizational life, it also effectively slows it down. This makes it much easier to see what is going on and how one department behaves in response to another, for instance. The amount of learning and decision-making the process can produce in a day can be immense. It has been estimated by participants that in a one-day Simu-Real they have enacted as much as a year or 18 months of real-time work (Klein, 1992, p. 577).

7. Learning from doing

The reflection periods are a key part of the process that allow participants to reflect on their lived experience in the organization. This may be something that they rarely have time to do, and certainly not in the company of other interested parties with the opportunity to test out new ideas immediately. The Simu-Real process can be seen as action learning at a whole system level.

8. Exposing the hidden

Much of organizational life takes place behind closed doors for all sorts of good or purely functional reasons. By effectively stripping out the walls, Simu-Real allows people to see how other groups function, to listen in to conversations, to see how information is interpreted in a different setting, and to see how decisions get made. Directors get to see into the union office and vice versa.

Critical Success Factors

1. Selecting the topic

The topic needs to be "a systemic issue or problem that has implications for everyone who attends" (Bunker & Alban, 1997, p. 163). Please note they say *systemic*, not systematic, that is, an issue where each action influences other actions. A systemic issue is a deeply connected system-wide pattern of inter-actions that is often hard to see. It is also possible to use Simu-Real for future-oriented activity, to road test or pilot proposed changes. The topic needs to be important, engaging, and something that, if improved, will have positive impact for everyone. I was once persuaded, against my better judgement, by someone who really wanted to see the process in action, to do a Simu-Real event on a topic that did not meet these criteria and for which Simu-Real was not really the appropriate way forward. While the event achieved some benefit it didn't have the feel or the impact of events such as that described in the introduction to this chapter, where the topic under consideration cried out for this whole system approach. I learnt a valuable lesson.

2. Preparatory work with the planning group

More than for any of the other interventions explored here, the preparatory work is key to a successful event.

The planning group needs to:

- design or decide the tasks that will be performed during the action period
- identify who needs to be there
- design the simulation "organizational map" and work out how to represent it in the working space (i.e., work out where to put the different organizational groups in relation to each other to best reflect the lived experience of the organizational relations and geographical realities)
- gather information from the organization about the issue under consideration (i.e., work out how the workflow process, for example, actually works on the ground at present – this work in itself can be very revealing)
- decide which tasks will be tackled during the three action periods
- design the questions for the "analysis" periods (e.g., at the beginning of the analysis period you might direct the questions towards what they learnt from the action session just completed, while towards the end you might, given their reflections, direct questions towards what they want to implement, do differently, or negotiate with other groups in the next action session)
- think about how to create good group norms that will militate against the danger of blame and humiliation
- design and issue invitations, explaining the nature and purpose of the event
- agree on the decision-making process
- attend to other logistical issues of the day (e.g., refreshments and timings)
- gather data beforehand to inform the day
- act as ambassadors, exciting others
- identify any "hot spots" of frustration or anger in the system that might need careful attention.

3. Clarity on the decision-making process

The potential for fast, informed, on-the-day decision-making is one of the most exciting aspects of this approach. There are three main alternatives.

a) Executive decision-making
This option means that the existing management structure remains responsible for determining what course to follow regarding the task or

issue under discussion. If working to this model, it is suggested that at that end of the day the executives have a real meeting in a "fishbowl" format in the middle of the rest of the event participants. This means they sit in an inner circle and hold their meeting while everyone else sits in a circle outside, able to hear but not to join in. The executive circle should include an "empty chair" which any other participant can use when they want to express their views. The executive team then make real decisions in real time.

Klein suggests that this works best when the decisions made on the day will be binding on the organization; members of the organization are generally satisfied with how top management works; there is no particular desire to experiment with decision-making; and the decisions will be implemented by the senior managers (Klein, 1992, p. 573).

b) Ad hoc decision-making

This means that decision-making power is vested in a representative body, drawn from the different organizational groups. The representative group is selected in advance and known to everyone. They need to be easily identifiable at the event. They use the decision-making table during the day as well as being members of their home groups. They discuss their observations and ideas with the consultant during coffee or lunch breaks. Ultimately, the process is similar to the executive decision-making process in that they hold the end-of-day discussion, and ratify the decisions made, in a fishbowl, in a manner observable and audible to all.

If you are to use this process you need to be very clear and confident that the senior people in the event and the organization will abide by the decision-making of this group. Klein says that this appears to work well when the senior group is comfortable with delegating decision-making power; the decisions will affect all levels of the organization involved in the simulation; the implementation depends on everyone following through on what has been decided; and the focus of the Simu-Real is on generating better coordination between groups (1992, p. 574).

c) The decision-making table

This means that a "decision-making table" is created in the middle of the action room with a given number of chairs. There is no designated decision-making group at the beginning of the exercise. The decision-making group is a flexible, emergent, and changing group. People need to be urged to keep an eye on what is going on at the table if they are interested in influencing the future of the organization. Generally 12 chairs are about the right number for a group of 40–50 people. It needs to be a small enough number to create some energy and tension, so well less than 50% of the group number.

The criteria for decision-making are that all the chairs must be occupied and that the decision is a consensus decision. In this case the decision made is made for the organization. Effectively, this is for the duration of the rest of the exercise and allows ideas for change to be instantly implemented in the simulation so their effects on system relations and the topic under exploration can be instantly experienced and assessed. The decisions can be ratified at the end of the event by the group as a whole. Klein suggests that this process works particularly well for comparatively small and non-bureaucratic organizations; where members are used to making decisions at staff meetings and so on; or in very hierarchical situations where there is a desire to increase engagement, proactivity, and empowerment among staff previously regarded as "hired hands" (1992, p. 574) (see Box 9.1).

Whatever the formal decision-making process, it is worth noting that as people become more connected, and as their analysis of the situation becomes more complex and sophisticated, it is highly likely that ideas emerge that are consensual (e.g., it becomes evident that an adjustment here or a reconfiguration there will improve things). One of the magic

---

Box 9.1 Deciding on the Decision-Making Process

When trying to decide which decision-making process is most appropriate, questions to ask that might help include the following:

Are the decisions taken during the Simu-Real to be advisory or binding?
How are decisions ordinarily made in the organization?
Should the organization use Simu-Real to explore a different approach to decision-making?
Should decision-making be delegated to executives or to a representative subgroup?
Is it preferable to give all participants in the Simu-Real event an equal opportunity to influence and participate in the decision-making?

Adapted from Klein (1992, p. 572)

outcomes of this co-creative process in particular is the number of small improvements that emerge that work to increase and improve inter-departmental alignment. Many of these never get recorded in the formal record of the event.

4. Participants

As usual with these methods, you want to invite the people relevant to the system under consideration. This may include people beyond the depart-ment that first invited you into the organization, or indeed people from outside the organization. It is sometimes helpful to have people not directly involved to be "on alert" to supply information quickly to the group if they need it to aid decision-making.

5. Establishing ground rules

There are some standard ground rules that help the simulation to run well.

- You may communicate with other groups in writing or by sending messages.
- Representatives of two or more groups may meet together anywhere in this space.
- Joint meetings of two or more groups are OK.
- If for any reason you want to call a meeting of the entire organization, the space marked "assembly area" is there for your use (e.g., the reflection area).

And, of course, if you are using a decision-making table you need to explain how that works.

6. Introducing the session

At the beginning, it is a good idea if the host explains the purpose and anticipated outcomes for the event before introducing the facilitator who will run the event. The facilitator should explain how the process works (i.e., the switch between action and reflection periods). It can be helpful to emphasize that in the first they need to be thinking and acting from the perspective of "you in your usual work role," while in the second it's helpful to think more as "you as a member of this community" (i.e., holistically).

The facilitator will also need to clarify and explain the decision-making process and their role as facilitator.

Explain that all they are being asked to do is to do the best they can to arrive at an end result that will satisfy them and others and will work well for the organization. As they work on the task, they're encouraged to gather information, explore viewpoints, and develop possibilities. While the action is going on, they need to act as an observer as well as a participant, in preparation for the reflection time. During the analysis and reflection time, they focus on identifying actions that were either helping or hindering the organization's work. The purpose of the analysis is to help them better understand factors that contribute to, and interfere with, the organization's work on the task.

7. Giving instructions

Simu-Real, while not difficult for people to engage with, is unusual. So it is helpful to give fairly clear, action-oriented instructions. We mentioned some when discussing establishing ground rules (point 5). It can also be helpful to say something like: "During action periods it's up to you, individually and with others, to decide how best to tackle the task. You'll probably want to do some planning in your groups. You will also need to be paying attention to the need to communicate with other groups to figure out how to work across group lines" (Klein, 1992). Even with this express permission it can, take people some time to break out of the habitual organizational norms of trying to solve all challenges within their usual limited, local environment.

8. Senior managers are open to receiving the data this event might produce

As ever, don't ask questions if you are not willing to hear the answers they produce. During this event lots of information about how things are "actually" done, rather than how senior management fondly believes they are done, is likely to come to light. Senior management need both to be prepared for this and to be able to appreciate the honesty and goodwill of those sharing this information, rather than focused on seeking to establish the past path of deviance and the allocation of blame. Even if they sign up to this before-hand, in the event the disbelief and dismay at reality can overwhelm the best of intentions and a segue into the blame game can quickly start. A key part of your role as facilitator is to deflect this before it gets started and to bring people's attention back to the usefulness of the information and to help them refocus on how things can be made better from here, not how they got to this state in the first place.

9. Effective simulation

The more the action work space is a good simulation of the organization the more convincing it will seem as a simulation, and the easier it will be for people to see it as their working organization. One factor to pay attention to is the arrangement of the groups. The arrangement needs to reflect the actual and the psychological realities. So have the "satellite" offices on the very edge of the space, while maybe the executive suite needs to be partially "screened off," reflecting the fact that the executive can't directly see what is happening on the shop floor. By the same token, use props to create a psychological reality for different spaces (i.e., bits of kit on the shop floor, order forms in the sales department, and Tonka trucks in the loading bay, for example!). These props also help people to demonstrate and act out ideas they are having or to explain how things work to each other. Each group space needs to be labelled so people can find their "home" space, and provided with chairs. Have a few flipcharts available in the "meeting spaces."

Key Skills

1. Creating good questions for both the action and the analysis period

As with all these co-creative methodologies, question formation is key to the process. For the action period, we want to suggest questions that will encourage groups to interact with other groups to seek answers and that will simulate their thinking and produce learning conversations or experiences. During the reflection sessions, we want to elevate and connect that learning. Klein suggests a generic "connector" question for concluding an analysis period: "Given what you have learnt during this analysis session, think about what you might do to help the organization work more effectively on the task (or issue) during the next action period" (Klein, 1992, p. 577). The case study at the beginning of this chapter shows how the broad principles were adapted for this particular situation.

2. As facilitator

a) Holding the space

I find the way these events unfold fascinating. As others have noted (Bunker & Alban, 1997), in the initial action round people can be very reluctant to come out of their own spaces. You can see groups trying to solve systemic or system-wide challenges without involving others. This is likely to be a reflection of what is happening in the organization. It makes the "silo mentality" that is so often a challenge for organizations highly visible. Generally, the pace changes after the first reflection period as it becomes clear that groups will have to actively coordinate their activity to achieve change. People may be somewhat confused, disoriented, and at sea to begin with in this unusual activity where they are much more visible to others than usual. As facilitator, you need to not panic if you don't see much happening initially. By the end of the event, in my experience, the energy in the room is electrifying!

b) Running action phase

Help people adhere to the ground rules. Listen in to conversations and check out what is happening during the action phase. Wander around the space, observing and feeling how things are. Keep time. The role of the facilitator is likely to vary in the different rounds as the energy and the pace warm up.

c) Running reflection phase

While Klein's advice is to work in one large circle, I have also found that working in smaller groups in parallel can work very well. Ensure the groups are mixed by function. Either way, the role of the facilitator is to ask questions, allow intra-group discussion, and then facilitate inter-group discussion.

d) Concluding the event

Towards the end of the day, bring everyone together – for this a large circle is a necessity – and conduct a review of the events, progress, and learning from the day. Usually, a key purpose of this period is to review the decisions made during the exercise and to "formally" ratify them to be implemented; starting from today whenever possible. What form this takes depends on the decision-making process that has been adopted for the day. This period is also used to decide how those ideas that need more work will be carried forward and by whom. Since, by definition, you should have the senior organization decision-makers in the room, this should not be a contentious part of the programme as they have been able to influence all the decisions during the event. Rather, the final discussion process is a consolidation of the change produced by the event as a firm foundation on which further improvement can be built.

Origins of the Methodology

Simu-Real was designed by Donald C. Klein in the 1970s. It emerged from his awareness of how difficult it was for many organizational members to know about the roles of other people in the organization and to appreciate the "complexity-beyond-grasp" dilemma (Klein, 1992, p. 568). This is the idea that so many things are going on in an organization at any one time that no one can take it all in. As he puts it, "I became increasingly fascinated by the seemingly impossible challenge of making client systems intelligible to the groups and individuals of whom they were composed" (1992, p. 566). Klein noted that this complexity-beyond-grasp issue tended to lead to the belief that it was impossible to change anything; as indeed, if you are trying to solve a system-wide issue without involving the whole system, it usually is.

Long-Term Effects

In my experience, the effects continue well after the event because the learning is of such a profound nature. People have a much improved understanding of the organization as a whole, they are better connected to other groups, and they understand their needs much better. This means that as they make decisions back in their own space they are much more likely to have other groups "in mind" and to think to consult with them about anything that might impact on them. People leave these events with new awareness, real work progress, and an improved mental map of the organization or the process. In addition, there is usually huge energy, as demonstrated in the case study, to immediately make changes. As in the example here, it is often the little things that never get attended to, even though many people know they are a problem, that emerge as being key factors in the challenge at hand. Simu-Real can be great at helping to identify the little things that make a big difference.

When to Use and When Not to

Simu-Real is appropriate when you want to create an intensely focused situation in which people can bring their creativity, energy, and problem-solving ability together to apply to a predetermined problem or issue. It's appropriate when you want to illuminate in a single day and a single space something of the complexity of relationships and connections that exist over time and space. Simu-Real acts to compress time, bringing these connections into view for the whole group. Our case study clearly identified how small initial errors in data, due to "quick and dirty" weight assessments combined with some dodgy weighing equipment, escalated and amplified into major problems such as short orders being delivered or packages being mislabelled. No one intended these outcomes and no one was being negligent; on the contrary, they were busting a gut to get the orders out, but still these problems regularly arose. While people's initial instinct in these situations is often to blame other people, the Simu-Real showed that many factors that caused the problems were beyond any one individual's control. At the same time, everyone left with a much clearer understanding of the high-risk impact of seemingly small inaccuracies in data.

Simu-Real creates the opportunity for self-reflection by the organization. In my experience, this allows for a completely different quality of learning about "the system." People leave literally unable to carry on as before now that the unhelpful unintended consequences of positively intended action is so clear to them. Or now they know how a small effort on their part can make a huge difference to someone else's job further down the line. They may have always kind of known this, but now they really know it and it matters to them. The main counter-indication is if senior management don't see the value of engaging their staff in the problem-solving, or if the problem is not appropriate to the method.

Conclusion

Simu-Real is a great process for calling on the collective intelligence of the system to solve system-wide problems or to explore system-wide options for change and development. It is highly practical and concrete as it brings the system to life in the moment and so adds a visceral component to the learning that takes place. In this way, it lends itself to the idea of "prototyping" in the design stage of Appreciative Inquiry. It takes a fair bit of setting up and, like all the co-creative methodologies, is labour intensive at the event. However, the effectiveness of the process and the speed with which coordinated change can occur should make this investment more than worthwhile. The greatest skill is probably in assessing when it is the appropriate methodology.

10

Pulling It All Together

Introduction

This chapter is about how to pull all the ideas, activities, and methodologies presented in this book together to create unique events that create sustainable change. First we will examine why planned approaches to organizational change are so dominant and ineffectual, then we will summarize key concepts and key methodologies from positive psychology that support the alternative approach presented in this book. Next we will consider why this is the right time for these approaches. Then we'll explore some general principles for bringing this understanding of change to more conventional change processes. And finally we will explore David Cooperrider's latest exposition of the positive change revolution.

Rise of Planned Change Approaches

From the 1980s onwards the field of organizational change has been dominated by consultant-generated models of "planned change," loosely based on Lewin's original work (1951). These approaches are generally acknowledged to have a high rate of failure. Kotter (1996), Keller and Aiken (2009), and Blanchard (2010) all estimate the failure rate to be 70%. Despite this, these methodologies are frequently called upon by organizations facing, or contemplating, making changes in their organization.

There are a number of reasons for this; in particular, people don't know about the alternatives, and planned change approaches are very attractive

Positive Psychology and Change: How Leadership, Collaboration, and Appreciative Inquiry Create Transformational Results, First Edition. Sarah Lewis.
© 2016 John Wiley & Sons, Ltd. Published 2016 by John Wiley & Sons, Ltd.

to practitioners and mangers. Collins refers to planned change management methodologies as "N-step guides for change" (1998, p. 82). Coming at the challenge of organizational change from a sociological perspective, he finds that "many of the accounts of change and much of the advice which is offered on planning and managing change is based on a limited, mechanistic and overly-rational view of organizations and of social interaction" (p. 82). One can only nod one's head wisely and agree. But if people are drawn to these pragmatic change recipes, transferable without much modification from one context to another, we have to ask why. He suggests their attraction lies in the fact that they are rational, sequential, and upbeat. They appeal to our desire for the clarity of logic over the messiness of human emotion, the simplicity of sequential activity over the complexity of simultaneity, and the attraction of apparent predictability over the gamble of an emergent change.

He notes that these planned change models present change as controllable, a problem of formal logic, something with a clear beginning and end, and something that offers a way to draw a clear line under the past. In other words, change is presented as a linear unidirectional process. He notes that within these models either conflict is not acknowledged or it is problematized. That is to say, resistance can be discounted either as a lack of comprehension or as the problem of the person (e.g., they don't "get" it, or they are "dinosaurs, constitutionally against change"). At the same time, he notes that there is no explicit recognition of the management agenda of control: change is presented as inevitable, the only answer, not as a choice made by those in power. And very importantly, he notes that there is an implicit guarantee of success: do the change right and you will reap the rewards. By an inversion of logic this also means that if you don't reap the rewards you didn't do the change right; you were at fault, not the model. Collins outlines a "generic" model of change of this nature (see Box 10.1).

The dream of problem-free, pain-free, error-free, progressive, organizationally in-step change is precisely that: a dream. Human change just doesn't work like that. We are messy, iterative, forgetful, slow to learn, and creatures of habit. We are also creatures of insights, of leaps of imagination, of bold risks and impatient shortcuts. We're in a hurry to get where we're going; we are prepared to act on hunches and guesses and "good enough" analyses. I'm not saying this makes for great organizational practice; I'm just saying this is the way we are, and fighting it is a waste of organizational time and energy. A much better investment might be to work out how to get the best from the human way, to work out how to work with these crazy, illogical, emotionally driven creatures, to work out how to utilize their imaginative

---

Box 10.1   Collins's Generic Planned Approach to Change

Collins helpfully provides a generic model of the planned approach to change.

1. Develop strategy
2. Confirm top-level support
3. Use project management approach
   Identify tasks
   Assign responsibilities
   Agree deadlines
   Initiate action
   Monitor
   Act on problems
   Close down
4. Communicate results

Collins (1998, p. 83)

---

abilities, their boldness, and their social ties to achieve great things together. This is what co-creative approaches, informed by positive psychology insights, offer us.

This is not to suggest that we throw the baby out with the bath water. PRINCE2 and project and programme management offer value to organizations. They provide clear and coherent accounts of what will happen and how. They facilitate monitoring and tracking. They assign clear accountability and they help identify areas of commercial risk during the change process. Many project managers are highly skilled at working with and understanding the characteristics of the social systems with which they work, as Charles Smith discovered in his research (2007). Yet maybe we can shift from seeing programme and project work as the *driver* of change to recognizing it as a *support* to co-creative energized change.

Co-creative Approaches to Change

Fortunately, alternative approaches to change have emerged or have been developed over the last 25 years. They are predicated on a different understanding of organizations and so of organizational change. They recognize organizations as social phenomena, co-created by their members. By working with this process of co-creation of organization, so we work with the process of organizational change, development, and growth.

Co-created change processes offer an alternative to the imposed change model outlined above. By working closely, from the beginning, with those who will be affected by any proposed change, it becomes possible to sidestep some of the challenges associated with the old model, and to release additional benefits. This book has been dedicated to exploring this co-creation approach to change and organizations. Some of the distinguishing features of co-created change approaches supported by positive psychology theory are outlined below.

Features of Co-created Change

1. *Tapping into collective intelligence*

Participative co-creation taps into the collective intelligence of the organization at the point where the application of that intelligence can have the most effective impact at the least cost: by involving those who know the area under consideration inside out from the very beginning. Co-creation change processes offer organizational members the opportunity to contribute their wealth of experience about how the organization actually works (as opposed to how the organizational "map" says it should), and to help identify the sweet spots for effective intervention, while ideas are still being formulated and considered.

They can also road-check solution ideas for feasibility before they have become invested with the weight of being the right and only answer. Co-creation approaches to change lead to better solutions, arrived at in a cost-effective manner.

2. *Creating active participation*

When people are involved in discussing and defining the problem or challenge, and in the selection and the design of the solution, they start to make changes in their behaviour immediately. Being an active participant in the processes of understanding, sense-making, and decision-making affects their mental maps of the organization and so how they are motivated to behave. In addition, once formal plans are issued, or projects started, they already understand why and don't need to be persuaded of, or sold on, the rightness of the action. The likelihood of "resistance to change" is much reduced. Co-creation approaches to change lead to faster change implementation.

3. *Offering direct involvement in decision-making*

When people have direct involvement in decision-making, they are much more likely to accept the outcome. As long as their views have been genuinely appreciated and considered, they are likely to accept the evolving nature of the solution. People can track their particular contributions as the answer evolves. Such involvement inspires a sense of ownership of, and commitment to, decisions made. Co-creation leads to a high level of commitment.

4. *Building social capital*

People who have worked together in a positive way on something that is important to them form stronger social bonds. Collectively, the strength of these internal relationships is known as the "social capital" of the organization. High social capital means a high level of trust across the organization, good information-sharing, and easy information flow. It also facilitates problem-solving at the level of the problem. Investment in social capital helps to ameliorate the well-known problems of "silo mentality." Good social capital facilitates low-level, quick and effective, peer-to-peer problem-solving, vital when new unfamiliar systems are being implemented. Increasing social capital leads to coherent, coordinated action.

Sten Smith

5. *Leveraging organizational strengths in change*

Co-creation processes that focus on identifying existing strengths and core values as part of the change process help people link the need for change with success and personal integrity. They also create positive emotion that is energy for the change. Aligning the future with the past along the lines of what is best about the current organization makes it more likely that people will feel hopeful and optimistic about the change and the future. Co-creation based on existing strengths and clear values is likely to be implemented with hope and enthusiasm, leading to a smoother implementation process. Leveraging strengths and values leads to hope and optimism.

Many of the research areas of positive psychology chime with and build on these distinguishing characteristics. They can be expanded to help us think about organizations, and business, differently.

6. *Understanding strengths as the key to a new organizational economy*

The idea of individual natural strengths, and the advantages of knowing and using them, is becoming more widely accepted. While in 2007 Buckingham could state that 87% of people believed that finding your weaknesses and fixing them was the best way to achieve outstanding performance, today Polly is able to state that 64% of people believe that strengths enable success (2015). Strengths were first located in the positive psychology field by Peterson and Seligman (2004) as an attempt to create a counterweight to the extensive detailed listing of 297 human psychological ailments outlined in the *Diagnostic and Statistical Manual of Mental Disorders*, fifth edition (DSM V). Peterson and Seligman were interested to delineate the best of the human condition. Their pioneering work identified 26 character strengths that they declared to be universal and timeless since they had assembled their list from an extensive trawl of world current and historic literature, seeking out universally admired human characteristics (see Box 10.2). Since these early days, a plethora of competing classifications has emerged and a supporting industry of measures and tools (Lewis, 2012).

We can build on this by considering the idea of "the organization as an economy of strengths." This phrase "economy of strengths" featured in the call for papers for the 2012 World Appreciative Inquiry Conference held in Ghent, Belgium. Jem Smith and I put together a paper to begin to explore what this phrase might mean, looking particularly at the word "economy." The presentation can be found on the Appreciating Change website,

Box 10.2   Peterson and Seligman's Virtues and Character Strengths

Wisdom and knowledge
  Curiosity
  Love of learning
  Judgement
  Originality
  Social intelligence
  Perspective
Courage
  Valour
  Perseverance
  Integrity
Love and humanity
  Kindness
  The capacity to love and be loved
Justice
  Citizenship
  Fairness
  Leadership
Temperance
  Self-control
  Prudence
  Humility
Spirituality and transcendence
  Appreciation of beauty
  Gratitude
  Hope
  Spirituality
  Forgiveness
  Humour
  Zest

Taken from Seligman (2003)

along with a report of the session (www.acukltd.com). The session was very exploratory. The main benefit that people identified was that the phrase seemed to act as a very useful bridge between the "fluffy" world of psychology and the "hard" world of business. We might say it helped to bridge the language gap. I find that the question "How would we think differently about our organizations if we thought of them as economies of strengths?" helps to promote thinking that goes beyond a process improvement; for instance, from the performance appraisal refocus on strengths as suggested in Chapter 5 to potentially transformational thinking about how organizations are organized. Recently, Cooperrider and Godwin have extended this thinking about the transformational power of elevating strengths into an understanding of organization and world change based on "the entire systemic strengths spectrum"(2015, p. 10). We examine this in more detail at the end of the chapter.

In this way, the emerging networked economy has the potential to become an economy of strengths rather than an economy of exploitation. Pioneers of effective utilization of our interconnected economy, such as Ferris (2011), point the way to how such an economy could work. While the author's emphasis is on accessing a network of cheap skills, the potential exists for the emergence of a network, and an economy, of strengths. At its simplest, the idea of an economy of strengths is predicated on everyone spending most of their time doing what they do best and love doing, with a supporting structure that allows people to find people with complementary strengths to their own. In our interconnected world this, theoretically, has never been easier. Enterprises of the sharing economy such as Airbnb offer a model. Most importantly, these pioneer commercial enterprises have cracked the two key challenges to a global networked economy: those of smooth financial transactions and trust between strangers.

Note that this is in sharp contrast to the still dominant idea that "a good worker" can cover the whole range of their "job" equally well regardless of their personal strengths profile, and that to ask for help with any aspect of that role is a sign of weakness. Please don't for a moment believe this is dead and buried. Only recently, some strengths identification work I did with a senior team led to exactly this conversation and to the tentative admission by one brave soul both of some areas of less than excellent performance and of the disinclination to ask for help in the "macho" culture of this high-performing organization. This attitude leads to enormous inefficiency as people procrastinate, hedge, hesitate, fudge, ignore, or execute resentfully, badly, and/or with enormous effort the parts of their "job" for which they are, as we might say, by nature ill-suited. Moving organizations towards the idea of an economy of strengths is a key positive psychology idea that one can bring to all these interventions.

7. Understanding social networks as the heart of organizations

Another key concept that underpins all these approaches is that of the organization as a social network. It sounds obvious, but the language of the organization as a "well-oiled machine" or "a bureaucracy" or "an org. chart" can easily obscure this essential reality. A continual focus on people and their patterns of interaction and communication is a key focus of these approaches. Positive psychology research into patterns of relationship and interconnectedness, such as the work by Baker, Cross, and Wooten into positive energy networks in organizations (2003) and that by Dutton and Heaphy into high quality connections (2003), is relevant here. This research is discussed in more detail in Lewis (2011).

8. Recognizing the importance of dialogue as words create worlds

In these approaches, a key area of focus and concern is language and dialogue. It matters both what people say to each other and how they say it. Keen attention needs to be paid to how people are framing their experiences of change in language. I had an interesting conversation with a potential client the other day who had attended a previous workshop I ran on Appreciative Inquiry where I had used the expression "words create worlds." Since then his department had undergone huge change which had involved a redesign of some key roles. He was noticing that people were having to find new ways to talk about "what they did all day" and that the language being used was developing a somewhat negative tone. Further reflection on his observations led us to consider that the staff concerned were essentially struggling to create a "narrative" about their new role. It seemed that without time, space, and help to think about this they were perhaps inadvertently reflecting the "negativity bias" that afflicts us all in the accounts that they were creating (Cohn, 2013). We recognized that creating an opportunity for those concerned to co-create a more purposeful, forward-oriented, positive account of their new role, and to create opportunities to broadcast this new narrative more widely, could be very beneficial.

9. The importance of narrative for sense-making in action

We have considered narrative in some depth (Chapter 3), so I won't reiterate it here. This is just to emphasize the point that the accounts we create of the world and what goes on it are our best guides to appropriate action.

They are our reality. They aren't immutable. A key factor in the success of these approaches in achieving change is that they facilitate conjoint shifts in narrative, allowing the team or organization as a whole to create new accounts of "what is going on" that allow new meanings to emerge, or sense to be made, which in turn liberates new possibilities for action.

10. Recognizing the energizing effects of positive emotions

I have discussed the contribution of positive emotions to the workplace in other contexts (Lewis, 2011). Since then I think my key realization has been how central hope and courage are to the process of change, as explored in Chapter 3. Cooperrider and Godwin also mention hope in their observation that "Over the years we have been struck by the constructive 'change power' of emotions such as hope, inspiration and joy, and especially feelings of awe, when combined with experiences of collective empowerment" (2015, p. 8). All of these can be damaged or reduced during change processes, and a key focus of all these appreciative and positive methods is the re-ignition or regeneration of positive emotional states in general, and these in particular. Positive emotional states are a key component of resilience, an attribute also much in demand during times of change. People sometimes find it hard to reconcile the need to create positive mood states with news or a current state of affairs that seems to appropriately warrant a doom and gloom reaction. Yet actually it is the ability to create positive emotional moments during the doom and gloom that is key to creating the energy and motivation to make real differences. The expression "If I didn't laugh, I'd cry" is a pithy expression of the experience of resilient behaviour.

11. Utilizing imagination as the pull for change

As has been emphasized throughout this book, we can push people towards change or we can pull them towards change. The former can seem easier and quicker and leads to the desire to create, find, or build "burning platforms" for change. The latter is slower, and, since the imagined future is often less immediately available to the imagination than the all too real undesirable present, can be harder to access. However, it creates a more sustainable energy for change. Appreciative Inquiry as a methodology is particularly alive to and focused on this. Appreciative "dream" questions can be used in the other methodologies to help create pulls towards change.

12. Calling on the whole power of systems

I hope an appreciation of the importance of considering a whole system when attempting to achieve change has permeated this book. However, I thought it might be worth emphasizing at this point. The whole system relevant to any particular topic, challenge, or change is not predetermined by the existing organizational structure that will have been organized with other considerations in mind. Rather, the relevant system needs to be identified in each instance using the ARE IN guidelines (see Chapter 6).

Linking Theory, Research, and Practice

The field of positive psychology offers extensive research evidence and theoretical thinking that both underpin and explain the efficacy of these dialogic approaches to change. As the emerging era of "evidence-based practice" in leadership, management, and human resource or organizational development activity emphasizes, we need to be investing in what works rather than the current fads or fashions. Figure 10.1 below gives some idea of how the ideas presented in this book work together to create a platform of evidence-based practice.

While we have covered Appreciative Inquiry, World Café, Open Space, and Simu-Real in some detail, this is not an exhaustive list of these types of co-creative change methodologies. Others that deserve an honourable mention include Future Search (Weisbord & Janoff, 2000) and Search Conferences (Emery & Devane, 1999). The reader interested in extending their repertoire of approaches to call on or integrate into their practice is

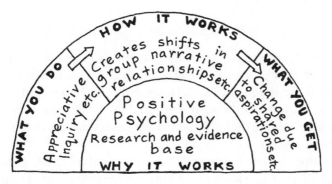

Figure 10.1 How it all holds together.

referred to the excellent *Change Handbook* (Holman, Devane, & Cady, 2007). For the theoretically minded, Bushe and Marshak's recent compilation of Dialogic Organization Development theory and practice will prove a rich treasure trove of ideas and models (2015b). We are in the second decade of the twenty-first century. The time is ripe for these positive, co-creative approaches to change; here are some reasons why.

Time for Something Different

1. Change is changing

Traditional, top-down, change that is designed then implemented takes too long and is too hard to push through an organization. The plan is out of date almost as soon as it's made. People resist. Change needs to be fast, flexible, and proactive and focused on maximizing tomorrow's possibilities rather than rehashing yesterday's mistakes. Change needs to be a simultaneous system phenomenon, taking everyone with it.

2. The future exists only in our imagination

Imagination is more powerful than forecasting in an unpredictable world. The past does not predict the future; it suggests possible trajectories. Using our imagination, we can create other, more attractive, more creative, more inspiring trajectories, to inspiring and attractive futures. Collective imagining has the power to create dreams that pull people to work together to achieve them. We can use our analytic powers to analyse data; we can use our creative powers to imagine pictures of the future that pull us towards it.

3. The best organizations positively flourish

Positive psychology research demonstrates that positive workplaces, where people feel hopeful, encouraged, and appreciated, reap many benefits. People are likely to be more creative, more generative, share information better, grow and learn better, be more energized, be bolder and braver about innovating, be able to deal with more complex information, and to respond better to change.

Interestingly, research shows that being good and doing well go together. The organizations that focus on creating positive cultures and leading with values, where people thrive and where the organization flourishes, where there is a bias towards the positive and where there is a sense of abundance, often also do very well commercially. Timberland, Merek Corporation, Cascade, Synovus Financial Corporation, FedEx Freight, Southwest Airlines, The Green Mountain Coffee Corporation, Fairmount Minerals, and the Marine Corp are all a testament to the possibility of doing the right thing and doing well. The current edition of *Firms of Endearment* lists 28 US publicly funded companies, 29 US private companies, and 15 non-US companies that fit the bill. The general definition of a firm of endearment is one that is led by "resolute and highly successful business professionals who augment their human-centred company vision with sound management skills and an unswerving commitment to do good by all who are touched by their companies" (Sisodia, Seth, & Wolfe, 2014, p. xxiii). This is augmented by 16 defining criteria (p. 8). These companies have outperformed "the best of the rest," as identified as the good to great companies, by a factor of at least 6 and has surpassed the general average, as identified by the Standard and Poor's 500 Index, by a factor of over 10 over the last 15 years (p. 20). While the stock market, judging by the prices to earnings ratio, appears to view them as the best bet for the future (p. 115). Meanwhile, the World Inquiry into Business as an Agent of World Benefit (http://aim2flourish.com) is busy collating accounts of exceptional sustainable innovation.

4. Social capital is a source of sustainability

Relational reserves are what see organizations through difficult times as much as financial reserves. Relational reserves are the goodwill your people feel towards you, the trust they have in what you say, and the willingness they demonstrate to forgive leadership errors, or accept bad luck, and to work with you to put things right. Social capital and goodwill are earned over time through good leadership and management.

5. Speed is of the essence

The world is constantly changing; organizations need to be nimble and flexible, able to recast themselves to meet new challenges – and quickly. Cascading change takes too long. Change needs to happen simultaneously from top to bottom. These approaches work with the whole system simultaneously, so the need for change is experienced, absorbed, and understood from top to bottom. Ideas for change are designed and tested for impact by, and on, those they affect before the money is spent.

6. Resistance costs too much

Planned change frequently induces resistance. Resistance slows down change and diverts managerial energy and attention. It also frequently illuminates unforeseen problems and obstacles to the change that cost money to put right at a late stage in the change process. Resistance to change costs both negatively (wasting time and energy) and positively (helping the organization make necessary corrections). These co-creative approaches can work positively with all reactions to change to co-create a sustainable, valued, endorsed, and appreciated approach to change. Resistance need no longer be part of the change conversation.

7. Change is not a commodity to be bought

Organizations put a lot of energy into getting "buy-in" to their plans for the future. This activity comes after the plans have been made, when other people have to be persuaded of the rightness of the plans. Co-creative methodologies bring those affected by change in from the start, so that they are helping to co-design change, bringing their expertise to bear at an early stage, being heard, being valued, having a role in shaping their destiny, and co-creating a future that holds attraction for them. It means that people have built it themselves and don't need to be sold it.

8. We need to use our intelligence

The world is more interconnected that ever before. Everything affects everything else. We need all the intelligence we can get to keep up and get ahead. Treating most of the organization as "hired hands" and only the top echelons as the brains of the business wastes a huge amount of organizational intelligence. Co-creative change brings all brains, all experience, all skill, and all knowledge in the system to bear on the challenges of keeping up, getting ahead, doing right, doing well, and flourishing.

9. Strengths are a source of competitive advantage

Organizations spend too much time trying to fill gaps in people's profiles, adapting people's personalities, and helping them become better at things they aren't good at, and not enough time on building on strengths and abilities. Positive psychology research demonstrates that the more time spent working to their strengths, the more productive, fulfilled, and energized people are likely to be. Building on the strengths of individuals and on the strengths of the organization creates a strength-based organization. Such an organization has a competitive advantage.

Bringing Emergent Change Insights to Planned Change Projects

While each of these co-creative methods works well as a stand-alone, bringing them together can create additional value. The whole appreciative frame can be applied to World Café or Open Space in the form of the questions asked, while parts of the Appreciative Inquiry process can be facilitated through holding an Open Space or a World Café. Simu-Real can be seen as an Appreciative Inquiry process with a strong emphasis on design through prototyping. Sometimes, however, we have to bring our insights and methodologies to a change ship that has already sailed.

When organizations decide they need to make changes in the way they work, their culture, or their IT system, they often default to a planned change approach. Typically, lean management specialists and programme managers, if not already present, are hired and the organizing of a change process that is driven from the top down begins. This approach has its strengths. It often reveals scope for improved efficiency, but more tellingly, it presents change as a problem of data and logic and makes change look manageable, sequential, and what I can only describe as "tidy." Unfortunately, it also leads straight to the "how to get buy-in" and "how to overcome the resistance to change" conversations.

Planned change approaches inadvertently encourage people to give up trying to contribute to the change conversation or to influence how it happens. They can become passive, demotivated, and demoralized, waiting to be told what to do. It is when the downsides of this approach become apparent that people find their way to "alternative" change practitioners, presenting their challenge as a problem of disengagement, of poor morale, and of people needing support during change.

We know that emergent, dialogic, psychological, and co-creative approaches to change such as Appreciative Inquiry, World Café, and Open Space act to motivate, engage, and energize people. They also connect to their desire to influence their own futures and to be part of the change process. The challenge is how to bring these approaches to the party when the planned change process is already in full swing. There is an art to bringing value from our perspective under these circumstances. We need to work at the interstices, in the gaps that emerge in the planned change process. In working with this challenge, there are some principles for engaging that I have found useful.

1. Work with who you can, where you can

You may not be able to get "the whole system in the room"; that doesn't mean you can't work in these ways with the bits of the system to which you can gain access. Use all opportunities available to help people start to understand change as an emergent phenomenon that they can influence, even as planned change is unfolding all around them. Bring your appreciative questioning style and your positive focus on strengths and positive emotions to all opportunities. Work wherever you can, with whomever you can, to move the focus to what we *can* do and what we *can* influence.

2. Adapt processes to fit the opportunities

a) Multi-events for one process

I have used Appreciative Inquiry when it has proved impossible to collect the whole system together into one space at one time. Instead, I have worked with different parts of the system over a series of events and then held other events combining people from the previous events to pull things together.

b) With a whole system over a time period

I have used Appreciative Inquiry with a small system where we could only negotiate a couple of hours together at a time. In this case the process is split over the different events. The key is to reconnect with the previous event (and part of the process) each time you come together again.

c) One-day events

I have developed one-day "roadworthy" Appreciative Inquiry processes when unable to negotiate the longer time I would have desired. I have found Appreciative Inquiry to be an incredibly robust process that acts to re-energize, re-motivate, and re-engage the disillusioned, disengaged, and demotivated time after time. I have also run short World Café sessions or Open Space afternoons to fit to the available opportunity.

3. Encourage awareness of possibilities of local influence and control

Help people and groups focus on what they can influence. Usually, the idea that top management "has got it all planned out" is a myth. Top management don't have brain space to attend to every last detail. If people want good decision-making in their own area, they need to seize the initiative and start presenting ways forward. Help groups focus on what is important to them in the change and on how they can influence the wider system. Once again, Appreciative Inquiry is great for this. It is these conversations that start to rekindle hope, optimism, and motivation to engage.

4. Keep bringing key ideas to the fore

These are some of the ideas that need encouragement and reinforcement as planned change swings into gear, and that you can bring to any conversation or situation to which you are able to negotiate entry.

a) Volunteerism
People are being pushed around enough already; try to make any specific events you are able to run optional (and very attractive!).

b) Co-creation
Always ask, "Who else can we usefully involve in this?" Encourage leaders to take questions to their teams in a co-creative (i.e., not just consultative) way. I find using the phrase "drawing on the collective intelligence" often helps me negotiate more involvement by lower-level staff in the event. In the same way, it can help negotiate the involvement of more of the wider system in the event.

c) Positivity
Focus on emotional states; it really helps create resilience during a difficult time. Encourage others to recognize the continuing importance of positive mood boosts. Many "rewarding" experiences disappear during change as people go "heads down" and pleasurable interactions can lessen.

d) Strengths

People are more energized, engaged, motivated, and so on when they can use their strengths to achieve their objectives. Help groups focus on identifying these and working out how to draw on them: individual strengths, group strengths, and organizational strengths.

e) Hope and optimism

In my experience, these can be early casualties of planned change. Using appreciative techniques helps people focus on the best of the past and on their hopes for the future. Hope is also part of the "building resilience" challenge.

f) Proactivity

Encourage people to take responsibility for how they are engaging with the change and the effect they are having on others around them. It's the anti-dote to the "being done to" feeling that can be so strong during planned change.

g) Leaders' face

Be mindful always of leaders' face. They are (usually) doing their best to do the best for the organization, and they are doing it the only way they know how. As we help people make sense of what is going on, we need to help them recognize this.

h) Story and choice

Unhelpful stories often emerge during change about the motivation for change in general and to explain leaders' behaviour in particular. These are often stories of blame, inadequacy, deficit and deceit, nefarious motives, and so on. We can remind people that there are many truths about a situa-tion, and situations are often paradoxical. We can remind them that they have a choice about the story they choose to tell, both to themselves and to others, and that the telling of stories has impact for action.

i) Amplifying success

In change, people get so focused on what isn't working they lose sight of the fact that they are still achieving things. Bringing these to the fore helps with morale, pride, and other positive emotions.

POSITIVE: The Whole Strengths Spectrum
Approach to Change

Increasingly, an invitation to work with a whole system is being recognized as an invitation to have impact not just on the organizational system, but also on the larger system of which it is part. It is this realization of the interconnectedness of organizations and other aspects of human life that creates the strong connection to the sustainable world agenda. It is increasingly recognized that organizations have a huge impact on all aspects of quality of life across the world. By being invited to work with an organization, we are also being invited to help improve the world's chances of survival! Guides for what more planetary-aware organizations might look like are beginning to emerge. I have a pile of books awaiting my attention; for example, *Conscious Capitalism* (Mackey & Sisodia, 2014), *Reinventing Organizations* (Laloux, 2014), and *Leading from the Emerging Future* (Scharmer & Kaufer, 2013), all of which have been recently recommended to me by people whose opinions I value.

David Cooperrider is the pioneer in creating such opportunities out of the invitations he has received. In partnership with the participants, he created innovative ways of being together (radically different meeting structures and processes that resulted in radically new conversations and relationships) both at the United Nations and at the World Religious Forum. He has been the driving force behind Business as an Agent for World Benefit for many years (2015). As the originator of Appreciative Inquiry, he has had more first-hand experience of the transformational effect of these ways of working than most. Recently, with Lindsay Godwin, he has devised an eight-step platform for change (note platform, not process) called P.O.S.I.T.I.V.E. (see Box 10.3).

This is the codification of everything they have learnt about "non-deficit, life-centric and full spectrum strengths-powered change" (Cooperrider & Godwin, 2015 p. 10). He argues that we change best when "we experience the magnified and resonating power of every relevant resource available to us across the entire systemic strengths spectrum inside and outside the system" (p. 10). He creates an image of change taking place in a "surround sound" of strengths (p. 10) because we now know beyond doubt that positive states produce optimal change capacities.

He offers this as "an early articulation of an affective theory of social constructionism that is to meaning-making human systems what genetic change is to biological systems" (Cooperrider & Godwin, 2015, p. 9). It is

Box 10.3   P.O.S.I.T.I.V.E.

Pre-frame

This is about creating the call to action. We need to ask: What do we most want to create? Given the best of who we have been and who we are, what is the world calling for to which we can respond? This is at the heart of creating positive, purposeful organizations; the answer elevates change from a technical possibility to an inspirational opportunity. So we move from "Fixing our rustbelt problems" to "Creating a green city on a blue lake."

Open-innovate

Here we are thinking about creating the *conditions for change* in the wider system of which we are part: a platform rather than a programme. We invite others to work or join with us. Cooperrider and Godwin use the metaphor of the artificial reef, whereby the deliberate placing of an object on the seabed can lead to its rapid colonization and the emergence of a flourishing eco-system.

Strengthen

The work on savouring has helped us understand that by really focusing on the strengths identified in the discovery process we can produce a concentration of strengths energy. As we savour our individual or organizational strengths so we are increasing our awareness and understanding of them and expanding their potential impact.

Imagine

This is the dream stage of Appreciative Inquiry. Positive future images call to the best of us. They activate the power of hope. By creating positive emotional attractors of the future, we attract the investment of ourselves and others; we release that motivational energy.

Translate

Here we translate the dreams and designs into willpower and waypower. We create ideas of what we can be doing now to move us towards that future; what we need to do that is different, what we need to do differently, or what we need to stop doing. We identify ideas and design artefacts to help us, as prototypes for the future. Seeing the future in the texture of the actual creates the attitude of "we know it's possible" because we are living it now, even if only an early prototype.

Improvise

Rather than issuing a detailed plan of implementation of change, we release our early prototypes of futures (and the supporting artefacts and ideas) into the organization and encourage people to experiment with them and to improvise around them. In this way, we recognize the live dynamic nature of change as an emergent process. Everyone can be invited into prototyping iteration, rapidly creating substantial engagement.

Value

This is about the need to notice and capture changes that are emerging; to put a spotlight on progress and success, in order to value it. We need to spot early changes and amplify them into wider visibility.

Eclipse

By creating the new, we can eclipse the old. Change happens when a newer life force or urge emerges that eclipses the old. In the light of the new life attractor, what was formally seen as a problem is eclipsed. The problem is diminished and dissolved as part of the wider pattern of activity focused on achieving the attractive future, responding to the stronger life force.

Drawn from Cooperrider (2015) and Cooperrider and Godwin (2015) with permission

focused on conscious co-elevation. That is elevation in both senses of the word: strength in lifting up and transcendental spirit rising. The authors offer us a new equation of change:

$$\text{Positive change} = \frac{\text{Experience of elevation}}{\text{Experience of deficit}}$$

The experience of elevation is about "the strengths density of the change initiative" and it is made up of wholepower (the power of the whole systemic strengths system) + willpower + waypower (Snyder's two elements of hope

(Snyder, Rand, & Sigmon, 2005)). The experience of deficit is diagnostic definition + deficit despair. I understand this to mean the classic approach of mechanistic problem and deficit approach combined with the despair that can be induced by such diagnostic techniques. This thinking is still new to most of us and certainly to me. I wanted to introduce it here to give you a sense of where this thinking is going. I understand a book is forthcoming. For now, I recommend the article for a fuller explanation of the thinking and experience behind the model. Meanwhile, while we await a fuller articulation of this model that promises to offer us a truly transformational concept of organizations and organizational change, I hope you find this book a useful guide along the way.

Conclusion

That's all, folks. In this book I have attempted to bring together positive psychology thinking with co-creative practice to demonstrate that together they create a more effective, and respectful, way of creating change in organizations. Conditions are never perfect, and I hope I have shared some of my personal learning about how to bring the benefits of those approaches to people, groups, and organizations in less than ideal situations. I wish you every success in your attempts to find ways of creating change that reflect the realities of work in the twenty-first century.

References

Achor, S. (2011). *The happiness advantage: The seven principles of positive psychology that fuel success and performance at work.* New York, NY: Random House.

Adams, V. H., Snyder, C. R., Rand, K. L., King, E. A., Sigman, D. R., & Pulvers, K. M. (2002). Hope in the workplace. In G. A. Giacolone & C. L. Jurkiewicz (Eds.), *Handbook of workplace spirituality and organizational performance* (pp. 367–377). New York, NY: Sharpe.

Avolio B., Griffith, J., Wernsing, T. S., & Walumbwa, F. O. (2010). What is authentic leadership development? In P. Linley, A. S. Harrington & N. Garcea (Eds.), *Oxford handbook of positive psychology and work* (pp. 39–53). Oxford, UK: Oxford University Press.

Baker, W. (2004). *Half-baked brown paper bag presentation on positive energy networks.* Unpublished manuscript, University of Michigan Business School, Ann Arbour, MI.

Baker, W., Cross, R., & Wooten, M. (2003). Positive organizational network analysis and energizing relationships. In K. Cameron, J. Dutton, & R. Quinn (Eds.), *Positive organizational scholarship: Foundations of a new discipline.* San Francisco, CA: Berrett Koehler.

Barsade, S. G. (2002). The ripple effect: Emotional contagion and its influence on group behavior. *Administrative Science Quarterly, 47*(4), 644–675.

Ben-Shahar, T. (2015, June). *Making change last.* Paper presented at the World Positive Psychology Conference, Orlando, FL.

Blanchard, K. (2010, January). Mastering the art of change – Ken Blanchard offers some strategies for successfully leading change. *Training Journal,* 44–47. Retrieved from http://www.kenblanchard.com/img/pub/blanchard_mastering_the_art_of_change.pdf

Positive Psychology and Change: How Leadership, Collaboration, and Appreciative Inquiry Create Transformational Results, First Edition. Sarah Lewis.
© 2016 John Wiley & Sons, Ltd. Published 2016 by John Wiley & Sons, Ltd.

Bolino, M. C., Turnley, W. H., & Bloodgood, J. M. (2002). Citizenship behaviour and the creation of social capital in organizations. *Academy of Management Review, 27*(4), 505–552.

Boniwell, I., & Zimbardo, P. (2003). Time to find the right balance. *The Psychologist, 16*(3), 129–131.

Bouskila-Yam, O., & Kluger, A. N. (2011). Strength-based performance appraisal and goal setting. *Human Resource Management Review, 21*(2), 137–147.

Brown, J., Isaacs, D., & The World Café Community (2005). *The World Café: Shaping our futures through conversations that matter.* San Francisco, CA: Berrett-Koehler Publisher.

Brown, J., Homer, K., & Isaacs, D. (2007). The World Café. In P. Holman, T. Devane, & S. Cady (Eds.), *The change handbook: The definitive resource on today's best methods for engaging whole systems* (pp. 179–195). San Francisco, CA: Berrett Koehler.

Brown, N. J., Sokal, A. D., & Friedman, H. L. (2013). The complex dynamics of wishful thinking: The critical positivity ratio. *American Psychologist, 68*(9), 801–813.

Bryant, F. B., Erickson, C. L., & DeHoek A. H. (2013). Savoring. In J. L. Lopez (Ed.), *The encyclopedia of positive psychology* (pp. 857–859). Chichester, UK: Wiley-Blackwell.

Buckingham, M. (2007). *Go put your strengths to work.* London: Simon & Schuster.

Bunker, B., & Alban, B. (1997). *Large group interventions: Engaging the whole system in rapid change.* San Francisco, CA: Jossey-Bass.

Burnes, B. (2005). Complexity theories and organizational change. *International Journal of Management Reviews, 7*(2), 73–90.

Burnes, B., & Cooke, B. (2012). Review article: The past, present and future of organizational development: taking the long view. *Human Relations.* Sagepublications. com. Retrieved from http://hum.sagepub.com/content/65/11/1395.short.

Bushe, G. R. (2001). Five theories of change embedded in Appreciative Inquiry. In D. Cooperrider, P. Sorenson, D. Whitney, & T. Yeager (Eds.), *Appreciative Inquiry: An emerging direction for organization development* (pp. 117–127). Champaign, IL: Stipes.

Bushe, G. R. (2007). Appreciative Inquiry is not (just) about the positive. *OD Practitioner, 39*(4), 30–35.

Bushe, G. R. (2010). *Clear leadership: Sustaining real collaboration and partnership at work.* Boston, MA: Davies-Black.

Bushe, G. R. (2013). Generative process, generative outcome: The transformational potential of appreciative inquiry. In D. L. Cooperrider, D. P. Zandee, L. N. Godwin, M. Avital & B. Boland (Eds.), *Organizational generativity: The appreciative inquiry summit and a scholarship of transformation (Advances in Appreciative Inquiry*, Vol. 4, pp. 89–113). Bingley, UK: Emerald Group Publishing Limited.

Bushe, G. R., & Fry, R. (2012). *Generative engagement: Going beyond the positive for transformational change.* Paper presented at the World Appreciative Inquiry Conference, Ghent, Belgium.

Bushe, G. R., & Marshak, R. J. (2015a), Introduction to the dialogic organization development mindset. In G. R. Bushe & R. J. Marshak (Eds.), *Dialogic organization development: The theory and practice of transformational change.* Oakland, CA: Berett-Koehler.

Bushe, G. R., & Marshak, R. J. (Eds.). (2015b). *Dialogic organization development: The theory and practice of transformational change.* Oakland, CA: Berett-Koehler.

Cameron, K. (2003). Organizational virtuousness and performance. In K. Cameron, J. Dutton, & R. Quinn (Eds.), *Positive organizational scholarship: Foundations of a new discipline.* San Francisco, CA: Koehler.

Cameron, K. (2008a). *Positive leadership: Strategies for extraordinary performance.* San Francisco, CA: Berrett-Koehler.

Cameron, K. (2008b). Paradox in positive organizational change. *The Journal of Applied Behavioral Science, 44*(1), 7–24.

Campbell, W., & Radford, A. (Eds.). (2014). Adaptable leadership. *AI Practitioner, International Journal of Appreciative Inquiry, 16*(1). Retrieved from www.aipractitioner.com.

Carlsen, A., Hagen, A. L., & Mortensen, T. F. (2012). Imagining hope in organizations. In K. S. Cameron & G. M. Spreitzer (Eds.), *The Oxford handbook of positive organizational scholarship* (pp. 288–303). Oxford, UK: Oxford University Press.

Cheung-Judge, M., & Holbeche, L. (2011). *Organizational development: A practitioner's guide for OD and HR.* London, UK: Kogan Page.

Cohn, M. (2013). Emotional asymmetry. In J. L. Lopez (Ed.), *The encyclopedia of positive psychology.* Chichester, UK: Wiley-Blackwell.

Collins, D. (1998). *Organisational change: Sociological perspectives.* London, UK: Routledge.

Cooperrider, D. (2015, June). *Mirror flourishing: Appreciative Inquiry and the designing of positive institutions.* Presented as keynote talk at Fourth World Congress on Positive Psychology, Orlando, FL.

Cooperrider, D., & Godwin, L. (2012). Positive organizational development: Innovation-inspired change in an economy and ecology of strengths. In K. S. Cameron & G. Spreitzer (Eds.), *The Oxford handbook of positive organizational scholarship* (pp. 737–751). Oxford, UK: Oxford University Press.

Cooperrider, D., & Godwin, L. (2015). Elevation-and-change: An eight-step platform for leading P.O.S.I.T.I.V.E. change. *AI Practitioner, 17*(3), 7–14.

Cooperrider, D., & Srivastva, S. (1987). Appreciative Inquiry in organizational life. In R. Woodman & W. Pasmore (Eds.), *Research in organizational change and development* (Vol. 1, pp. 129–169). Greenwich, CT: JAI Press.

Cooperrider, D., & Whitney, D. (2001). A positive revolution in change: Appreciative Inquiry. In D. Cooperrider, P. F. Sorenson Jr., T. Yaegar, & D. Whitney (Eds.), *Appreciative Inquiry: An emerging direction for organizational development.* London, UK: Stipes.

Cutuli, J. J., & Masten, A. S. (2013). Resilience. In J. L. Lopez (Ed.), *The encylopedia of positive psychology* (pp. 837–843). Hoboken, NJ: Wiley-Blackwell.

Damasio, A. (2005). *Descartes' error: Emotion, reason and the human brain.* London, UK: Penguin.

Davies, W. (2015). *The happiness industry: How the government and big business sold us well-being.* London, UK: Verso.

De Jong, J. (2011). The daily disciplines and practices of an appreciative leader. In S. Lewis & L. Moore (Eds.), *Appreciative Inquiry Practitioner, 13*(1), 22–24. Retrieved from www.aipractitioner.com.

DeRue, D. S., Ashford, S. J., & Cotton, N. C. (2009). Assuming the mantle: Unpacking the process by which individuals internalize a leader identity. In L. M. Roberts & J. E. Dutton (Eds.), *Exploring positive identities and organizations: Building a theoretical and research foundation* (pp. 217–236). Hove, UK: Routledge.

Ko, I., & Donaldson, S. I. (2011). Applied positive organizational psychology: The state of science and of practice. In S. I. Donaldson, M. Csikszentmihalyi, & J. Nakamura (Eds.), *Applied positive psychology: Improving everyday life, health, schools, work, and society.* Hove, UK: Routledge.

Dutton, J., & Heaphy, E. (2003). The power of high quality connections. In K. Cameron, J. Dutton, & R. Quinn (Eds.), *Positive organizational scholarship: Foundations of a new discipline* (pp. 263–279). San Francisco, CA: Berrett Koehler.

Dutton, J., & Ragins, B. (2009). Positive relationships at work: An introduction and invitation. In J. Dutton & B. Ragins (Eds.), *Exploring positive relationships at work: Building a theoretical and research foundation* (pp. 3–29). Hove, UK: Routledge.

Dutton, J. E., Roberts, L. M., & Bednar, J. (2011). Prosocial practices, positive identity and flourishing at work. In S. I. Donaldson, M. Csikszentmihalyi, & J. Nakamura (Eds.), *Applied positive psychology: Improving everyday life, health, schools, work and society.* Hove, UK: Routledge.

Emery, M., and Devane, T. (1999). *Search conference: Collaborating for change.* San Francisco, CA: Berett-Koehler.

Ferris, T. (2011). *The 4-hour work week.* London, UK: Vermilion.

Fredrickson, B. L. (2003). Positive emotions and upward spirals in organizations. In K. S. Cameron, J. E. Dutton, & R. E. Quinn (Eds.), *Positive organizational scholarship: Foundations of a new discipline* (pp. 163–175). San Francisco, CA: Berrett Koehler.

Fredrickson, B. L. (2015, July). *Locating us in the space.* Paper presented at the World Appreciative Inquiry Conference, Johannesburg, South Africa.

Fredrickson, B. L., & Losada, M. (2005). Positive affect and the complex dynamics of human flourishing. *American Psychologist, 60*(7), 678–686.

French, W., & Bell, C. (1999). *Organizational development: Behavioural science interventions for organizational improvement* (6th ed.). New Jersey, NY: Prentice Hall.

Gable, S. L., & Gosnell, C. L. (2011). The positive side of close relationships. In K. M. Sheldon, T. B. Kashdan, & M. F. Steger (Eds.), *Designing positive psychology: Taking stock and moving forward* (pp. 265–279). Oxford, UK: Oxford University Press.

Gable, S. L., Reis, H. T., Impett, E. A., & Evan, R. A. (2004). What do you do when things go right? The intrapersonal and interpersonal benefits of sharing positive events. *Journal of Personality and Social Psychology, 87*(22), 228–245.

Gastaldi, M. (2011). New leaders: How conflict transforms into distributed leadership producing organizational fitness. In S. Lewis & L. Moore (Eds.), *AI Practitioner, International Journal of Appreciative Inquiry, 13*(1), 24–31. Retrieved from www.aipractitioner.com.

George, J. M. (1995). Leader mood and group performance: The case of customer service. *Journal of Applied Social Psychology, 25*(9), 778–794.

Gergen, M., & Gergen, K. (2003). *Social construction: A reader.* London, UK: Sage.

Gittell, J., Cameron, K., & Lim, S. (2006). Relationships, layoffs and organizational resilience: Airline industry responses to September 11th. *The Journal of Applied Behavioral Science, 42*(3), 300–329.

Greene-Shortridge, T. M., & Britt, T. W. (2013). Leadership. In S. Lopez (Ed.), *Encyclopedia of positive psychology.* Chichester, UK: Wiley-Blackwell.

Hammond, S. (1996). *The thin book of Appreciative Inquiry.* Lima, OH: CSS Publishing.

Harter, J. K., Schmidt, F. L., & Keyes, C. L. M. (2003). Well-being in the workplace and its relationship to business outcomes: A review of the Gallup studies. In C. L. M. Keyes & J. Haidt (Eds.), *Flourishing: Positive psychology and the life well-lived* (pp. 205–224). Washington, DC: American Psychological Association.

Hefferon, K. (2013). *Positive psychology and the body: The somatopsychic side to flourishing.* Maidenhead, UK: McGrawHill.

Hochschild, A. (1997). *The time bind.* New York, NY: Henry Holt.

Holman, P., Devane, T., & Cady, S. (2007). *The change handbook: The definitive resource on today's best methods for engaging whole systems.* San Francisco, CA: Berret Koehler.

Hoogendijk, C. (2015). *Appreciative inquires of the 3.0 kind: How do we connect, share and co-create for tomorrow's human wholeness?* Rijswijk, Netherlands: OrgPanoptics.

Ibarra, H. (2003). *Working identity: Unconventional strategies for reinventing.* Cambridge, MA: Harvard Business School Press.

Jones, E. E., & Harris, V. A. (1967). The attribution of attitudes. *Journal of Experimental Social Psychology, 3*(1), 1–24.

Justice, T., & Jamieson, D. (1998). *The complete guide to facilitation: Enabling groups to succeed.* Amherst, MA: HRD Press.

Kahana, E., & Kahana, B. (1983). Environmental continuity, futurity, and the adaptation of the aged. In G. D. Rowles & R. J. Ohta (Eds.), *Aging and milieu* (pp. 205–228). New York, NY: Howarth Press.

Kahneman, D. (2011). *Thinking fast and slow.* London, UK: Allen Lane, Penguin.

Keller, S., & Aiken, C. (2009, April). The inconvenient truth about change management. *McKinsey Quarterly*, 1–18.

Kelm, J. B. (2005). *Appreciative living. The principles of Appreciative Inquiry in personal life.* Wake Forest, NC: Venet Publishers.

Kimball, L. (2011). The leadership sweet spot. In S. Lewis & L. Moore (Eds.), *AI Practitioner, International Journal of Appreciative Inquiry, 13*(1), 36–51. Retrieved from www.aipractitioner.com.

Klein, D. (1992). Simu-Real: A simulation approach to organizational change. *Journal of Applied Behavioural Science, 28*(4), 566–578.

Kline, N. (1999). *Time to think: Listening to ignite the human mind.* London, UK: Ward Lock.

Kluger, A. N., & Nir, D. (2010). The feedforward interview. *Human Resource Management Review, 20*(3), 235–246.

Kotter, John P. (1996). *Leading change.* Cambridge, MA: Harvard Business School Press.

Kubler-Ross, E. (1969). *On death and dying.* New York, NY: Scribner.

Laloux, F. (2014). *Reinventing organizations: A guide to creating organizations inspired by the next stage of human consciousness.* Brussels, Belgium: Nelson Parker.

Lewin, K. (1947). Frontiers in group dynamics: Concept, method, and reality in social science, social equilibria and social change. *Human Relations, 1*(1), 5–41.

Lewin, K. (1951). *Field theory in social science.* New York, NY: Harper and Row.

Lewis, M. (2010). *The big short: Inside the doomsday machine.* New York, NY: Norton.

Lewis, M. (2011). *Boomerang: Travels in the new third world.* New York, NY: Norton.

Lewis, S. (2011). *Positive psychology at work: How positive leadership and Appreciative Inquiry create inspiring organizations.* Chichester, UK: Wiley-Blackwell.

Lewis, S. (2012). Have we reached the tipping point for strength-based approaches to organisational challenges? *Assessment and Development Matters, 4*(1), 10–13.

Lewis, S. (2014). How positive psychology and Appreciative Inquiry can help leaders create healthy workplaces. In C. Biron, R. Burke, & C. Cooper (Eds.), *Creating healthy workplaces* (pp. 223–235). Farnham, UK: Gower.

Lewis, S. (2015). *How to work with skeptics.* Retrieved from https://www.youtube.com/watch?v=Re6Pn77_l5k.

Sisodia, J., Sheth, J., & Wolfe, D. (2014). *Firms of endearment: How world class companies profit from passion and purpose* (2nd ed.). Upper Saddle River, NJ: Pearson Education.

Smith, C. (2007). *Making sense of project realities: Theory, practice and the pursuit of performance*. Farnham, UK: Gower.

Snyder, C. R., Rand, K. L., & Sigmon, D. R. (2005). Hope theory: A member of the positive psychology family. In C. R. Snyder & S. J. Lopez (Eds.), *The handbook of positive psychology* (pp. 257–277). New York, NY: Oxford University Press.

Spreitzer, G. M., & Sonenshein, S. (2003). Positive deviance and extraordinary organizing. In K. S. Cameron, J. E. Dutton, & R. E. Quinn (Eds.), *Positive organizational scholarship: Foundations of a new discipline* (pp. 207–224). San Francisco, CA: Berrett Koehler.

Stacey, R., Griffin, D., & Shaw, P. (2002). Complexity and emergence in organizations [series preface]. In P. Shaw (Ed.), *Changing conversations in organizations: A complexity approach to change*. Hove, UK: Routledge.

Stellnberger, M. (2011). *Evaluation of Appreciative Inquiry interventions. Longer-term impact, critique and reflection across case studies*. Saarbrucken, Germany: Lambert Academic Publishing.

Surowiecki, J. (2004). *The wisdom of crowds: Why the many are smarter than the few*. London, UK: Abacus.

Sutcliffe, K. M., & Weick, K. (2007). *Managing the unexpected: Resilient performance in an age of uncertainty*. San Francisco, CA: Jossey-Bass.

Taleb, N. N. (2008). *The black swan: The impact of the highly improbable*. London, UK: Penguin.

Taylor, F. W. (1912). Scientific management. Reproduced in D. Pugh (Ed.) (1997). *Organization theory: Selected readings* (4th ed.). London, UK: Penguin.

ThinkReliability. (2014, January). *Flight 1549 'Miracle on the Hudson' – Cause Map*. Retrieved from http://www.thinkreliability.com/CM-Flight1549.aspx.

Watkins, J. M., & Mohr, B. J. (2001). *Appreciative Inquiry: Change at the speed of imagination*. San Francisco, CA: Jossey-Bass/Pfeiffer.

Waugh, E. (2003 [1938]). *Scoop: A novel about journalists*. London, UK: Penguin.

Weisbord, M. R., & Janoff, S. (2000). *Future search: An action guide to finding common ground in organizations and communities*. San Francisco, CA: Berrett-Koehler.

Weisbord, M. R., & Janoff, S. (2007). *Don't just do something, stand there!: Ten principles for leading meetings that matter*. San Francisco, CA: Berrett-Koehler.

Wheatley, M. (1999). *Leadership and the new science: Discovering order in a chaotic world*. San Francisco, CA: Berrett-Koehler.

Whitney, D., Trosten-Bloom, A., & Rader, K. (2010). *Appreciative leadership: Focus on what works to drive winning performance and build a thriving organization*. London, UK: McGraw Hill Professional.

Zern, E. (2004). *The best of Ed Zern: Fifty years of fishing and hunting from one of America's best-loved outdoor humorists*. Guilford, CT: The Lyons Press.

Zimbardo, P. G., & Boyd, J. N. (1999). Putting time in perspective: A valid, reliable individual-differences metric. *Journal of Personality and Social Psychology, 77*(6), 1271–1288.

Zimbardo, P. G., & Boyd, J. (2010). *The time paradox: Using the new psychology of time to your advantage*. London, UK: Rider.